Modern Epistemology
A New Introduction

Modern Epistemology
A New Introduction

Nicholas Everitt
University of East Anglia

Alec Fisher
University of East Anglia

McGraw-Hill, Inc.

New York   St. Louis   San Francisco   Auckland   Bogotá   Caracas   Lisbon
London   Madrid   Mexico City   Milan   Montreal   New Delhi
San Juan   Singapore   Sydney   Tokyo   Toronto

This book was set in Palatino by ComCom, Inc.
The editors were Cynthia Ward and Tom Holton;
the production supervisor was Diane Ficarra.
The cover was designed by B. C. Graphics.
R. R. Donnelley & Sons Company was printer and binder.

Cover Photo
Wedding Chapel IV *by Louise Nevelson, Bridgeman Art Library, London.*

MODERN EPISTEMOLOGY
A New Introduction

 This book is printed on recycled, acid-free
paper containing 10% postconsumer waste.

1 2 3 4 5 6 7 8 9 0   DOC   DOC   9 0 9 8 7 6 5 4

ISBN 0-07-021214-7

Library of Congress Cataloging-in-Publication Data

Everitt, Nicholas.
    Modern epistemology: a new introduction / Nicholas Everitt,
Alec Fisher.
        p.   cm.
    Includes index.
    ISBN 0-07-021214-7
    1. Knowledge, Theory of.   2. Philosophy—Introduction.
I. Fisher, Alec.   II. Title.
BD161.E53   ˙ 1995
121—dc20   94-23289

About the Authors

NICHOLAS EVERITT took his first degree at Christ's College, Cambridge, and his second at Wadham College, Oxford. He taught briefly at the University of Sussex before taking up his current post as Lecturer in Philosophy at the University of East Anglia, and for a number of years he has been a part-time philosophy tutor with the Open University of the UK. He is interested in, and has taught across, a wide range of philosophical areas and is the author of articles in epistemology, the philosophy of mind, the philosophy of religion, and moral philosophy. In 1979, he was Visiting Professor at Fairfield University, Connecticut.

ALEC FISHER teaches logic, philosophy, and critical thinking at the University of East Anglia, Norwich, Great Britain. Other books include *Formal Number Theory and Computability* (Oxford University Press, 1982), *The Logic of Real Arguments* (Cambridge University Press, 1988), and, with Michael Scriven, *Critical Thinking: Defining and Assessing It* (Sage: Corwin, 1994). For some years he has been an academic adviser to the University of Cambridge Examinations Board on how to assess the quality of students' reasoning and critical thinking. During 1993–94 he was a Visiting Professor of Philosophy and Assistant Director of the Center for Critical Thinking, Sonoma State University, California, and he is currently Director of the Centre for Research in Critical Thinking at the University of East Anglia. His current research deals mainly with questions about reasoning from the perspectives of logic, epistemology, and teaching and assessing critical thinking.

To the Women in Our Lives

Contents

Chapter 13 Rorty on Philosophy and the Mirror of Nature   196

Logic Appendix   209

Preface

We have enjoyed writing this book. For the last few years we have been teaching an epistemology course together, and this book has arisen from that collaboration. Initially, our approaches to many of the problems discussed in the book were quite different, but we have spent many pleasurable hours attempting to resolve those differences. In the process, we have both learned a great deal, we have both changed our views on a number of the issues, and we have reached substantial agreement on most of them. Academic collaboration is a difficult and risky process, but we have enjoyed it, and we look forward to continuing to resolve the disagreements that still remain between us.

Many people have helped us in the course of writing this book, and it is a pleasure to thank them here. Our own university, the University of East Anglia at Norwich, has supported us by giving us the time to write, and some of our philosophical colleagues at UEA have read and commented on earlier drafts of our material. We are particularly grateful to Martin Hollis and Angus Ross for their time and help. Our students over the years have also been willing guinea pigs, and they too deserve our thanks. Mary Robinson, our secretary, is always very helpful; she knows how much we have counted on her, but we want to thank her publicly. Cynthia Ward and Pattie Rodney, at McGraw-Hill, have also been understanding of our delays, instructive in their comments, and supportive throughout, and it is a pleasure to thank them. Appreciation is due the publisher's reviewers who helped refine the manuscript: Claude Macmillan, Onondaga Community College; Bonnie Paller, California State University, Northridge; Jefferson White, University of Maine; and Frank Wilson, Bucknell University.

Finally affectionate thanks to all the women in our lives, to whom the book is dedicated.

Nicholas Everitt
Alec Fisher

Introduction

As we remarked in the Preface, this book is a result of our collaborating on teaching an epistemology course in recent years. The content of the course has changed quite radically as we have worked together, and it may help the reader to know some of the influences that have shaped the book. The starting point was a set of fairly standard empiricist ideas about how knowledge is to be defined, how it rests on foundations, how the propositions that we know fall into such classes as the necessary and the contingent, the empirical and the a priori, and how the inferences that we draw can be classified as deductive or inductive. To this standard brew were added some less orthodox ideas about reasons and reasoning. However, as this mixture fermented over time, we felt impelled to give increasing weight to components alien to standard empiricism and ultimately destructive of it, components that derive principally from the work of Quine and to a lesser extent from Wittgenstein. Although many of these more subversive ideas go back 40 years or so, their implications are seldom taken seriously, even by those who pay lip service to them. Even less are they taken seriously in most introductory texts in epistemology. We aim in part to make good that deficiency.

Although the book is written from a certain standpoint, with a conviction that some views are demonstrably better than others, it is not meant to be narrowly polemical. We have written for those who are beginners in epistemology and indeed in philosophy as a whole, and we therefore go to some lengths to make plausible even those views that, ultimately, we think should be rejected. Because of our intended audience, we have also tried to keep the text as lucid and simple as possible even when we have been dealing with some quite difficult topics (such as non-Euclidean geometries and Godel's Theorems in Chapter 6, or Goodman's and Hempel's Paradoxes in Chapter 10).

In Chapter 1 we outline a number of questions that epistemologies have traditionally been supposed to answer and describe how epistemology relates to other areas of philosophy, such as metaphysics and ontology. This is followed by a fairly lengthy examination of recent attempts to pin down the concept of knowledge (Chapters 2 and 3). The aim is both to introduce readers to a central concept of traditional epistemology and to give them a thorough grounding in one of the principle methods of that tradition: the search for definitions or analyses of concepts in terms of logically necessary and sufficient conditions. Although we are ultimately skeptical about the value of this method, its explanation should enable readers to understand better the contrasting ideas proposed in some of the later chapters.

Chapter 4, a transitional chapter, argues that it is the concept of justified belief, rather than of knowledge, on which epistemology ought to concentrate. The central chapters of the book (5, 6, 7, and 8) then discuss at length the two dominant schools of thought about the structure of our total system of knowledge or justified belief, namely, foundationalism and coherentism, concluding that the latter is more plausible. Chapter 5 outlines, in a fairly orthodox manner, the foundationalist position in respect of empirical knowledge; this is followed in Chapter 6 by something unusual in epistemology texts, namely, a parallel account of foundationalism about the a priori. The rival theory, coherentism is then presented in Chapter 7; in this discussion we argue that Quine was right to reject the analytic-synthetic distinction and the allied contrasts between the a priori and the empirical, the necessary and the contingent. The success of the resulting coherentist position is then defended in Chapter 8 against a range of powerful objections, including those based on the incorrigibility of pain reports and the unrevisability of the law of noncontradiction.

Chapter 9 then takes up an issue that has so far been left in abeyance, the nature of the inferences that we draw from one belief to another. This topic is pursued through the (relatively unfamiliar) "problem of deduction" (Chapter 9) and the (more traditional) "problem of induction" (Chapter 10). In Chapter 11 we present a conception of inference that rejects the traditional deductive/inductive dichotomy in favor of an account that coheres nicely with the coherentist position that emerged at the end of Chapter 8.

In the final two chapters, we turn to two of the major influences in recent epistemology, Quine and Rorty. Over the last 40 years, Quine's work has consistently provided a source, albeit an oblique one, for revolutionary changes in epistemology. One of his central claims has been that epistemology needs to be "naturalized," and in Chapter 12 we examine what this claim means. We identify as importantly true one conception of naturalized epistemology that, we claim, is implied by his earlier rejection of the analytic-synthetic distinction. More recently, Rorty has championed the view that epistemology (or even philosophy in general) has suffered from deep misconceptions. In Chapter 13, we consider this claim, especially in connection with the thought that epistemology must have a social dimension.

An unusual feature of the book is the inclusion of a Logic Appendix. There are several reasons why we believe that such a section is desirable. First, we (like all philosophers) concentrate from the outset on *arguments*, in a sense of that term familiar to philosophers but often not to those coming to the subject for the first time. So it is essential for the reader to know something about what arguments are, how they can be identified, and how, traditionally, they have been classified and assessed. Second, theories of argument (i.e., logic) have historically exerted a profound influence on epistemology, for example, in providing a kind of ideal *certainty* to which other varieties of knowledge should aspire, or in suggesting that an axiomatized *structure* is what any genuine knowledge should display. Third, the material in the Appendix enables us to understand the thought, fundamental to the argument of this book, that we could have reason to revise what we currently accept as laws of logic.

At the end of each chapter, the reader will find a set of exercises. It is worth explaining that the purpose of the exercises is to help the reader engage in critical reading (a probing, reflective, questioning reading), rather than the kind of passive reading in which we often indulge. Though many of the questions are simply comprehension questions, which require readers to check their understanding of the ideas in the text, others require them to produce their own examples, to draw out implications, to evaluate arguments, and to assess the material they have read. These questions should be helpful in guiding the thinking of students who read the book as a self-study course and should also provide useful material for instructors. However, they do not go much beyond what is in the text, and many instructors will no doubt wish to supplement these exercises with questions of their own.

The material published in the area covered by this book is huge, and the recommended Further Reading at the end of the book presents no more than an initial foray. Full details of the works referred to both in the Further Reading section and in the text itself are given in the bibliography.

On the vexed question of personal pronouns, we have opted throughout for "she" in preference to "he." This was a choice prompted of course by political not grammatical considerations. Even if it pleases some readers, it may irk others. But we have found the consequent sense of surprise and even strangeness in our examples both enjoyable and also revealing. We hope that our readers will share these responses.

CHAPTER 1

What Is Epistemology?

1.1 What Sort of Theory Is a Theory of Knowledge?

The term "epistemology" derives from the two Greek words, "episteme," meaning "knowledge," and "logos," meaning "logic" or "rationale." So in modern English, epistemology has come to mean the theory of knowledge. But what is a theory of knowledge? We are accustomed to scientists formulating theories and testing them, theories for example about the cause of earthquakes or the structure of the atom, and even if we do not know enough science to understand the details of these theories, we can understand what sort of thing a theory about the cause of earthquakes might be. But how could there be a theory of knowledge? What would be the data which the theory was trying to explain? What would be the test of the correctness of the theory? Why should we need such a theory anyway? Our answers to these and related questions will become clearer as the book proceeds. However, let us begin by explaining eight problems which epistemology would traditionally tackle.

1.2 Eight Problems of Traditional Epistemology

(i) What is knowledge?

First of all, epistemologists have tried to offer an account of what knowledge is. We will find that in modern epistemology, this task has typically taken the form of trying to provide a definition of the word "know" (or more accurately of sentences containing the word). It might seem surprising that an inquiry into the nature of knowledge should focus on the word rather than the thing or state which the word denotes. After all, scientists developing a theory about the cause of earthquakes do not spend a great deal of time talking about the word "earthquake." Why philosophy has taken this linguistic turn is a large question. But part of the reason is that modern philosophers have come to feel that the way in which the old question "What is knowledge?" could best be answered was by focusing on the *concept* of knowledge; they then interpreted talk of concepts as being a shorthand way of referring to certain facts about language. Hence the old question "What is knowledge?," which seems to be about a phenomenon in the world, becomes transformed at least partly into a linguistic question, a question about the definition of the word "know." As we will see in Chapter 2, the definition sought is of a rather peculiar kind, and not at all the sort of thing which you might find in a dictionary.

(ii) What kinds of knowledge are there?

Secondly, epistemologies have historically tried to tell us something about the kinds of knowledge that there are. Most epistemologists, for example, have drawn a major distinction between empirical knowledge and a priori knowledge. Exactly what these terms mean is something that will occupy us later (see Chapter 5, section 2), but for the moment we can take it that empirical knowledge is knowledge derivable only from experience, and a priori knowledge is knowledge gained by reason alone. Are there really these two kinds of knowledge? It is easy to produce examples which seem to show that there must be. If I come to know that a particular flower is red by looking at it, surely that is knowledge that I have gained by experience, in this case by my visual experience. And if I know that if A is greater than B and B is greater than C, then A is greater than C, or that no statement can be both wholly true and wholly false at the same time, surely that is something that my reason tells me when I simply reflect on what it is that the statement is saying. Yet some philosophers have wanted to deny that experience by itself can be a source of knowledge, and others have denied that reason alone can be.

Descartes (1596–1650), the French thinker who is generally regarded as the founder of modern philosophy, is an example of someone who denies that the senses alone can be a source of knowledge. In a famous passage in his *Meditations*, he considers the knowledge that we have of a piece of a wax, and writes:

> . . . the perception I have of it is a case not of vision or touch or imagination.
> . . . but of purely mental scrutiny. (Descartes, Vol. 2, 21)

Here we have a contrast between the senses of vision and touch on the one hand, which, according to Descartes, do not by themselves give us knowledge of the wax, and "purely mental scrutiny" on the other. What he means by this phrase is not made explicit, but what is clear is that he thinks that our knowledge of the wax comes from the mind and not from the senses alone. No doubt Descartes would also have said in connection with the flower mentioned previously that my knowledge that it is red comes not from the senses but from "purely mental scrutiny." At the end of his discussion of the wax example, Descartes generalizes what he has been saying about the wax to cover our knowledge of all physical things:

> I now know that even bodies are not strictly perceived by the senses or the faculty of imagination but by the intellect alone, and that this perception derives not from their being touched or seen but from their being understood. (Descartes, Vol. 2, 22)

Again, we have an explicit contrast between the senses, which are declared not to be a source of knowledge, and something else (in this case, the intellect or understanding), which is a source of knowledge. So Descartes would be one philosopher who would deny that there is any empirical knowledge, if that term is understood as knowledge derivable only from experience.

By contrast, John Stuart Mill (1806–1873), the leading British philosopher of his day, took the opposite line. He thought that *all* knowledge was empirical, and hence denied the existence of any a priori knowledge. Speaking, for example, of the law of noncontradiction (which we quoted previously as saying that no statement can be both wholly true and wholly false), he had this to say:

> I consider it to be, like other axioms, one of our first and most familiar generalisations from experience. The original foundation of it I take to be, that Belief and Disbelief are two different mental states, excluding one another. This we know by the simplest observation of our own minds. (Mill, Bk. II, ch. 7, sec. 5, 183)

So Mill thinks that even the principle of noncontradiction is known empirically. And he goes on to make clear that he thinks, *contra* Descartes, that all of our knowledge is derived from experience. So that is a second task for our epistemology: what are the arguments for and against claiming that there are two kinds of knowledge, and what are the implications of accepting either view?

(iii) What are the sources of knowledge?

A related task, though one that is worth listing separately, is to consider what the sources of knowledge are. It is natural when we first start reflecting on where our knowledge comes from to pick on sense experience as the main and perhaps the only source of knowledge. We know about the things around us because we can use our senses to see them, touch, hear them, and so on. So, again in spite of what Descartes was saying, it looks as if sense experience has a good claim to be a source of knowledge. But how many senses are there? Common thought recognizes five, but some thinkers have suggested that we ought to recognize more, such as a sense of balance, or the sense which enables us to know without looking where our limbs are (usually called proprioception). And if we are recognizing new senses, where (if at all) does a moral sense fit in? But even if we recognize the existence of a number of other senses, there are still many things which we know about ourselves without having senses of any kind. To know what I am thinking, for example, or what emotions I am feeling, I do not have to use any of my senses; some philosophers have consequently postulated a faculty of introspection as a source of knowledge about the contents of our own minds.

Another favored source of knowledge has been reason or the intellect or the understanding. We saw how Descartes claimed, rather surprisingly, that our knowledge of a piece of wax was attributable not to our senses but to our intellect. More commonly, philosophers have argued that it is our intellect that tells us of the truths of logic and mathematics. We just "see" (in a nonvisual sense of the term) that certain things are true, or that one thing follows from another.

Should memory be counted as a source of knowledge? It seems in some ways to be like one. In answer to the question "How do you know?," we might reply "I can remember it," just as we might reply "I can see it," suggesting that memory functions like the sense of sight in supplying us with knowledge. But on the other hand, it seems unlike other sources of knowledge, in that it does not enable us to know anything new: memory is simply the retention of knowledge which is provided by some other source.

Testimony (and its more specific variety, authority) are other possible sources of knowledge. It seems that the great majority of the things we know about, we know because we have been told of them by other people, or because we have read what other people have said about them. If we focus on the idea of authority, we find that at different times in our intellectual history, different degrees of emphasis have been placed on the deliverances of persons and texts in special positions of authority. Sometimes authority has been contrasted with what our own senses tell us, and regarded as a superior source of knowledge. At other times, the pendulum has swung the other way, and the deliverances of authority have been treated as one branch of our sensory knowledge.

Beyond testimony come other alleged sources of knowledge, such as revelation, or parapsychological powers, such as telepathy, clairvoyance, and precognition. In mentioning these, we are not of course endorsing at all the claim that they do give us knowledge. Rather, we are saying that one of the tasks which has occupied epistemologists at different times in the past is trying to adjudicate between the claims made on behalf of *all* of these alleged sources of knowledge: what makes something a source of knowledge, what makes two sources of knowledge two rather than one, and so on? (Some of these questions will be taken up again in Chapter 13.)

(iv) What is the structure of our body of knowledge?

A fourth task concerns the structure of our total body of knowledge. We are familiar with the thought that one piece of knowledge can presuppose another. For example, I could not know that John's wife is a doctor unless I also know that John has a wife. But epistemologists are interested in a more general kind of dependence than this. For example, it is clear that in general our knowledge of the future depends on our knowledge of the past and present. Or, to give another example, if we have any knowledge of what other people are thinking and feeling, this must depend on our knowledge of their behavior. Some philosophers, in thinking about these dependencies, have thought that our knowledge is like a building, in that it rests ultimately on some "foundational" knowledge. If so, what would this foundational knowledge be like? Other philosophers, however, have argued that our knowledge is more like a spider's web where each strand in the web plays a part in supporting all the other strands, which in turn play a part in supporting it. There have been advocates for both of these views and also for other ways of seeing the structure of our knowledge; and we shall spend a good deal of time discussing this issue.

(v) What are the limits of what can be known?

A fifth task which has concerned epistemologists is to demarcate the limits of the knowable. Putting the matter like this may make it sound rather abstract, but the idea of the distinction is familiar in ordinary conversation and is often appealed to by people with no philosophical training. Here are three examples of it in action.

Suppose that there is an argument between a pacifist and someone who takes the more common view that killing, though in general wrong, is sometimes morally justified. Let us call this second person the traditionalist. We can easily imagine in some detail how a debate between these two might go. The pacifist will say that in her view, it is human life that has supreme value; that killing someone is an irreversible process, so that one can never undo the harm one does to one's victim; that no one is morally perfect, and that therefore no one is morally entitled to deprive another person of her life; that killing brutalizes the killer; that violence breeds only further violence; and so on. The traditionalist, however, is likely to say that killing is sometimes necessary to avoid a greater evil, that one has to weigh the life of the victim against the lives and welfare of many other people, that what is important is not mere life itself, but the quality of life, and so on. After some argument along these lines, they may reach an impasse, when one of them says "Well, that's just your opinion" or "You cannot prove it" or "It's only a subjective judgment anyway," or some such similarly dismissive phrase. Someone who says this is implicitly assuming the truth of a particular theory of knowledge. They are assuming the existence of a distinction between what is knowable and what is not knowable, and placing in the category of what is not knowable the class of moral judgments.

A second example concerns disputes about the existence of God. Throughout Western intellectual history, there have been many attempts to prove that God exists. Some of these arguments can seem very convincing, but to each of them there is a counterargument which seems to have roughly equal force. Thus we find Descartes defending the ontological argument, and Kant (1724–1804) attacking it, Butler (1692–1752) defending the argument to design and Hume (1711–1776) attacking it, and so on. This sort of seemingly irresolvable conflict has led some people to say that no one can really know whether or not God exists. They often mean by this not just that no one has up to now succeeded in proving the matter one way or the other, but rather that in principle the issue cannot be conclusively settled. And if they do take this view, they are again tacitly adopting a particular theory of knowledge. They are drawing a line between the knowable and the unknowable, and putting assertions about God into the unknowable category.

A final example concerns the sensations of other people. Can I know exactly what your sensations are? Or, a more difficult case, perhaps, can I know exactly what a dog's sensations feel like to the dog? Of course, I might have a more-or-less reliable guess at what you or the dog feel. If the dog's leg has just been broken by a passing car, and it is whining and whimpering, and resists all attempts to touch its leg, then *very* probably it is in pain. But would it be possible to *know* that this was so? And would it be possible to know exactly what kind of pain it felt? Many people have thought that the answer to these questions is "no." This means that once again, they are operating with a tacit distinction between the knowable and unknowable. As epistemologists, we would want to investigate this distinction. Is it the same distinction which is being appealed to in each of these types of cases? What is it that determines which category a given type of assertion should be placed in? This, then, is a fifth task which falls within the field of traditional epistemology.

It is worth emphasizing that the contrast here is between what is knowable in principle and what is not knowable in principle. There are many things which we do not currently know. But these do not count as unknowable in the sense in which we are here using the term. For science advances, our instruments of detection improve, and what today is in practice unknowable, tomorrow is known. When people say, however, that moral judgments are a matter of opinion not knowledge or that the existence of God is a matter of faith not knowledge, what is meant is not just that we do not now have enough evidence to achieve knowledge. The thought rather is that no conceivable evidence which we might hope to acquire in the future will enable us to gain knowledge in these areas.

(vi) What are the mechanisms by which we gain knowledge?

A sixth aim can be summarized as the task of finding mechanisms for knowledge, or at least making sure that such mechanisms are possible. What this means can best be shown with an example. Take the case that we mentioned earlier of seeing a red flower, and thereby coming to know that it is red. We know that there is a causal link between the flower and the knower. Light waves are reflected from the flower and enter the eye of the observer. They there produce chemical changes in the cones of the retina of the observer, and these changes in turn cause electrical impulses to flow up the optic nerve to the visual cortex in the brain. The end result is that the observer gains some knowledge about the flower. The details of this causal chain are not important for the philosopher, although obviously they are important for the physiologist. What is important for the philosopher is that the existence of some such causal chain as this, linking the flower to the observer, helps to make intelligible how an observer can come to have knowledge of an object that may, for example, be at a considerable distance from her. If we take the common sense view that looking at a flower can sometimes give you knowledge of what color it is, then we know that there is a causal mechanism which could explain *how* the knowledge is gained.

Contrast this with a different case. Some people believe that they have precognitive powers. They believe that they can see into the future, where this does not mean that on the basis of evidence from the past and present, they can infer more-or-less reliably some facts about the future, as the meteorologist tries to infer what tomorrow's weather will be like. The idea of precognition is rather that without the need for any evidence, they just know what the future will be like. There are several puzzling features to precognition, and one in particular that is relevant here is that there does not seem to be any mechanism which could explain how what is going to happen tomorrow could bring it about that today I know about tomorrow's events. If we reject the possibility that the future might cause the past and present, then it seems impossible that today's knowledge can be based on tomorrow's events. In other words, if someone claims to know things in a particular way, but there is no mechanism to explain how such knowledge is possible, then we would doubt their claim to have knowledge in this case.

So, a sixth task for traditional epistemology is to ensure that for each kind of knowledge admitted by our epistemology, there is some mechanism that makes it intelligible how there could be knowledge of that kind. As mentioned previously, the full details of the mechanism need not concern the philosopher. But what she must take care to avoid is countenancing a kind of knowledge, while having no idea at all of how knowledge of that sort is possible.

(vii) How is knowledge related to belief and justification?

So far in our listing of the tasks of epistemology, we have concentrated on the concept of knowledge. But epistemology is concerned with other related concepts as well, and in particular with the two concepts of belief and justification. As we will see shortly, on virtually every traditional account of knowledge, belief and justification are components of knowledge, and that is one reason for an epistemologist to be interested in those concepts. A second reason is that there are certain areas where knowledge is difficult to come by, and yet where some well-founded or justified belief is possible. In such areas, justified belief takes on for us the action-guiding role that knowledge can play for us in other areas. Indeed, some philosophers, such as Bertrand Russell (1872–1969), who are in general doubtful about the possibility of many kinds of knowledge, would maintain that the idea of justified belief is of more importance and interest than the idea of knowledge itself. Subsequent chapters will deal extensively with these issues.

(viii) How ought we to proceed in order to acquire knowledge?

A number of epistemologists in the past have not merely wanted to describe what knowledge is, what its limits are, and so on, they have wanted to *improve* the ways in which people think and reason. Thus, there has sometimes been a normative element in epistemological writings: the author has told us how we *ought* to conduct our search after knowledge, and what would be *right* for us to accept, and hence what we would be *justified* in believing. This task clearly requires some grasp of what knowledge is, what its limits are, what its sources are and hence is intimately related to the epistemological concerns we have previously outlined.

A good example of this is provided by Descartes. As we saw in section 1.2 (ii), he was firmly opposed to a reliance on the senses alone as a source of knowledge and regarded such a reliance as a major obstacle to intellectual progress. Accordingly, a number of his epistemological writings have a strongly normative content, an element of his thinking which is reflected in the titles of some of his works, such as *Discourse on the Method of Rightly Conducting One's Reason and Seeking Truth in the Sciences*.

This concern with how we *ought* to think can be found in many later epistemologists, including those writing in our own day. The contemporary philosopher of science Karl Popper (b. 1902), for example, has sought to change the ways in which (some) scientists formulate their theories and interpret the results of tests of those theories. As we shall see in section 10.5, Popper thinks that scientists ought to take seriously only those theories which are in principle falsifiable. He accordingly dismisses some allegedly scientific theories (such as Marxism and psychoanalysis) not because they have, as it were, got their facts wrong, but because they are unfalsifiable and hence are the wrong *sort* of theory to embody scientific understanding. One of the most recent examples in this tradition can be found in the work of the modern philosopher Stephen Stich, especially in his book *The Fragmentation of Reason*.

1.3 Epistemology and What There Is

Those, then, are the main tasks which epistemology has been concerned with in the past. But it will be helpful for later study to mention two other areas which are adjacent to epistemology and to which we will occasionally refer. These are metaphysics and ontology.

(i) The terms "metaphysics" and "ontology" explained

The term "metaphysics" originates in Greek philosophy with the writings of Aristotle (384 B.C.–322 B.C.). Aristotle produced a work dealing with the nature of the physical world, entitled the *Physics*. When his work was being collected and edited, included in the same volume as the *Physics* were a number of untitled writings. These came to be known as the *Meta-physics*, from the Greek "meta ta physika" (after the things of nature). Later commentators took the term to refer not just to the relative position of the writings, but rather to their content; in their hands, "metaphysics" came to mean something that was beyond or above the physical world, or existing apart from the world of nature. This is a sense (though not the only sense) which the term has retained into the twentieth century. In the contemporary usage which we shall be concerned with, metaphysics covers the realm of ontology.

"Ontology" comes from the Greek "ontos," meaning "being," and "logos," meaning (as we said earlier) "logic" or "rationale," and means literally "the study of being" or "the study of existence." But that by itself is not a very helpful definition. Surely, it might be objected, many other subjects are concerned with existence. Astronomers study the being or existence of heavenly bodies, biologists study the being or existence of living things, chemists study the being of chemical substances, and so on. What, then, is peculiar to the philosopher's concern with existence? The answer is that the philosophers have been concerned to list and describe the most basic kinds of things that exist.

(ii) Material objects

Let us illustrate this idea further. We know that the world contains both suitcases and telephones, and that they are very different kinds of objects. But nevertheless from one point of view, they are the same kind of thing, since they are both material objects. They are both composed of the same sorts of stuff (subatomic particles, etc.) differently arranged. Similarly with other objects that in ordinary life we think of as being very different from each other, such as pins and mountains, airplanes, and baseballs. Given that all these things do exist, it seems that we have to admit to our ontology the category of material thing. But do we have to admit anything else? Does the universe consist exclusively of material things?

(iii) Minds

Many philosophers have thought that the answer to this cannot be "yes," and have sought to show that our ontology must include other fundamental kinds of things. Let us consider briefly some favored additions. First, many philosophers (and many nonphilosophers too) have claimed that minds are a kind of entity irreducibly different from anything physical. They have argued that although minds may be causally dependent on bits of material stuff, like brains or central nervous systems, they are not actually identical with those physical entities. They have claimed that a mind is not itself a physical or a material thing, but has to be classified as nonphysical or nonmaterial. Part of what is meant by this claim is that minds do not have any spatial properties: they do not have a size or a shape or a location in space. So if this line of thought is right, we have to accept a fundamental dualism in our ontology: the world consists of the collection of all physical things and of nonphysical minds as well.

(iv) Abstract objects

Some thinkers have claimed, however, that we need to recognize the existence of a third kind of object, irreducibly different both from material things and from minds. Think, for example, of the number 1. Is that a material thing? If so, where is it, and what are its physical properties? Certainly the *numeral* "1" is a physical thing—or at least particular inscriptions of the numeral are. It makes sense to ask where a particular inscription of the numeral is located, how big it is, what its chemical composition is (i.e., in terms of the ink used), and so on. But of course the number 1 is not the same as the numeral which we can write or print. The number is what is denoted by the numeral, and once we have distinguished numbers and numerals, it seems clear that the number cannot itself be a physical thing. Are numbers then mental things? Some people have thought so. But if they are, they must be mental in a very different way from the way in which, for example, a feeling of anger is mental. The feeling of anger comes into someone's mind at a particular time, lasts for a certain length of time, and then ceases. If that particular person had never existed, that particular feeling of anger would never have existed either. By contrast, the number 1 does not come into existence at a particular moment when someone has a thought and then cease to exist when she starts to think about something else. We could not sensibly ask "Did the number 1 exist yesterday?" as we could ask "Was anyone angry yesterday?" The existence of the number 1 does not depend upon the existence of any particular person, in the way in which that person's feelings depend on that person: the number would still have existed even if the person had never been born. Indeed, even if nobody had ever been born, and hence there had never been any minds, it seems that it would still have been true that $1 + 1 = 2$. So it looks as if numbers cannot be mental items after all. And if they are not mental things at all, then we shall have to admit to our ontology a third kind of entity that is neither physical nor mental but abstract. Abstract entities will differ from both physical and mental ones, in that they will exist and yet not be in space or time.

(v) Space and time

Mention of space and time brings up a further puzzling item. Is space a material thing or a mental thing or an abstract thing, or does it belong to a fourth category of existence? Some thinkers have thought that space was a sort of unique nonmaterial stuff, independent of matter (this was roughly the view of the great physicist Isaac Newton [1642–1727]), while others have held that it does not exist in its own right at all, but is simply a set of relations holding between material things (this was roughly the view of the German philosopher Leibniz [1646–1716]). Similar conflicts persist over the nature of time. Should we think of it as a kind of thing in its own right, or is it just a set of relations holding between events? And if we say that space and time are just sets of relations, what sort of entity is a relation? Presumably it is not itself a material or a mental thing. So is it another abstract thing, and if so, is it the same kind of abstract thing as a number?

We do not need to answer these questions here. We raise them in order to illustrate the sorts of issues which concern an ontologist. But there are also links here with epistemology. Recall, for instance, what we said a moment ago about the sixth task for our epistemology, the issue of a causal mechanism for knowledge. Suppose that in reflecting on the nature of numbers, we took the view that they are indeed mind-independent objects that have a nonspatial and nontemporal existence. This is a view which can seem very plausible. It seems to account for the objectivity which arithmetic has, and for the fact that we discover arithmetical truths, we do not arbitrarily make them up as we go along. But if we take that view, we have a great problem in explaining how we could ever come to know about numbers. For if numbers are not in space or time, they presumably cannot interact with us causally in the way that physical objects can. How then can we ever get to know about them? It seems that our epistemology and our ontology are in conflict here. What this shows is that although epistemology and ontology are two separate concerns, when we undertake one, we will be well advised to keep an eye on the other.

Exercises

1. Without rereading the chapter, explain in half a page the traditional tasks of epistemology.
2. Without rereading the chapter, check how carefully you read it by *briefly* answering the following questions:
   a. what is the difference between empirical and a priori knowledge? (give an example of each)
   b. describe *two* structures which our body of knowledge might be thought to have
   c. give two examples of things which might be thought to be unknowable
   d. what are metaphysics and ontology?
   e. list three basic categories of object which philosophers have countenanced
3. Before reading Chapter 2, write in no more than one page your own account of what knowledge is. To help you do this, ask yourself the following questions:
   a. can you know something to be true if in fact it is false?
   b. if you know something, can you also believe it? do you *have to* believe it if you know it?
   c. if you claim to know something, do you have to be able to justify that claim?
   d. if you know something do you have to be *certain* of it?
   e. what would you have to know to know that Smith was the murderer?

CHAPTER 2

Propositional Knowledge as Justified True Belief

2.1 Capacity Knowledge, Knowledge by Acquaintance, and Propositional Knowledge

The things that we know form an enormous and very heterogeneous collection. We claim to know people, places, events, facts. We claim to know why things happen, who performed a particular action, where a given event occurred, how certain things are possible. We say that we know how to do things, like ride a bicycle or prove Pythagoras's theorem. Very often, our knowledge is not easily expressible verbally. A person can show that she knows the way to the library simply by taking the best route whenever she wants to get there. If we think of animals, and take for granted that they can know things (a dog knows how to find its way home, a cat knows that there is food in the bowl), then clearly there can be knowledge which the knower cannot express in words at all. If the animal example is unconvincing, there are plenty of instances of human knowledge which the knower might be unable to express in words. A person might know what his or her partner looked like, without being able to put the knowledge into words.

Faced with such tremendous variety, philosophers have tried to impose some order by distinguishing different kinds of knowledge. In this connection, we shall follow tradition in distinguishing between what we will call capacity knowledge, knowledge by acquaintance, and propositional knowledge. *Capacity knowledge* covers all those cases in which a person (or animal) knows how to do something (knows how to swim, how to mend a fuse, how to make people laugh, etc.). This is sometimes referred to as "knowing how," but this description is misleading. Capacity knowledge is knowing how *to do something*—and this is different from merely knowing how. I can know how old someone is, or how far it is to New Orleans, or how many there are in a baker's dozen, without knowing how to do anything.

The second kind of knowledge, *knowledge by acquaintance,* covers all those cases in which we are said to know some particular thing, a thing which exists in space and time, and to know it by personal acquaintance. Thus, I might know a person, a country, a building, a river, a painting. It is characteristic of knowledge of this kind that it is expressed by the verb "know" followed by a direct object. Thus I might speak of knowing New York, or knowing the Mississippi, or knowing the *Mona Lisa.*

The third kind of knowledge, *propositional knowledge,* covers all those cases in which a person (or animal) knows that some sentence or proposition is true. Notice that different kinds of sentences are used for different purposes. For example, "Are you loyal to the flag?" asks a question, "Please pass the salt" makes a request, "Stand at ease" issues an order. By contrast, "President Kennedy was assassinated in 1964" makes a statement which, unlike all the others, is either true or false. A proposition is customarily defined as whatever can be true or false—hence the term propositional knowledge. Thus, Bill's knowledge that Washington was the first president of the United States, that $E = mc^2$, and that the next eclipse of the sun will be in the year 2004 are all examples of propositional knowledge.

There are clearly some complex interconnections between these three types of knowledge. It may well be the case that when I know how to do something, I also have some propositional knowledge. For example, when I know how to get to the library, I may know a set of truths of the form "You must first go down the steps, then you must turn right at the deli, and then you will find the library straight ahead of you." It may be indeed that I acquired my knowledge of how to get to the library by first memorizing a set of truths like this, describing the different stages of the route. In other cases, capacity knowledge may have no accompanying propositional knowledge. I may know how to swim, without knowing any truths about the techniques which enable me to do so. When I know something by acquaintance, it is very likely that I will know some truths about it, and perhaps also have some capacity knowledge. If I know New York, I am likely to know some truths such as that Manhattan is in New York, that Central Park is in Manhattan, and so on. If I know New York, then I am likely to have some knowledge of how to find my way around New York—in other words some capacity knowledge. It may be that if I am to have any propositional knowledge, I must first of all have some knowledge by acquaintance. Conversely, it may be the case that knowledge by acquaintance is somehow reducible to propositional knowledge.

Historically, it is propositional knowledge which has attracted most attention from philosophers, probably because it connects with such philosophically interesting concepts as rationality and truth (remember that our initial explanation of propositional knowledge was knowledge of truths). We shall follow this tradition and focus on propositional knowledge.

To make the object of our attention a little more precise, let us specify the kind of sentence that expresses it. The kind of sentence will have the form "S knows that p," where "S" is replaced by a word referring to a person (or animal) and "p" is replaced by a proposition the truth of which S is said to know. (We here follow the usual philosophers' convention of using the lower case letters p, q, and so on, to represent propositions. Strictly speaking, they are propositional *variables*, that is to say, they mark the place where a proposition can be inserted. The important thing to remember is that they can be replaced only by whole sentences, not by parts of a sentence such as a name or a description.) Thus, "Jim knows that Paris is the capital of France" is an example of the type of knowledge sentence we have specified. So is "Mary knows that 25 × 25 is 625," "The man next door knows that the earth is flat," and "My friend knows that it is now raining in Chicago." By contrast, "Mary knows what 25 × 25 is" is not of the same form as "S knows that p," since "what 25 × 25 is" is not a complete sentence, and hence cannot be used to replace "p." Notice that it does not matter, from the point of view of identifying the sort of knowledge we are talking about, whether the sentence that replaces p says something true or false. Since the earth is not flat, it must be false to say that the man next door knows that it is flat. But that the statement is false makes no difference to the question of whether the statement has the form "S knows that p." Another way of putting this point would be to say that a sentence has the same meaning and structure whether it says something true or false. Other sentences, like "S wonders whether p," "S hopes that p," "Does S know that p?," "Make sure that S knows that p," do not have the form which interests us and so are not under discussion here.

So far, we have singled out a class of sentences (sentences of the form "S knows that p") which express claims to propositional knowledge, and we shall focus on *those* in order to say what propositional knowledge is. To tackle this question, we need to investigate under what conditions sentences of our favored sort say something true. Thus, we aim to give a logical analysis or a conceptual analysis of the concept of propositional knowledge.

2.2 The Idea of Logical or Conceptual Analysis Explained

(i) A logical analysis of "X is a bachelor"

Since the idea of a logical or conceptual analysis has been a fundamental one in philosophy and is still very influential, it is worth illustrating exactly what it involves, using a simple example. Suppose that someone wondered what being a bachelor was (or to use the grander language deriving from Plato, what the essence of bachelorhood was). If we were giving a logical or conceptual analysis, we would focus on a specific sort of sentence, a sentence that had the form "X is a bachelor." Sentences of this form would be what is sometimes called the "analysandum" (from the Latin, meaning "the thing to be analyzed") or sometimes the "definiendum" ("the thing to be defined"). An initial attempt at providing an analysis might be as follows:

> X is a bachelor if and only if (a) X is male, and
>
> (b) X is unmarried

What goes on the right-hand side of the "if and only if" is what is sometimes called the "analysans" or "definiens," meaning the thing that is offered as the analysis or definition of the analysandum.

Before we explain and criticize this analysis, it will be helpful to explain what necessary and sufficient conditions are. In short, "A is a *necessary* condition of B" means that A cannot be true unless B is; and "A is a *sufficient* condition of B" means that if A is true, then B must be too. Thus, in the above example, "X is male" is a necessary condition of X being a bachelor, and if X is a bachelor, this is sufficient to guarantee that X is male.

In this analysis, it is being claimed that each of our two conditions (a) and (b) is necessary to being a bachelor (you cannot be a bachelor unless you are male, and you cannot be a bachelor unless you are unmarried). Neither by themselves is sufficient for being a bachelor, since you could be a male without being a bachelor (if you were a married man) and you could be unmarried without being a bachelor (if you were an unmarried woman). But the aim of the analysis would be to produce a set of conditions each of which was necessary to being a bachelor, and which taken together were sufficient for being a bachelor. In fact, although conditions (a) and (b) above are certainly necessary for the truth of "X is a bachelor," it would be very plausible to claim that they are not sufficient. For there are cases where X is an unmarried male, but X is not a bachelor. Suppose, for example, that X is a dog who is male but unmarried (since dogs are not the sorts of beings who can be married). Such a dog could not properly be called a bachelor. That fact shows that conditions (a) and (b) above are not sufficient. We need to add another clause to our analysis, as follows:

> (c) X is human

For the truth of "X is a bachelor," (c) is a further necessary condition. Are (a), (b), and (c) jointly sufficient? In other words, if you are an unmarried male human, does that guarantee that you are a bachelor? Arguably not: an unmarried human male who is a newly born baby meets conditions (a), (b), and (c), but surely does not count as a bachelor. So we need to add a fourth condition:

> (d) X is of marriageable age

Of course, what counts as being of marriageable age (just as what counts as marriage) will vary from society to society. But this is no weakness in the analysis. It shows only that the concept of a bachelor is relative to one's society, that is to say, you might count as a bachelor in one society but not in another, because the two societies had different criteria for being of marriageable age.

(ii) How to critique a proposed logical analysis

Whether the four conditions that we now have are jointly sufficient for being a bachelor need not concern us. What we needed to illustrate was the *general technique* for constructing an analysis. There are four points in particular that we need to notice. First, the aim of a logical or conceptual analysis is to provide a set of conditions, each of which is necessary for the truth of the analysandum and which collectively are sufficient.

Secondly, notice how it is possible to critique a proposed analysis. What you must do is to show that it is possible for the left-hand side of the "if and only if" to be true when the right-hand side collectively is false, or vice versa. Thus we show that being a bachelor cannot be analyzed as being an unmarried male by showing that (a) and (b) on the right-hand side can be true even though the left-hand side is false. This is one place where philosophers appeal to the notion of "intuition," in a technical sense of the word. It does not mean some nonrational feeling, but rather refers to what we feel is the right way to describe something before we have engaged in any philosophical theory. Thus, we might say that intuitively, we would not call a dog a bachelor, so that in constructing our analysis of the concept of bachelor, we would want to arrive at an analysis which took account of that intuition (which is exactly what the analysis above does).

But thirdly, when we consider concepts more complex than that of bachelor (such as the concepts of knowledge, justification, identity, cause, etc.) it is often very difficult to find a set of necessary and sufficient conditions which will accommodate *all* the intuitions we have, and in that case, philosophers often settle for what is sometimes called a reflective equilibrium. One might be able to accommodate more of one's intuitions, but only by making the analysis extremely complex. In that case, there is a trade-off between the scope and the simplicity of the analysis. What counts as an equilibrium is a matter of judgment: the wider the scope, the better, but also the simpler the analysis the better; but these two aims can pull in opposite directions.

Fourthly, because the technique for criticizing proposed analyses asks if it is possible for one side to be true when the other side is false, philosophers who engage in this sort of conceptual analysis have a particular interest in possible cases as opposed to actual cases. This will become clearer when we come on to analyses of the concept of knowledge.

(iii) *"Logically"* necessary and sufficient conditions?

Two final remarks before we leave our example of bachelorhood. We have so far spoken simply of necessary and sufficient conditions. Many philosophers speak in this context of logically necessary and logically sufficient conditions. What does the word "logically" mean here? Unfortunately, it is difficult to say clearly and noncontentiously. The idea is of a contrast between what logic makes so and what the laws of nature make so. It is clearly necessary that if

X is a bachelor, then he can breathe. Nature makes this so, for people who cannot breathe cannot live, and hence cannot exist as a bachelor or as anything else. But "X breathes" would not be regarded as a *logically* necessary condition of "X is a bachelor," because it does not constitute part of the essence of bachelorhood. The main point is that "logical" as used by philosophers is virtually always a technical term and practically never has its ordinary everyday meaning of "reasonable."

(iv) A historical note on logical analyses

In the earlier years of this century, providing an analysis of the kind we have been discussing was deemed a major part, or even the sum total, of proper philosophical activity. The aim was to provide analyses of a wide range of philosophically puzzling concepts, such as the concepts of knowledge, causation, free will, the self, and so on. In recent years, the pendulum has swung very much the other way, and some philosophers (influenced by such writers as Wittgenstein and Quine) are skeptical about the possibility of providing any philosophically illuminating analyses of this kind. Though we start with an open mind on this issue, the reader will see later that we share this skepticism.

2.3 The "Justified True Belief" Analysis of Propositional Knowledge

Bearing in mind the method of logical analysis which we explored in our bachelor example, let us return to the task of giving an analysis of "S knows that *p.*" What we are looking for is a set of conditions which are individually necessary and jointly sufficient for the truth of "S knows that *p.*" We will start by considering what has come to be known as the traditional or justified true belief (JTB) account of knowledge. According to this, there are three conditions only which are individually necessary and jointly sufficient for the truth of "S knows that *p.*" They are:

1. *p* is true
2. *S* believes that *p*
3. *S* has adequate justification for believing that *p*

Let us examine these in turn.

The first condition, generally called the truth condition, says that you cannot know that something is true if in fact it is false. So if you are to know that *p*, then *p* must be true. Of course, *p* can itself be a claim that something else is false. For example, *p* might be "It is false that arsenic is nourishing," and I can certainly know that it is false that arsenic is nourishing. But here, what I know (namely that it is false that arsenic is nourishing) is something that is true. You can believe that something is true when really it is false; and you can also wrongly take yourself to know that something is true when in fact it is false. However, you cannot, according to this first condition, really know something to be true if in fact it is false.

It is true that people sometimes speak as if they thought that when you know something to be true, it could still be false. But we can make sense of such remarks only by treating them as ironic or elliptical. Thus, if a historian says "Hitler's problems stemmed from the fact that he knew that the German army would conquer the Reds," we can make sense of this only if we assume that she means something like "Hitler was absolutely certain (though wrongly so) that the German army would conquer the Reds." This truth condition is the least controversial of the three conditions in the JTB account. It is accepted by all sides in the debate about knowledge, and we shall henceforth regard it as not in question.

The second condition calls for a little more explanation. The mere fact that p is true does not guarantee that S knows it. There must be some connection between S and p. S must have some sort of mental relation to p. But this relation has to be of a certain kind. It is no use, for example, if she wonders whether p, or fears that p, or hopes that p. These are all attitudes which she might have toward p, but they are incompatible with her knowing that p. If she is to know that p, she must accept that p is true, or, as the second condition says, she must believe that p.

It is easy to misunderstand this second condition because in ordinary life we often seem to contrast knowledge with belief as if they were mutually exclusive. Mary might reasonably say "I don't *believe* that my name is Mary, I *know* that it is," and this seems to imply that knowledge and belief are incompatible states. The term "belief" in ordinary use often carries suggestions about the inconclusive nature of the evidence which we have, as when people contrast matters of belief with matters of fact. Sometimes it carries religious connotations. A person who describes herself as a believer does not mean that she holds beliefs of some kind or another. She means that she accepts some religious claims. But none of these ordinary associations of the word "belief" is present in the second condition of the JTB analysis. The condition is not implying that S is uncertain of the truth of p, or that she lacks evidence for p, or that p has a religious content. All it is saying is that she accepts p—what her grounds are, if any, and what the strength of her conviction is, is left undetermined by the second condition. In this usage, believing something covers the spectrum of cases ranging from thinking that it is more probable than not to being absolutely certain of it.

Are these first two conditions by themselves sufficient for the truth of "S knows that p"? Can we, in other words, equate knowledge with true belief? Our technique for criticizing suggested analyses tells us what we must do. We must see if it is possible for someone to hold true beliefs without thereby having knowledge. If it is possible, then true belief cannot be logically sufficient for knowledge. According to the JTB analysis (and indeed to the great majority of thinkers), there are possible cases which show that true belief is not sufficient for knowledge. For sometimes a person's belief is true just by chance or by luck. If a person bets regularly on horses, and says "I just know that one day I'm going to have a big win," we would not say that she knew what she claimed to know, even if one day she did have a big win. We might say that she believed that she would have a big win, or that she was sure that she would have a big win. But intuitively we think that such a case would not be an example of knowledge.

What further condition, then, is needed to turn true belief into knowledge? It seems that something is needed to prevent it being the case that a knower's true belief is true just by chance, or just as a matter of luck. There must be, to put it generally, some sort of connection between the fact that the knower believes that *p*, and the fact that *p* is true. According to the JTB account, this connection is supplied by the idea of a good justification. The trouble with the gambler (from the point of view of knowledge) is that she has no justification for her belief that she will win. Unless she has a good justification for her belief, she is guilty of wishful thinking. Suppose, for example, that it transpired that the woman was involved in a criminal conspiracy which involved doping heavily all the favorites in a race while backing very heavily some rank outsider. Then we might be prepared to concede that she knew that she would win. Perhaps we feel that even in such a case, her justification is not good enough for knowledge. Perhaps we think that an adequate justification would have to be something like the following: it turns out that the woman is a millionaire, and in one particular race, she owns all the horses which are running, so that whichever horse wins, she knows that she will collect the winnings. Here surely we should admit that she knew that she would win, for her belief is not merely true, and not merely the product of wishful thinking, it is one which is backed up with an excellent justification.

2.4 Veritable, Consequential, and Epistemic Justification

We have spoken of the need for justification. But the idea of justification covers a number of different concepts, and we need to specify which one is supposed to be relevant to the concept of knowledge.

Sometimes, people are said to be justified in their beliefs simply because their beliefs have turned out to be true. A teacher may say of an ex-pupil "Trish's later successes have fully justified my early confidence in her." Here, the sole justification for the teacher's belief that her pupil had a bright future lies in the fact that the belief turned out to be true. There is no suggestion that at the time the teacher formed the belief, she had good or adequate reason for thinking that the belief was true. There is no suggestion that she was rational or reasonable in holding the belief. She may or may not have been rational or reasonable: the mere fact that her belief was justified, in this sense of "justified," is no evidence for or against her reasonableness. Let us call this "veritable" justification.

Sometimes a person is said to be justified in holding a belief because the consequences of her doing so are very beneficial to her or to the world at large. Suppose, for example, that I find the thought of ill health and death very depressing, and that my life would become utterly miserable if I thought that I were ill and dying. If, on the other hand, I believe that I am in good health, I can lead an active, vigorous, and enjoyable life. It would then be very sensible of me to believe, so far as it was within my power, that I was in good health. I might, for example, take care not to have medical check-ups which might prove to me that I was ill. I might seek out the company of friends who, I know, will assure me how well I am looking. But the fact that the consequences of my believing that I am in good health are beneficial is no reason to think that the belief is true, nor does it constitute evidence that it is true. I may be reasonable or justified in holding on to the belief, even though the belief is not true (and hence I lack veritable justification) and even though I have no reason to think the belief is true. Some writers call this "prudential" justification, but a better name for it is "consequential" justification, since it makes the justification for a belief depend on the consequences of holding the belief.

Neither of these two sorts of justification is being invoked by the suggestion that knowledge is justified true belief. The sort of justification which is thought to be relevant to knowledge is what is usually called "epistemic" justification. The thought here is that you are justified in holding a belief if and only if you have some good reason to think that the belief is true, and indeed a better reason to think that it is true than that it is false. It is this sort of justification which connects the ideas of evidence and truth. In this sense, a justified belief could turn out to be false (and hence to lack veritable justification) and could be one which had disastrous consequences for the believer (and hence be one which lacked consequential justification).

It is, then, epistemic justification which is being invoked in the JTB analysis. But within this general sort of account, there is room for variation. Some writers, for example, say that the second condition should not invoke the very wide concept of belief that we were noticing earlier, but rather should speak more narrowly of *certainty* or sureness. They would claim that you cannot know something unless you are sure of it. This line of thought, deriving ultimately from Plato, has found modern defenders in writers like Ayer and Unger. Other writers, instead of speaking of justification, prefer to speak of having a reason for one's belief, or of having evidence for the belief. Clearly, too, the idea of a good justification is one which needs to be explained in more detail. How good is good? Is it the same in all contexts, or does it depend on the sort of thing that is known? Can degrees of justification be measured, and if so, how? But rather than explore these other issues that would arise if we wanted to defend the JTB analysis, we shall mention one very influential line of criticism that has convinced most philosophers that the JTB account cannot be accepted as it stands.

2.5 The Gettier Objection: There Are Examples of Justified True Belief Which Are Not Knowledge

This line of criticism can be found in Russell but was brought to prominence in more recent epistemology in a very short but very influential paper by Gettier. What Gettier did was to provide examples of beliefs which were both true and apparently adequately justified, but which did not amount to knowledge. If his argument is correct, then we know that the traditional account as it stands will not do as a complete analysis of propositional knowledge, for it would not be giving sufficient conditions for the truth of "*S* knows that *p*" (the conditions could be met and the knowledge claim would still be false).

Let us see what a Gettier-style example is like. Suppose that Mr. Smith's daughter tells her father that she has just bought a car. Mr. Smith knows that his daughter is an honest person and can think of no reason why she should be deceiving him in this matter. So on the basis of what his daughter has told him, Mr. Smith comes to believe that his daughter has just bought a car. So when Mr. Smith meets his neighbor Mr. Brown, and Mr. Brown says to him "I hear that someone in your family has just bought a car," Mr. Smith replies "Yes, I know [that someone in my family has just bought a car]." But there are two facts unknown to Mr. Smith. The first is that, very unusually, his daughter on this occasion was lying: she had not just bought a car. The second fact unknown to Mr. Smith is that his wife, Mrs. Smith, has just bought a car—but secretly. The question now is: when Mr. Smith says to Mr. Brown "I know [that someone in my family has just bought a car]," is what he says true? Does he really have knowledge?

We can see in this simple example that the three conditions specified by the traditional analysis are all met. First, it is true that someone in Mr. Smith's family has just bought a car, namely Mrs. Smith. Secondly, Mr. Smith certainly believes that someone in his family has just bought a car. Thirdly, it appears that Mr. Smith has adequate justification for his belief, since his source of information is his daughter, who we are told is very honest and who, further, has no motive that Mr. Smith knows of for being deceitful in this particular case. So Mr. Smith does have an adequately justified true belief that someone in his family has just bought a car; and yet, so Gettier's objection goes, Mr. Smith does not know this. So knowledge cannot be equated with justified true belief.

Before we look at possible philosophical responses to this type of objection, notice two points of technique. First, the objection pursues exactly the strategy for criticizing proposed analyses which we mentioned earlier. The aim of the objection is to show that the three conditions offered by the traditional account are not sufficient for knowledge. It does this by trying to show that there can be cases (our *intuition* tells us that there are *possible* cases) in which the three conditions are met and yet in which we still do not have a case of knowledge. Putting the same point slightly differently, the objection tries to show that the right-hand side of the analysis can be true when the left-hand side is false, which would at once show that the left- and right-hand sides could not be equivalent.

Secondly, in order for the objection to be effective, it does not have to say that there are actual cases in which the right-hand side is true and the left-hand side is false. All it has to do is to claim that it is *possible* for the right-hand side to be true and the left-hand side to be false; and to show that this is possible, a fictional case will do just as well as a real one. Indeed, the whole story of Mr. Smith and his family is fictional: it was invented precisely to illustrate an objection to the JTB account, and the fact that it was made up is no weakness in the objection.

2.6 A First Response to Gettier-Style Objections

(i) "Good" justification is not enough

Let us consider then what responses might be made to Gettier-type objections to the JTB analysis. A first response might be to argue that the requirement of a good justification is too weak, at least if Mr. Smith counts as having a good justification for his belief that someone in his family has just bought a car. What is needed for knowledge, it might be argued, is complete justification; and Mr. Smith, although he has some justification for his belief, does not have complete justification. He has simply relied on what he has been told by his very honest daughter and has not checked whether his daughter is being honest on this occasion in particular.

Although this is a response which might seem prima facie attractive, it turns out to be one which it is very difficult to defend. The main problem is to explain what can be meant by "complete" justification. There are two related aspects to this problem. The first is to make the concept of completeness sufficiently demanding to rule out Gettier-type cases (if the concept does not do this, there is no point in switching from good justification to complete justification). The second problem is not to make the concept so demanding that we virtually never have complete justification, and thus virtually never know anything.

These difficulties are nicely illustrated precisely by the situation in which Mr. Smith found himself, namely one in which he is being told something by a reliable source. One of the most striking features about human knowledge, which must be taken seriously by any adequate epistemology, is that we learn most of what we know by being told it by someone else, either through the spoken or written word. But in the great majority of cases (perhaps in all cases) when we are told something by someone else, it is possible that person is mistaken (either they are lying or they have been misinformed, or they are mis-remembering, etc.). Now if our justification for believing something consists solely in the fact that we have been told it by a normally reliable authority whom we have no reason to believe is mistaken in this particular instance, and if it is nevertheless possible that what they are telling us is wrong, does this mean that our justification is less than complete, and hence that we do not acquire knowledge of what they are telling us?

(ii) "Complete" justification will not do either

If the answer to our question above is "no," then there are *no* grounds for deny-ing that Mr. Smith has complete justification for his belief. It would then fol-low that even if we accepted that knowledge requires complete and not merely good justification, the Smith example would still show that our analysis was faulty: there could be cases of completely justified, true belief which were not cases of knowledge.

If the answer to our question above is "yes," then we will have defined knowledge in such a way that we will know very much less than we thought we did. It will have the consequence for example that most people do not know what their own name is. Our knowledge that we are called Samantha or Genghis or whatever our name is, is derived from what other people have told us. We take our informants to be generally reliable sources of information, just as Mr. Smith takes his daughter to be a generally reliable source of informa-tion. And just as he did not check whether his daughter was telling the truth on that particular occasion, so most of us have not taken steps to check whether our parents were telling us the truth when they brought us up recognizing a particular name as our own. We have not checked that bureaucrats made no mistake, intentional or otherwise, when they issued our birth certificates, pass-ports, or other identity cards, which bore the name that we take to be our own.

It might be asked what would be wrong with analyzing knowledge in such a way that we knew very much less than common sense would suggest that we know. After all, it might be said, common sense has been wrong in the past (about whether the earth goes round the sun, about the distance of the stars, about the origin of life, etc.). Why should we give it any special status and assume that its deliverances must be regarded as sacrosanct? Why shouldn't it be the case that in fact we know very much less than common sense would hold that we know? Indeed, isn't this precisely what skepticism maintains? How can we dogmatically assume that skepticism is mistaken?

(iii) A conceptual analysis should not diverge greatly from standard usage

This question raises large and interesting issues of methodology, and we will have to return to them later. We would claim that skepticism, and the attempt to refute skepticism, should not be central concerns of epistemology. It cannot *seriously* be doubted that we do know a great many things (including, for most of us, what our own name is!). Serious questions can be raised about *how* we can know the things that we know, and how the total fabric of knowledge hangs together. But the starting point must always be that we do indeed know a great many things. More specifically, in relation to the above objection to the "complete justification" solution to the Gettier problems, we need to note the following: that we have no means of specifying which concept we are talking about if we totally ignore our common sense judgments. Of course we can say that the concept we are discussing is the concept of knowledge— but which concept is that? The answer must be that the concept is pinned down by the judgments which we make using it. It is by reference to our judgments using the concept that we try to construct our analysis of the concept. We pin the concept down by appeal to the intuitions which we have as to what knowledge is, what possible examples would count as cases of knowledge, and so on. So if we produced an analysis according to which most of our judgments using the concept were mistaken, there could be no grounds for saying that we had correctly analyzed that concept. The analysis would have failed because it would not have captured any (or perhaps enough) of our intuitions about the nature of knowledge. Suppose, to revert to our earlier discussion of the concept of a bachelor, someone were to propose an analysis according to which X is a bachelor if and only if X has four legs and a tail. Such an analysis would make very many of our judgments using the concept of a bachelor false, so the analysis must be wrong. What a correct analysis must do is try to extract from our uses of a term a set of explicit conditions which could explain why native speakers use the term as they do. Of course, the best analysis that we can find may not provide us with a perfect fit between our prephilosophical uses of the concept, and our set of explicit conditions. But the better the fit, the more plausible the analysis. So an analysis which had a very bad fit with the judgments we make using the term would be for that reason a bad analysis. And so, finally, if the requirement of conclusive justification, interpreted in a very demanding way, meant there was a bad fit between a proposed analysis of knowledge and our actual practice, that would be a good reason for thinking the analysis to be mistaken.

It appears, then, that the appeal to complete justification will not solve the Gettier-type cases. Interpreted weakly, the requirement will not show that Mr. Smith lacked a justification for his belief that someone in his family had just bought a car; interpreted strongly, it will indeed rule out Mr. Smith and others like him as knowers, but it will have the unacceptable consequence that nearly all our knowledge claims are false, false because we lack the complete justification which knowledge requires. But is there perhaps some other way in which the concept of justification can be interpreted, which avoids the problems associated with the notions of good and complete justification? That is the question which we will take up in the next section.

2.7 A Second Response to Gettier-Style Objections

(i) "Good" justification is not enough: justification must be indefeasible

We can lead into this alternative interpretation of the idea of justification by focusing on what it is about Mr. Smith's situation which prevents him from having knowledge. The crucial fact is that he is unaware that his daughter is lying to him. If he became aware of this fact, then he would no longer be justified in believing that someone in his family has just bought a car. His belief (that *someone* in the family has bought a car) would, of course, still be true (remember that it is Mrs. Smith who has bought a car). But it is his belief that his daughter has just bought a car which functions as his justification. If he were to discover the truth about his daughter, that would undermine or *defeat* the justification he has for thinking that someone in his family has bought a car. Perhaps, then, what knowledge requires is not just that one should have a well-justified true belief, but further that one's belief should not be susceptible to being undermined or defeated by any truths of which one is currently unaware, in short that one's justification should be "undefeatable" (or "indefeasible" to use the philosophers' term). More formally, we can define indefeasible justification in this way:

> S's belief that *p* is *indefeasibly* justified if and only if there is no further fact *q* such that if she came to believe *q*, she would no longer be justified in believing that *p*.

Notice that on this account, what prevents S's having knowledge is simply that *q* is true, whether or not S is aware of *q*. By contrast, what prevents S's having a justified belief is not simply that *q* is true, but that S is aware of the truth of *q*. So if S remains in ignorance of *q*, she can still have a justified belief that *p*, although not knowledge that *p*. An example will help to illustrate this.

Mary Anne claims to know that the burger bar is open. Her grounds for this belief are that today is a normal Saturday, when the burger bar is always open. Unbeknown to her, the owner was shot by an angry customer that very morning. This would normally have led to the closure of the bar, but it has remained open because the police have laid a trap. Thus, Mary Ann has a true belief for which she has good justification. However, the death of the owner is a defeating condition: it prevents Mary Anne's justified belief that the bar is open from being a case of knowledge, and it has this power whether or not Mary Anne knows that the owner has been killed. But the death of the owner does not in itself prevent Mary Anne from having a *justified belief* that the bar is open: she still has good reason for that belief, and no evidence that tells against it. It is only if she became aware that the owner had been killed that she would have counterevidence, and hence no longer be justified in believing that the bar was open.

Although convoluted, this is a promising suggestion. It allows us to hold on to the thought that knowledge is indeed a species of justified true belief; but it also explains why some cases of justified true belief do not count as knowledge. It explains why Mr. Smith, and others who find themselves in a similar situation do not really know what they think they know. Mr. Smith lacked knowledge that someone in his family had bought a car because unbeknown to him there was a fact which undermined his claim to know, namely the fact that his daughter was lying when she told him of her purchase of a car.

(ii) A defeated justification can be reinstated, redefeated, reinstated . . . ad infinitum

But once we start thinking about the concept of indefeasible justification, we can see that the account needs to be made a little more complicated. Let us give the label "counter" to any fact which is such that if I were to come to believe it, it would undermine my justification for holding a particular belief. The undermining might consist in either a total destruction or a partial destruction of my justification. Let us label these "total" and "partial" counters. The former would cover the case where the counter showed either that my justification was false, or that although it was true, it did not have *any* justificatory force. The latter would cover the case where the counter showed that even if the justification was true and had some justificatory power, it did not provide sufficient justification for my belief to count as adequately justified, and certainly not enough to make my belief a case of knowledge. The complication that we now have to take account of is that I may be adequately justified in holding on to a belief, even though there are total counters for my belief. To see how this can be so, consider the three following scenarios.

Scenario 1: I know my next-door neighbor Mr. Klein very well. We frequently socialize together, and I know exactly what he looks like. One day as I am coming out of my house, I see going into his house someone who looks exactly like Mr. Klein. We exchange a few words, and I go on my way convinced that I have just seen my neighbor going into his house. In fact, it was Mr. Klein, and there are no further facts which, were I to come to learn of them, would undermine my justification for believing that it was Mr. Klein. There are, in other words, no counters, total or partial. I thus have an indefeasibly justified true belief, and (on this account of knowledge at least) I have knowledge.

Scenario 2: This starts just like scenario 1 but in this case, there is a counter. Unbeknown to me, Mr. Klein has an identical twin. So alike are they that I would not be able to tell which was which, even if I saw them at close range and spoke to each of them in turn. The existence of the twin must clearly count as a total counter to my justification for believing that it was Mr. Klein whom I saw entering the house. The justification that I have (what the person looked like, how he spoke) fits Mr. Klein's brother just as well as it fits Mr. Klein. So if I came to know of the existence of the brother, my justification for thinking that it was Mr. Klein I had seen would be completely undermined. Hence, my justification is defeasible, thus I do not have indefeasibly justified belief, and so I do not have knowledge either, even though I may be right that it was Mr. Klein whom I just saw.

Scenario 3:   This starts just like scenario 2. I have seen a Klein-like person going in next door. The existence of Mr. Klein's identical twin is a total counter to my justification for thinking that it was Mr. Klein whom I saw. But, also unbeknown to me, there is a counter for the counter. For it happens to be true that if I were to ask Mrs. Klein where her brother-in-law is at the moment, she would tell me that he is currently in Australia. If I were now to learn both that Mr. Klein has an identical twin, and that Mrs. Klein would affirm that this twin is now in Australia, my justification for thinking that it was indeed Mr. Klein whom I had seen entering the house would remain intact. There is a counter for that justification (the existence of the twin), but there is also a counter for that counter (Mrs. Klein's claim that her brother-in-law is now in Australia).

A consideration of the three scenarios shows that if we are going to define knowledge as indefeasibly justified belief, we have to understand the notion of indefeasible justification in a certain way. What makes a belief indefeasibly justified is not, as we first suggested, that there is no counter for it. We need to incorporate the fact that my justification may still be indefeasible, even if there is a total counter for it, provided that there is also a counter for the counter! But now it becomes clear that in principle there could be a counter of a counter of a counter. This may sound like a joke, but consider a fourth scenario.

Scenario 4:   This is the same situation as in scenario 3 where Mrs. Klein's testimony is a counter to a counter. But now suppose that unbeknown to me, Mrs. Klein is a pathological liar. If I were to become aware of that fact, it would undercut the undermining power of her testimony that Mr. Klein's brother is now in Australia. It would hence leave uncountered the countering power of the fact that Mr. Klein has an identical twin. That fact would then be an uncountered counter to my original justification for thinking that it was Mr. Klein whom I had seen. So if Mrs. Klein is a pathological liar, that fact would be a counter of a counter to a counter. The counter is that Mr. Klein has an identical twin; the counter to the counter is that Mrs. Klein, if asked, would tell me that the twin is currently in Australia; the counter to the counter to the counter is that Mrs. Klein is a pathological liar. Let us give the label "second-level counter" to the counter to the counter, "third-level counter" to a counter to a counter to a counter, and so on.

So what the notion of indefeasible justification needs to incorporate is the thought that for knowledge, the justification for my belief must be *ultimately* indefeasible, where being "ultimately" indefeasible means either that there is no counter for my justification, or that if there is a counter, there is a second-level counter; and that if there is a third-level counter to that second-level one, then there is a fourth-level counter; and so on.

(iii) Sherlock Holmes was familiar with defeasibility

This account may sound very strange and remote from ordinary concerns. But it is easy to see how it is simply describing and ordering, in a rather strange language, some very familiar facts. Think of a detective, say Sherlock Holmes, gathering evidence about a crime. There are lots of bits of evidence that he collects (alibis, cartridge cases, eyewitness reports, etc.). On the basis of his evidence, he forms a hypothesis that a certain person is the criminal. But he knows that not all of the evidence he has will point in the same direction. Some evidence that he gets later in his inquiry will disprove the hypothesis that he formed at an earlier stage of the inquiry. The later evidence will show that the original hypothesis is no longer justified. But then still later evidence may swing the balance back again and reinstate the hypothesis that had been abandoned. What Holmes is doing as he formulates, abandons, and then reinstates various hypotheses in the light of his increasing evidence is discovering counters, then counters to counters, then counters to counters to counters, and so on.

(iv) Knowledge without indefeasible justification

There are other refinements to the indefeasibility analysis which could be added. But we now have enough detail for an assessment of the account to be possible. Let us grant for the sake of argument that if you have an indefeasibly justified true belief, then you have knowledge, and ask whether the converse is true: are there any cases of knowledge which are not cases of indefeasibly justified true belief? We will argue that S can know that p even when S has *no* justification for her belief, and *a fortiori* does not have an indefeasibly justified belief. From this it will follow that the indefeasibility account does not specify necessary conditions for knowledge, even if it does specify sufficient conditions.

One common type of case which suggests that knowledge does not require indefeasibly justified true belief is that in which we know something but cannot remember how or where we came to believe it, or what evidence was presented to us in support of the belief. For example, I know (and hence have a true belief) that light travels at approximately 186,000 m.p.h. Call this belief L. What is my justification for this belief? I cannot remember who told me that L was true or even whether I was told it rather than, for example, reading it somewhere. Nor have I (or could I) conduct any experiments of my own to prove the truth of L. The point here is not just that I am not now *conscious* of any other beliefs which would confirm L. Nor is it that I cannot by an effort of memory *summon them to consciousness*. The point is rather that I now *have* no beliefs which confirm L. What makes it true that I know L is that I was told it by someone who knew, and I have not forgotten what I was told, although I have forgotten being told it (or reading it in some authoritative text, etc.).

It is true that I might be able to *acquire* justification for my true belief in L if I am challenged. If I have access to authoritative texts or people, then I can acquire further beliefs of the form "The distinguished physicist Dr. Spanos has confirmed that L is true," and I could then use this belief as part of a justification for L. Alternatively, if I am a very reflective (or even philosophical!) sort of person, I might reflect that I am a cautious and rational person, that I would not have acquired the belief in the first place unless at the time, I had good evidence for it (e.g., that I was being informed by an expert); hence that the mere fact that I, as rational believer, hold the belief, is in itself evidence that the belief is true.

But the possibility of acquiring these *ex post facto* justifications is not a precondition of my having knowledge. They may help me to convince other people that I have knowledge, but they are not necessary conditions of my having the knowledge in the first place.

A great deal of our knowledge fits this pattern. At school, we learn dozens of facts which we retain even though we do not retain any beliefs about the circumstances in which we acquired these facts, nor any other beliefs which justify our acceptance of them. If pressed, we say something like "I suppose that I must have learned it at school." In such cases, we do not confirm our initial belief by saying that we learned it from an authoritative source; rather, we infer that we must have learned it from an authoritative source from the fact that we hold the belief.

If this line of thought is correct, it shows that justification, whether good or complete or indefeasible, cannot be essential to knowledge. Accordingly, we will turn in the next chapter to consider some attempts to define knowledge which drop the justification requirement altogether.

Exercises

1. Without rereading the chapter, write no more than one page explaining what capacity knowledge, knowledge by acquaintance, and propositional knowledge are. Illustrate your answer using the following examples:
   a. Jill knows that person in the corner
   b. Susan knows that the person in the corner is the mayor
   c. Tom knows the way to cook a soufflé
   d. Frank knows what I know
   Check your answers against sections 2.1 and 2.2 for accuracy, clarity, and completeness.

2. Try to construct a logical analysis of
   a. X is an aunt
   b. X is a student
   Critique your attempted answers in the way the text critiques attempted analyses of "X is a bachelor." Write no more than one page.
3. Without rereading the chapter, explain briefly what epistemic justification is and how it differs from other varieties. Write no more than one page.
4. Construct two Gettier-type examples of your own which are counterexamples to the JTB analysis. Make them as different as possible from the examples in the text. Explain your example to a fellow student and assess each other's examples for appropriateness.
5. Without rereading the chapter, explain the notion of "indefeasibility," using as your example the case of an historian trying to discover who killed President Kennedy. (Quite hard.)
6. Argue the case for believing that "S knows that p" can be true, even though S has neither good, nor complete, nor indefeasible justification for believing that p. (Hard.)

CHAPTER 3

Further Attempts to Define Propositional Knowledge

So far we have looked at three attempts to define knowledge. These relied on the idea that knowledge requires our beliefs to be supported by a justification which is either good, or complete, or indefeasible, and each of these ran into problems. In this chapter, we look at three more attempts to define "knowledge," which drop the justification requirement. At the end, we shall be in a position to draw some provisional conclusions both about the nature of propositional knowledge and about the philosophical method which consists in searching for analyses of sets of necessary and sufficient conditions.

3.1 Knowledge Defined as True Belief Acquired by a Reliable Method

According to "reliabilist" accounts of knowledge, what makes a true belief a case of knowledge is *not* that the knower has a justification for it, but that it has been produced in a certain way:

> For a belief to count as knowledge . . . it must be caused by a generally reliable process. (Goldman, *Epistemology and Cognition*, 51)

Let us try to unpack what is envisaged here.

There are different ways in which people acquire beliefs about the world around them. Sometimes they look and see for themselves whether something is so or not. Sometimes they rely on what other people tell them, by word of mouth, in books, on television, or in some other way (cf., 1.2[iii] on the sources of knowledge). Sometimes they reason things out for themselves from the information that they already have. There are also other more esoteric methods of acquiring beliefs. The Romans used to examine the entrails of a sacrificial chicken in order to forecast the future! In our own day, Jehovah's Witnesses try to achieve the same end by scrutinizing the Book of Revelation.

Other religious people take the content of dreams to be a portent for the future. Water diviners rely on the twitching of a twig to tell them of the presence of water. Some people consult astrological charts, others rely on palm-reading or examination of tarot cards, or even the arrangement of tea leaves left in the bottom when the tea has been drained to the last drop! There is clearly no limit to the variety of ways in which we can seek to acquire beliefs about the world.

Confronted with this variety, most of us will think, to put the matter at its weakest, that not all of these methods are equally reliable! Most of us will think that some methods are more reliable than others or more reliable for certain kinds of information, and some of us will think that some of these methods are wholly unreliable and reveal only the gullibility of their practitioners. The thought of the reliabilist is that if we divide possible methods of belief acquisition into those that are reliable and those that are not, we can then *define* knowledge as *true belief which has been acquired by a reliable method.* Thus our definition becomes:

S knows that p if and only if (i) p is true

(ii) S believes that p

(iii) S's belief that p has been acquired by a reliable method

(i) Does a reliable method have to be infallible or only one which *generally* yields true beliefs?

The first task in making this analysis more precise is to explain what is meant by "reliable." One way of taking this term, which we mention in order to dismiss it at once, is when it means "totally reliable," that is to say, never leads to error. This is unpromising because any method could in principle lead us astray on any particular occasion. Suppose my method is relying on the evidence of my own two eyes, and I am looking at something on my desk right in front of me. I come to believe that it is a pen. I know what a pen is, and I am looking at the object under favorable viewing conditions (the light is good, the object is right in front of me, etc.). But it is still possible that I have acquired a mistaken belief. The object may be a torch which has been designed to look exactly like a pen, it may be a paperweight which looks like a pen. Alternatively, I may make one of those unexplained mistakes, simply fail to notice an object in front of me at all, and acquire the belief that my desk is entirely clear.

The only way of meeting the objection that none of the methods which we use is totally reliable would be to distinguish between the method itself and our use of the method. Thus, we might say that if we have to add five 99's, the method of adding five 100's and then subtracting 5 is in itself totally reliable. It will always give the correct answer. If people who use the method sometimes get the wrong answer, that shows only that they have misapplied the method. We can, then, draw a distinction in some cases between the method and the use of the method. But it is very difficult to do this in all cases. This in fact leads to the question of how methods are to be demarcated from each other, which we shall discuss shortly.

We seem forced then to recognize that a reliable method need only be one which in general yields true beliefs. But we might well wonder whether a method which is only reliable in general is good enough for knowledge. To see why, consider the following example. Let us accept that looking someone up in the phone book is a reliable method of finding a person's phone number. We know that it is not infallible, because there can be misprints, people can change their phone number, and so on. But the method is certainly in general reliable (if it were not, there would be no point in publishing phone books at all). Suppose that I look up Ms. Krupke, and see that her number is recorded as 12345. In fact, her number *is* 12345, so I have acquired a true belief by a reliable method. But there are two extraordinary facts of which I am unaware: (1) when the phone book was printed, Ms. Krupke's number was 54321, and it was simply a misprint in the telephone directory to record it as 12345; (2) since the telephone directory was printed, Ms. Krupke has moved to a different address and acquired a new telephone number, which by amazing coincidence happens to be 12345! There are thus two errors in my acquisition of the belief about Ms. Krupke's number, but the two errors cancel each other out. I certainly end up with a true belief, but it is a matter of luck that I do so, because it is a matter of pure chance that Ms. Krupke happens to have moved to a new address whose phone number exactly matches the misprint in the old telephone directory. In such a case, it would surely be wrong to say that I knew what Ms. Krupke's number was.

Thus, what we need is the thought not just that the method is in general reliable, but that it is reliable in the particular case at hand. However, reliability is not something that can characterize a single occasion. The reliability of a method is the *tendency or disposition* of the method to give right answers in general. So the reliability of a method attaches to the *run* of answers which the method yields; it cannot attach to any individual answer. What attaches to any individual answer is correctness (or incorrectness). And a method which is only reliable in general will on occasion give incorrect answers.

(ii) Even a method which *generally* gives right answers might not be a "reliable" method

It seems, then, that whether we require the method to be infallible or merely reliable, the reliabilist is faced with some awkward problems. Let us assume for the sake of argument that she can solve these, and that she opts for the requirement that the method need only give right answers in general. Is that sufficient for being reliable? Some reliabilists have said "yes." Others have said "no," arguing that to be reliable, a method must be such that it not only yields true beliefs in actual circumstances, but it must also be such that it would have yielded true beliefs if circumstances had been different. An example will make the point clear.

Beth wants to know what the time is each morning as she goes to work, and her method of finding out is to look at the town hall clock. The clock shows 8:00 this morning, and Beth acquires the belief that it is 8:00. It is in fact 8:00, so Beth has acquired a true belief. Further, since looking at clocks is a generally reliable way to find out the time, she has acquired a true belief by a reliable method. But unbeknown to Beth, the clock has stopped. It has in fact not been going for over a week. Suppose that Beth has consulted the clock several times in the past week on her way to work, and the time is in fact 8:00 every time she looks. Then the method she has used to find out the time (looking at the town hall clock) has given her true beliefs. And yet surely the method she has used is not a reliable method. It seems that for the method to be reliable, it must be the case not just that it does give true beliefs but also that it would have given true beliefs in slightly different circumstances. In Beth's case, if the circumstances had been very slightly different (say she had looked at 7:45 or at 8:15) she would have acquired a false belief. Indeed, had she looked at any time other than 8:00, she would have acquired a false belief. The moral, then, seems to be that in order to be reliable, a method must be such that not only does it generally lead to true beliefs, it must also be the case that it would have led to true beliefs if the circumstances had been slightly different. If the clock had been going, this requirement would have been met. It would have shown 8:00 if Beth had looked at 8:00. But it would also have shown 7:00 had she looked at 7:00, 9:00 if she had looked at 9:00, and so on. If the clock is going, then not only does it show the right time when people look, it would have shown the right time if Beth or other people had looked at other times when in fact they did not. It seems that this latter fact is essential if looking at the town hall clock is to be a reliable method of finding out the time.

(iii) How can the relevant hypothetical circumstances be identified?

There are, however, at least two problems with this development in the reliabilist account, one specific and one general. The specific one is that there seems no principle by means of which we can demarcate the relevant hypothetical circumstances which need to be taken into account in order to determine whether the method is reliable or not. In Beth's case, presumably the factors which are relevant to determining whether her method is reliable or not include what beliefs she would have acquired if she had looked at the clock at other times. But in other cases, the time at which a belief is acquired, and hence the question of what beliefs would have been acquired at different times, may have nothing to do with the reliability of the method used.

The second and more general problem arises from the invocation of hypothetical circumstances. Since this is a point of some importance which will recur in other contexts, let us examine it a little further. We can think of the history of the universe as a sequence of different states of affairs succeeding one another in time. We can imagine that this sequence could have been different from the way that it actually was. We can imagine it both as being only very slightly different (as, for example, if we think of Napoleon at Waterloo having his handkerchief in his left pocket instead of right pocket); or we can think of it as very different (as, for example, when we contemplate how the world would have been if Hitler had won the Second World War); and we can even think of it as radically different (as when we imagine what it would have been like, say, if the dinosaurs had never been wiped out or Homo sapiens had never developed). These different ways of imagining the world are contrary to what we know the facts actually to be, and so they are called contrary-to-fact, or counterfactual, assumptions. They are expressed in propositions which are known as counterfactual conditional propositions (sometimes counterfactual hypothetical propositions). These are "If . . . then . . ." propositions, which often take the form "If such-and-such had been the case, then so-and-so would have been the case" or "If such-and-such were the case, then so-and-so would be the case."

Propositions of this kind are philosophically puzzling. It is very difficult to develop a satisfactory account of their logical behavior (i.e., what they imply and what implies them)—witness the fact that the standard account of implication sketched in the Logic Appendix does not cover these cases. There are also puzzles over their epistemology (how we can come to know them to be true or have a reasonable belief in their truth). In general, then, if we are trying to elucidate a concept (such as the concept of knowledge), it is not a good idea to invoke counterfactual assumptions. This would be seeking to elucidate the less obscure by the more obscure. If we had a good account of counterfactuals, we should be able to answer the problem raised above about which hypothetical or counterfactual circumstances ought to be taken into account in determining the reliability of a method. Presumably the additional condition that the reliabilist account needs is that the method generally gives the right answer when it is actually used and would have given the right answer in counterfactual situations which are only slightly different from the actual situations. An adequate account of counterfactuals would enable us to be more precise about what counts as "only slightly different," and why.

(iv) The notion of a "reliable" method is vague in two more ways

There are two further problems with the notion of a reliable method. First, a method might have a poor record of reliability in general, but yet be a very good method over a small range of cases. If Lynn is an expert mathematician, then asking her is likely to be a highly reliable method of acquiring mathematical beliefs. But if Lynn is also very unworldly, asking her is likely to be a very unreliable method of acquiring information about the Stock Exchange. If, then, I have acquired the belief that p by a particular method M, and the question arises whether the method was reliable, are we asking how reliable M is in producing all the beliefs which it does produce, or how reliable M is in producing beliefs like p? It seems that it ought to be the latter, since that gives us the more discriminating assessment of reliability. But if we do take that choice, we will have added a further vagueness to the "reliable method" account. For the notion of "being a belief like p" (whatever belief p may be) is extremely vague.

The second problem arises from the vagueness of what is meant by a "method." This can be neatly illustrated by looking again at Beth. What method was she using to find out the time? Should the method be described as "looking at a town hall clock"? Or should it be described as "looking at a clock which had stopped"? Even if we grant that the first is a reliable method, the second is clearly a very unreliable method. And yet both descriptions apply to what Beth did. She of course did not know that the second description applied and would doubtless have referred only to the first. But why should we assume a person is the best guide to which method she is using? Nor is this a problem which arises only with a limited range of unusual examples. Suppose that Richard knows that there are mountains on the moon. When we ask how he knows, he replies "The woman I was speaking to at the party told me." Suppose the woman is in fact his neighbor, and is also a professor of astrophysics. Is the method which Richard is relying on "accepting what someone at a party tells him"? Or "accepting what his neighbor tells him"? Or "accepting what an astrophysicist tells him"? Each of these is a description of how Richard came to acquire his belief. Which description tells us the method he was using? More importantly, and more generally, given any believer, by what principle can we identify the description which picks out the method she was using? Unless we can do this, unless we can say what the method was, we are in no position to raise the question "Is that method a reliable method?"

(v) Vagueness apart, a reliable method may fail to yield knowledge

The position so far, then, is that the "reliable" part of the reliable method account of knowledge is confronted by unpleasant choices which push it in the direction of intolerable vagueness. The requirement of infallible success is too strong, the requirement of general success is too weak. Further, to assess reliability, we have to consider not just actual success rates, but also hypothetical success rates in nonexistent circumstances; furthermore, we have to assess them in relation to an ill-defined class of beliefs. And in relation to the "method" component, we have no principled means of telling what is to count as the method which a given believer has used.

However, even if these vaguenesses in the account can be removed, the account still does not look hopeful as an analysis of knowledge. For someone can be using a method which is reliable in both actual and counterfactual instances, and is reliable in relation to beliefs of the kind which she acquires, and yet even though she acquires a true belief, she does not gain knowledge. For it can still be the case that a belief yielded by a method which meets these demanding conditions for reliability is true just by chance. Suppose I wonder whether Anne has handled a gun that was later found at the scene of a crime. A reliable way of finding out is to see if her fingerprints are on the gun. I discover that they are on the gun, and I forthwith acquire the belief that Anne has handled the gun. Let us suppose that Anne has indeed handled the gun. So I have a true belief, acquired by a reliable method. But unbeknown to me, immediately after handling the gun, Anne wiped it clean of all her fingerprints. The fingerprints that I found on the gun had been discovered by a bent detective going through Anne's flat. He had taken the fingerprints from a glass in Anne's flat and transferred them to the gun in an attempt to incriminate Anne. If this is how Anne's fingerprints came to be on the gun, I take it that I do not know that Anne has handled the gun, even though my true belief was acquired by a reliable method. It is simply by chance that use of a reliable method has yielded a true belief in this case.

It seems, then, that we have still not found a satisfactory analysis of knowledge.

3.2 Knowledge Defined as Appropriately Caused True Belief

(i) The causal analysis of "S knows that p" explained

What is generally called the "causal analysis" of knowledge accepts the first two conditions laid down by the previous accounts we have looked at but differs on the third condition. What it offers us is the following:

S knows that p if and only if (i) p is true

(ii) S believes that p

(iii) what p is about is causally connected in the appropriate way with S's belief that p

What does this mean? It means that what distinguishes cases of knowledge from cases of true belief is *not* justification (as in the JTB account) but the causal connections of the belief. If a true belief has the right sort of causal connections, then it is knowledge; if it has the wrong sort of causal connections, it is merely true belief. And what makes the causal connections of a belief the right sort of causal connections is (very roughly and for many cases) that they connect the belief to the event which the belief is about. An example will make this clear.

Consider again the Smith family and their car. Mr. Smith's belief that someone in his family has bought a car is caused by his daughter's telling him that she has bought a car, in combination with his background belief that his daughter is very honest and reliable. Why the daughter lies in this case does not matter, but we are told for a fact that the daughter did not buy a car, and so it could not have been the event of the daughter's buying a car which caused Mr. Smith's belief that someone in the family had just bought a car. By contrast, the event which does make Mr. Smith's belief true (namely that Mrs. Smith has just bought a car) is causally *unconnected* with Mr. Smith's belief that someone has just bought a car. It is not because of Mrs. Smith's purchase that Mr. Smith holds the belief that he does.

We can represent the position as follows, using arrows to indicate causal connections (see Figure 1):

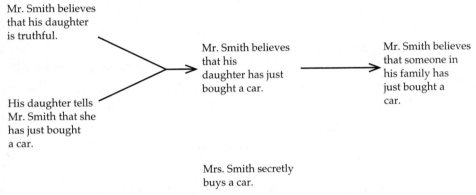

FIGURE 1 Read "➜" as " . . . is part of what brings it about that . . .," or (more briefly) "causes."

By contrast, imagine the position slightly changed. Suppose that Mr. Smith's daughter did buy a car and told her father so. Then given the honesty of the daughter and her lack of motive for lying in this particular case, we surely would say that Mr. Smith knew that someone in his family had just bought a car. On the causal analysis, Mr. Smith's true belief would amount to knowledge in this case because it is directly caused by the very event which makes it true. It is caused by what the daughter says to Mr. Smith, and that in turn is caused by the daughter's purchase of the car. So Mr. Smith's belief that someone in the family has bought a car is caused by someone in the family buying a car.

These two examples suggest that a causal analysis might be able to explain why some cases of true belief are cases of knowledge and some are not, by reference to the causal connections of the belief. It implies that the causal origin of a true belief is more important from the point of view of knowledge, than whether the believer has a justification for his belief. Of course it is quite possible both that the believer has a justification and that her belief has the right sort of causal connections. But such cases will be examples of knowledge in virtue of the causal connections of the belief, not in virtue of the believer's justification.

Let us see how the causal account will apply to other cases. I have a true belief that the Second World War started in 1939. Do I know that this is correct? Ordinarily we would not hesitate to say so. Suppose that I was told so by a reputable authority or read it in a very reliable textbook, and that at the time, I understood that this was not a matter of debate and controversy, but something accepted by every reputable historian. But suppose that I now cannot remember who first told me the date, nor what reputable sources later confirmed that the date was certain beyond dispute. It is then very difficult to see what justification I have for my belief, and hence very difficult to see how, on the JTB account, I could be credited with knowledge. But on the causal account, by contrast, given that my belief was caused by what reputable historians once told me (or told other reliable people who told other reliable people . . . who told me) and given that the historians' belief was itself caused by evidence produced by the outbreak of the war, my true belief will count as knowledge. For it will be a true belief caused by the event which makes it true. So if it is right to think (as surely it is) that I do know when the Second World War began, it seems that this is a judgment which can be accommodated much more easily by a causal analysis than by a JTB analysis. My knowledge could be represented as follows (see Figure 2):

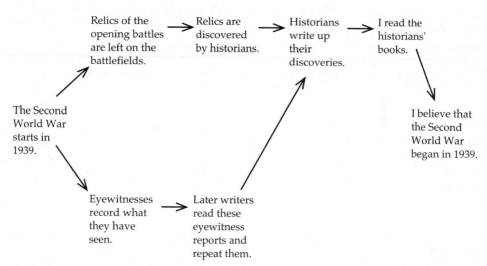

FIGURE 2

So far, the cases of knowledge we have considered have involved beliefs which were caused by the events which made them true. Mr. Smith's true belief that someone in his family had just bought a car was caused by the fact that someone in his family had just bought a car; my true belief that the Second World War began in 1939 was caused by the outbreak of the war in 1939. But what about cases of knowledge of the future? If we make the very plausible assumption that later events cannot be the cause of earlier events, it is clear that if I have a belief about a future event, my belief cannot be caused by the event which it is about: when I first hold my belief, the event which it is about has not yet occurred and hence cannot be what caused my belief. So if knowledge of the future is to be possible under the causal analysis, it will not do to say that what makes a true belief knowledge is that it is caused by what the belief is about. But even if the belief is not caused by what it is about, it can still be causally connected to what it is about. How is this possible? One possibility is that the belief and what it is about must both be the effects of some third factor which causes both of them.

Again, an example will make this clearer. Suppose that Jenny intends to go to Denver next week, and she tells you of her intention. Knowing her to be completely reliable on such matters, you acquire the belief that she will go to Denver next week. Sure enough, when next week arrives, she does go to Denver. So the first two conditions for knowledge are clearly met: you do have a true belief. The question is: did you know before Jenny went that she would go? Your true belief that she would go was not caused by her going, since at the time you acquired the belief, she had not gone. The case is thus different from the modified Smith case and the Second World War case. But your belief, and the event that made it true (namely, Jenny's trip to Denver) are both indirectly caused by the same thing, namely Jenny's original intention to go to Denver. Her intention to go caused her both to go to Denver and to tell you that she was going. Her telling you that she was going, together with your background belief in her reliability, caused you to believe that she would go to Denver the next week. We can represent this situation as follows (see Figure 3):

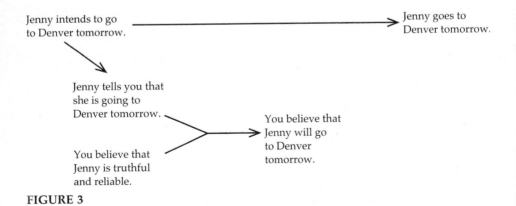

FIGURE 3

It is true that in this case, you do have an adequate justification for your belief that Jenny will go to Denver and it is true (let us suppose) that your justification is indefeasible. So on the JTB analysis of knowledge, and on some modified JTB analyses, this would count as a case of knowledge. But according to a causal account, the reason that this is a case of knowledge is not that you have a correct justification, but that your belief has the right causal connections. Even if you had no justification for your true belief, it would still have been a case of knowledge provided that your belief was caused in the right sort of way.

Does a causal analysis, then, provide us with a satisfactory account of knowledge? Critics have identified several problems which it faces. We will mention two of these, one concerned with the scope of knowledge, and the other concerned with so-called deviant causal chains.

(ii) First objection to the causal analysis: our mathematical beliefs cannot be causally connected with what makes them true

Let us take first the problem about scope. So far, we have been considering examples where a putative knower has a belief about some specific event, past, present, or future (someone in the family buying a car, the date a war began, a visit to Denver). The central fact about all events is that they take place at a time or over a period of time. There is a date at which they occur or a period during which they occur. Very often, when we speak of one thing causing another, we have in mind a causal connection between events, between kinds of things which happen in time. It is because we think of causal connections as holding between things in time that it makes sense to say that causes must precede their effects. If either a cause or an effect was not something that occurred at a time or during a period of time, it would not make sense to say that it must precede or follow anything. So if we are thinking of causal connections between beliefs and what makes them true, we are thinking of what makes our beliefs true as being events, as being occurrences in time. But (and this is where problems emerge for the causal analysis of knowledge) many of the beliefs we hold are not about specific occurrences at all. They are not about things which occur in time or over a period of time, and hence they are not about things which could be causally related to our beliefs. Insofar as we have knowledge in such cases, therefore, it is knowledge which is not appropriately caused true belief, and hence the causal analysis of knowledge must fail.

What are these beliefs which are not beliefs about occurrences in time? There are several kinds of such beliefs, but we will mention one kind to illustrate the problem. Consider Louise's true belief that 65,537 is a prime number. Her belief will certainly have a cause. Perhaps she knows the Fermat formula which would enable her to work it out for herself; perhaps she has been told it by an honest and competent mathematician. But one thing that will not have been the cause of her belief, nor even causally connected with her belief, is the number 65,537, for this is not an entity which exists in time. It is not something that starts to exist at a particular moment in time, it does not get older day by day. It is a nontemporal kind of thing, and as such it cannot act as the cause of any of our beliefs. To say this is not necessarily to say that we cannot have beliefs about 65,537, or that we cannot have knowledge about it. It is to claim only that when we do have beliefs or knowledge about it, our belief is not caused by the number itself.

(iii) Second objection: appropriate versus deviant causal chains

Let us turn now to the second of the standard problems that have been raised for the causal analysis, the problem of deviant causal chains. The causal analysis tells us that a true belief counts as knowledge if it has an appropriate causal connection with what makes the belief true. The problem is to say what is meant here by "appropriate" and to say how an appropriate causal connection can be distinguished from an inappropriate one. It can be illustrated with the following example. We are back with the Smith family again, but in a different scenario. In this new example, Mr. Smith's daughter tells both her parents that she has just bought a car, and Mr. Smith (knowing his daughter to be very truthful) acquires the belief that someone in the family has just bought a car. However, Mrs. Smith, being more perceptive than Mr. Smith, can tell that the daughter is lying, reasoning to herself that the daughter is really hinting how much she would like a car, and so Mrs. Smith secretly goes and buys one, intending to give it to the daughter in the near future. We can represent the situation as follows (see Figure 4):

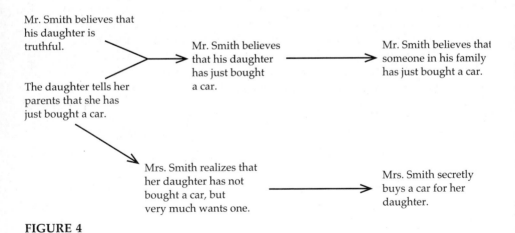

FIGURE 4

Here, Mr. Smith's true belief *is* causally connected to the event which makes it true. For his belief (that someone in his family has just bought a car) and the event which makes it true (Mrs. Smith's purchase of a car) are both caused by the daughter's original remark. They are coeffects of a third event which is their common cause. This is precisely the sort of causal connection which earlier we suggested should count as appropriate when we were talking about knowledge of the future. And yet surely in this case, we ought to say that Mr. Smith did not really know what he thought he knew. So what stops this being a case of knowledge cannot be that there is no causal connection between Mr. Smith's belief and what makes it true. It is rather that there is a causal connection, but it is the wrong kind of connection to turn true belief into knowledge. But given that it is the same kind of connection which we invoked to allow knowledge of the future, why does it count as the wrong kind of connection in the revised scenario illustrated above? So, the critic concludes, either we have to retract what we said about knowledge of the future, or we have to say that in this case, Mr. Smith does have knowledge, or we would have to produce a quite different account of what an "appropriate" causal connection is. Hence, she concludes, the causal analysis is either unable to accommodate knowledge of the future, or misclassifies some cases of true belief as knowledge, or is radically incomplete.

It is not clear how strong this second objection is. The problem of so-called deviant causal chains is one which confronts causal analyses of other philosophically important concepts (causal analyses of perception, of memory, of inference, etc.). Proponents of such analyses, while acknowledging that there is a problem, imply that it is not a serious one, and certainly not important enough to warrant abandoning a causal theory altogether. Critics of the analyses claim that on the contrary, the problem *is* an important one, and is one to which no solution is forthcoming.

Our own view is that the first of these reactions is correct. But rather than pursue the point here, let us turn to one final attempt at giving an analysis of propositional knowledge, to see if that can provide an unproblematic account.

3.3 Knowledge Defined as True Belief Which "Tracks" Reality: Nozick

(i) The "tracking" analysis of "S knows that p" explained

The last attempt to analyze the concept of knowledge which we shall look at is the so-called tracking account, associated particularly with the work of Nozick (1984). As with the previous accounts, Nozick accepts as unproblematic that the two necessary but not sufficient conditions for the truth of "S knows that p" are that

(i) p is true, and
(ii) S believes that p

What Nozick says we need to add to the two conditions is the idea that S's belief is somehow dependent on the truth of what it is that she believes, and that *she would not have believed* p *if* p *had not been true.* The causal account was trying to capture the same idea in saying that S's belief must be causally connected to the fact that p. But as we have seen, this creates problems about the possibility of certain types of knowledge, such as mathematical knowledge. What Nozick suggests as a third condition is something rather simpler in appearance, namely

(iii) if p were not true, S would not believe that p

Let us see how this condition applies in particular cases.

Suppose we think back to the very first of our examples (in 2.5) where Mr. Smith's daughter simply lies to her father, and Mr. Smith on the basis of what his daughter has said acquires the true belief that someone in his family has just bought a car. On the tracking account, this would not count as knowledge because it will not pass condition (iii). Even if nobody in Mr. Smith's family had bought a car, Mr. Smith would still have believed that someone in his family had just bought a car, because his belief is based on what his daughter has told him and not on what his wife has (unbeknown to him) done—and it is what his wife has done that makes his belief true. As long as his daughter tells her father that she has just bought a car, and as long as the father has no reason to distrust the daughter, the father will believe that someone in his family has just bought a car, whether or not they have. So the following statement is not true:

> If "someone in Mr. Smith's family has just bought a car" were not true then Mr. Smith would not believe that someone in his family had just bought a car.

So condition (iii) is not met, and that is why in this case Mr. Smith does not have knowledge. (There are some complications here which we shall have to come back to in a moment, but prima facie the tracking account could give us the result we want in this case.)

What about the modified example with the Smith family, discussed in section 3.2(iii), the example that proved fatal to the causal analysis? This was the case where Mrs. Smith is caused to buy a car by hearing the daughter tell her father that she (the daughter) has just bought a car. Here too it seems that the tracking account can explain why this is not a case of knowledge. It fails to be a case of knowledge because again the third condition is not satisfied. That is to say: it is not the case that if no one in Mr. Smith's family had just bought a car, Mr. Smith would not have believed that someone in his family had just bought a car. For Mr. Smith would have believed that someone in his family had just bought a car, provided only that his daughter tells him that she has bought a car. So, if Mrs. Smith had not bought a car, and no one else in the family had bought a car, Mr. Smith would still have believed that someone in the family had just bought a car.

To see how we might have a genuine case of knowledge under this account, consider a different scenario. Suppose Mr. Smith goes with his daughter when she buys a car. Mr. Smith actually witnesses the purchase of the car, and on the basis of what he has witnessed, believes that someone in his family has bought a car. Here condition (iii) is satisfied: Mr. Smith would not have held his belief that someone in his family had just bought a car, unless he had witnessed the fact, and he would not have witnessed the fact unless someone in his family had actually bought a car. So if it had been false that someone in his family had just bought a car, Mr. Smith would not have believed that someone had.

We can also see how on this account of knowledge, mathematical knowledge would be possible, or at least would raise fewer problems than it did on the causal account. Suppose that Jennifer calculates the square of 25 and arrives at the answer 625. She has a true belief that 25 squared is 625. Is this a case of knowledge? According to the three conditions we are currently considering, it would be knowledge if this condition were met:

If 25 squared had not been 625, then she would not have believed that it was.

This is admittedly a rather odd condition. Since we know that 25 squared is 625, and indeed has to be 625, it is strange to speculate about what would have been the case if 25 squared had been something else. But nevertheless, it surely is a condition which could be met. If someone is a competent arithmetical calculator, then it must surely follow that if a calculation had been incorrect, they would not have accepted it. And if this is true, then it must surely be right to assert the condition above which we described as an odd one.

(ii) A problem: being caused to believe the truth by electrical stimulation

Do these three conditions, then, give us an acceptable definition of knowledge? Nozick argues that by themselves they do not. There can be cases where all three conditions are met, and yet we would not have a case of knowledge. Here is an example of the type of case which Nozick has in mind: suppose that I am a supercompetent scientist of the future, and you are my victim. I have you strapped to a table, I attach myriads of wires to your cortex, so that by stimulating your brain, I can induce in you any set of beliefs and any set of experiences that I choose. I can make you believe, for example, that you are not strapped to an operating table, but are instead prowling through the Amazonian jungle. I can make you think that you are seeing, hearing, smelling, tasting, and feeling, precisely the sights, noises, scents, and so on, appropriate to such an activity. I can change all your memory beliefs too, so that while you believe you are prowling through the jungle, you also believe that you are a famous explorer, who has done this sort of thing many times before. Alternatively, I could make you think that you are sitting in a concert hall listening to a particular piece of music. I could make you believe that you see the orchestra playing, that you hear exactly the sequence of sounds for a rendition of,

say, Haydn's 85th symphony, and so on. In short, I can make you have any
set of beliefs I like. Now suppose that the set of beliefs that I make you have
is that you are strapped to my operating table, with electrodes stimulating
your brain, by means of which I am inducing beliefs in you. In other words, I
induce in you a set of beliefs which is in fact true. But I do not allow you to
acquire these beliefs in the ordinary way, for example, by letting you use your
eyes to see for yourself what your situation is. Instead, I feed the beliefs
directly into your brain via the electrodes. The question now is: given that you
have a true belief that you are strapped to a table, with electrodes stimulating
your brain, by means of which I am inducing beliefs in you, does this true
belief count as knowledge?

It is clear that the first two conditions of knowledge are met. It is true that
you are strapped to a table, and so on, and it is also true that you believe this.
It is also the case that condition (iii) is met. For if it had not been the case that
you were strapped to a table, I would not have been able to induce this belief
in you via the electrodes to your brain, and hence you would not have believed
that you were strapped to a table. But although our three conditions are met,
it seems wrong to describe this as a case of knowledge. The problem is, in Nozick's useful phrase, that while you are strapped to the table, your belief that
you are so strapped is not "sensitive to the truth." It is not because your belief
is true that you believe it; it is a mere coincidence that your belief and the truth
coincide in this particular case. I could have produced any belief in you by
simply altering the cortical stimulation I was giving you.

(iii) A further condition is necessary

What then is required for the "sensitivity to the truth" which Nozick speaks
of? He suggests a fourth condition:

(iv) if p is (were) true, then S believes (would believe) p

Condition (iii) tells us that for knowledge, S's belief must be sensitive to the
falsity of p (because it tells us that if p were false, S would not believe it); condition (iv) tells us that S's belief must be sensitive to the truth of p (because it
tells us that if p is true, S will believe it). What the two conditions are intended
to capture is the thought that when S knows that p, S believes that p *because* it
is true. When these two conditions are met, Nozick says that S's belief that p
"tracks" the fact that p.

If we accept condition (iv), we can now explain why your true belief that
you have been strapped to the operating table does not count as knowledge.
It is not true of you that if you are now strapped to the table in the manner
described, you will believe that you are strapped to the table. What is requi-
site for you to hold the belief is not just that you are strapped to the table, but
also that I choose to induce in you precisely the belief that you are so strapped.
So your belief that you are strapped down is not sensitive to the truth that you
have been strapped down and hence is not knowledge.

(iv) The tracking account fails for familiar reasons

But now we might wonder whether our four conditions are not too demanding. Consider the following case. Suppose that I acquire the true belief that my brother Jim has arrived, and I acquire it because my sister Lucy, who has seen Jim arrive, tells me so. But suppose that if he hadn't arrived, I would still have believed that he had because my other sister Hilary (who is normally completely reliable, but in this instance is intent on deceiving me) would have told me that he had, and I would have believed her. In such a case, condition (iii) is not met: it is not the case that if Jim had not arrived, I would not have believed that he had. And yet surely, we would say in such a case that I knew that Jim had arrived. After all, I had been informed by a reliable informant who herself knew that Jim had arrived.

A different example will suggest that condition (iv) is also too demanding. By chance I meet an old friend, and in the course of conversation, he tells me that he as just seen a recent production of *Hamlet.* Knowing my friend to be truthful, I acquire the true belief that he has just seen *Hamlet.* Do I know that he has just seen *Hamlet?* Surely I do. But this is a case in which condition (iv) of the tracking analysis is not met. For it is not in general true that if my friend has seen *Hamlet,* I will believe that he has. Whether I believe that he has depends also (a) on my chance meeting with him and (b) on what he happens to tell me. It would have been quite possible for him to have seen *Hamlet* and yet not met me, or for him to have met me and yet not told me that he had seen *Hamlet.* In either case, it would not have been true that if my friend saw *Hamlet,* then I will believe that he did.

To cope with the first kind of case, Nozick introduces the idea of a method of acquiring beliefs. In the case of my brother Jim, my method of acquiring my belief that he has arrived is reliance on the testimony of Lucy, not on the testimony of Hilary. So when the third condition says that if I am to know that Jim has arrived, it must be the case that if he had not arrived, I would not have believed that he had, we must understand this to be saying "I would not have believed that he had, if I were relying only on the method which in fact I relied on, namely the testimony of Lucy."

Nozick suggests that the same idea of a method of acquiring beliefs will also apply in the second kind of case. The thought here would be that if my friend has seen *Hamlet,* and I am to form any belief as to whether he has seen *Hamlet* or not, then *if I rely on what he tells me* (this is the relevant method), I will acquire the belief that he has seen *Hamlet.* Hence condition (iv) is satisfied.

But we may well feel that the tracking account is now beginning to lose its attractiveness. We saw in connection with reliabilism that it seems impossible to specify in any principled way what is to count as a method of acquiring beliefs, a way which will allow the concept of a method to do the work which is being demanded of it here. What general grounds could we have for saying that being told something by Lucy is one method, and being told something by Hilary is another method? Why don't they both count as cases of a single method, namely, being told by one's sister, or being told by a family member, or being told by a reliable informant? What is to stop us making the specification of the method arbitrarily more fine-grained, so that for example, being told something by Hilary in January counts as one method, and being told something by Hilary in February counts as a second method? The concept of a method is simply too vague to perform the tasks which Nozick is here expecting of it.

Further, even if we could get clear what is to count as the same method, and why, the fourth condition seems still too restrictive. Think again of my *Hamlet*-viewing friend, and suppose that my only method of acquiring a belief about whether he has seen *Hamlet* is by reliance on what he tells me when we meet. Even if he does tell me of his theater trip, and I thus acquire a true belief, it would clearly have been entirely possible for him not to have mentioned *Hamlet* at all. If he had not, then I would not have acquired the belief that in fact I did acquire. So it could easily have been the case that he saw *Hamlet*, without my believing that he had. So on the tracking account, condition (iv) is not met, and I do not have knowledge. But the fact that it *could* have been the case (although it was not in fact the case) that my friend kept quiet about *Hamlet* is surely insufficient to show that if he does tell me about his theater trip and I believe him, I nevertheless do not know that he has seen *Hamlet*.

Finally, the tracking account, like reliabilism before it, relies heavily on the notion of counterfactual possibilities. It requires us to utilize the idea of what would have been the case, if the facts had been different. Would I still have believed *p*, if *p* had been false? Would I still have believed *p*, if *p* had been true, but the world had been slightly different? Nozick recognizes that there is a problem here, but comments that "our purposes require, for the most part, no more than an intuitive understanding of subjunctives [i.e., of propositions of the form 'If *p* had been true, *q* would have been true too']" (Nozick, 1984, 680, n. 8). But it is not clear that this response is wholly adequate. One of the aims of a philosophical analysis is to pass beyond a merely "intuitive understanding" of a concept. We want to be able not just to use the concept correctly, but to have an explicit grasp of its logical and epistemological behavior. After all, we start off with an "intuitive understanding" of the concept of knowledge. If this kind of understanding were philosophically adequate, there would be no need for the tracking account or any of the other attempts to analyze knowledge which we have looked at.

3.4 Why No Satisfactory Analysis of "*S* Knows That *p*" Has Been Found

We have looked at five attempts to offer a definition or analysis of propositional knowledge of the kind that recent philosophers have favored, and none of the ones we have looked at has proved *wholly* satisfactory. The exercise has, however, been very instructive. First of all, we have learned that there is universal agreement that knowledge requires truth. Secondly, there is an almost equally widespread agreement that knowledge requires belief. The disagreement arises on what more is required for knowledge than true belief. We can certainly say in negative terms what more is needed. If I know that *p*, then it must not be merely by chance, or by accident, or by coincidence that my belief is true. It must be, in some sense of the word, *because* what I believe is true that I believe it. The differences between the accounts we have looked at derive from their different ways of interpreting this fact.

Is there, then, some perfect account waiting to be discovered, an account which will specify in unproblematic terms necessary and sufficient conditions for the truth of claims of the form *"S* knows that *p"*? It is certainly still possible to think so. Perhaps some future attempt will be successful. On the other hand, one cannot help viewing the repeated failure to provide a conceptual analysis of knowledge with a feeling of suspicion about the whole enterprise. Over the past thirty years, ever since the publication of Gettier's article, enormous efforts have been expended on this problem by large numbers of able philosophers. There have been literally hundreds of articles and books devoted to producing an analysis of knowledge. Why has no consensus emerged? Why has there not been a convergence of views on one particular type of theory?

A possible answer to this is that the search itself is misguided. It may be that analyses of the kind being sought are simply not available for most ordinary everyday concepts like knowledge. Many everyday concepts have vague boundaries or merge by degrees into something else (think, for example, of color concepts, or of terms like "fat" or "facetious," "bald" or "boring," "healthy" or "happy," "tall" or "tiring"). In a famous analogy, Wittgenstein likened the features of entities described by a word to the strands of which a rope is composed. It may be that no one strand runs the whole length of the rope. Instead, the rope is made up of a series of shorter strands each of which overlaps with its neighboring stands. Similarly, when we look at a cluster of objects all denoted by a single term, there may be no one feature or set of features which they all have in common, and which separate them off from entities of a different kind. Wittgenstein illustrated this in connection with the concept of game. Some have an element of competition, but not all (think of ring-around-the-rosy); some require more than one player, but not all (think of solitaire); some are played for fun, but not all (think of professional sports); and so on. The relationship between all the different things we call games is (Wittgenstein suggested) more like a family resemblance:

> I can think of no better expression to characterise these similarities than "family resemblances"; for the various resemblances between members of a family: build, features, colour of eyes, gait, temperament, etc. etc. overlap and criss-cross in the same way. And I shall say: "games" form a family (Wittgenstein, *Philosophical Investigations*, Pt. I, sec. 67)

It is a controversial question how far Wittgenstein thought that his remarks about family resemblance could be extended. Some commentators think that he was simply pointing out that some terms functioned like this, that we must not expect definitions in terms of necessary and sufficient conditions for all meaningful terms. Others argue that the family resemblance doctrine is meant to have universal application and hence to show us that no terms have necessary and sufficient conditions. This latter position certainly is too extreme, not just for technical reasons (every concept gives necessary and sufficient conditions for itself!) but also because ordinary language does contain concepts where the approach in terms of necessary and sufficient conditions seems successful (think of kinship terms like "brother" and "sister" [male and female sibling], "father" and "mother" [male and female parent]; or some status terms like "bachelor" or "spinster" [see the discussion in 2.2(i)]; or terms like "vixen" [female fox], "lamb" [young sheep], etc.).

Would it matter if there were no definitions for certain terms, even for philosophically important ones? The short answer is "no." It is a mistake to think that it is necessarily a defect in a term if it cannot be pinned down by a set of necessary and sufficient conditions. In some contexts (mathematics is the most obvious example) it may be a merit to have definitions available. In other areas, our vocabulary can function perfectly well without any such definitions (think here of terms defining musical genres, like "classical" and "romantic," "jazz" and "blues," "folk" and "rock").

Where, then, does that leave the search for the definition of knowledge? Does knowledge have a definition or not? Our conclusion here must be provisional, but at the moment the state of current research does not justify the belief that there is a definition to be found.

Exercises

1. Without rereading the chapter, write no more than one page explaining why a reliable method need not be infallible but needs to do more than usually yield correct answers. When you have done this, check your answers against (i) and (ii) for accuracy, clarity, and completeness.

2. Most people learn what they know about the activities of their government by listening to television reports. Bearing in mind the discussion of 3.1, assess whether this is a reliable method in the case of your own government. Write no more than one page.

3. Without rereading the chapter, explain how according to the causal account, a future event, like your next birthday, could be connected causally to a present belief in such a way as to yield knowledge. Write no more than one page.

4. Imagine an archaeologist trying to reconstruct how Stone Age people lived in a village which she is excavating. Describe ways in which her beliefs might be "appropriately" caused, and hence count as knowledge, and ways in which the same beliefs might be "inappropriately" caused, and thus not count as knowledge.

5. Imagine that a very skilled hypnotist is causing someone to believe whatever she (the hypnotist) chooses. Use this example to explain why Nozick's first three conditions are insufficient, and why his fourth condition is needed. Check your answer against 3.3.
6. Assess why attempts to provide a logical analysis of "S knows that p" have not been 100 percent successful so far, and say what you think the significance of this is. (Hard.)

CHAPTER 4

When Is a Belief Adequately Justified?

4.1 Why Focus on Justified Belief?

So far, the primary focus of our discussion has been the concept of (propositional) knowledge. This is an entirely traditional preoccupation of epistemologists and indeed in some cases has been their exclusive concern. But we now want to shift the focus from the concept of knowledge to the concept of justified belief. There are two reasons for doing this. First, if you have been persuaded that some version of the "justified true belief" account of knowledge is correct, you will naturally also think that you should have an understanding of what justified belief is. What is it that makes a belief *justified* and hence turns a true belief into knowledge? But secondly, even if you reject entirely the view that justified belief is partly constitutive of knowledge, you may well want to assign to it a central place in your overall epistemology. For in many areas where we would ideally like to have knowledge, we cannot get it, or if we can get it, the cost in time and energy is too great for it to be worth our while. In such cases, we make do with something less than knowledge: we make do with belief. Belief in such circumstances can play the same role in guiding our actions that knowledge plays in other cases. Suppose, for example, that I am contemplating launching a new magazine for chess players, and I wonder what the demand for it would be. I decide to do a little market research. In principle, I could find out for sure what the demand is by identifying every single chess player in the country and asking what their reaction to the new magazine would be. I could put myself in a position where I could say "I *know* what the demand will be." But of course such a procedure would be absurdly wasteful. In practice, what I will do is (say) identify 100, or 1000 chess players, ask them for their responses, and generalize from them to the population of chess players as a whole. The information that I end up with may not be *knowledge* of what the demand will be; it will be no more than a more-or-less well-founded belief. But given the cost of acquiring further information, the sensible thing is to be guided in my decision by my reasonable belief, rather than to persist in the search for knowledge.

4.2 Some Points about "Belief"

(i) There is propositional belief, object belief, and "belief in" things

We have spoken here of "justified belief," and both of these terms call for some comment. First, we need to notice that just as different kinds of knowledge can be distinguished (propositional knowledge, capacity knowledge, and knowledge by acquaintance), so we can distinguish between different kinds of belief. In particular, we can distinguish between what we will call propositional belief, object belief, and "in" belief. Propositional belief is parallel to propositional knowledge. It is believing that some proposition is true or false. It is expressed by sentences of the form "S believes that p" (where "S" stands for a believer and "p" for a proposition). As our discussion of knowledge will have made clear, this differs from "S knows that p" *at least* in this respect: that a belief can be true or false, but necessarily anything that we know is true.

By object belief, we mean those forms of belief which are expressed by "S believes x," where "x" stands for a person, or a text, or a body of assertions. Thus "Fred believes the President," and "George believes the Bible" and "Anne believes the prisoner's testimony" are all examples of object belief. Object belief can be seen as a derivative form of propositional belief. For to say that Fred believes the President is to say that Fred believes (the proposition) that what the President says is true; to say that George believes the Bible is to say that George believes (the proposition) that what the Bible says is true; to say that Anne believes the prisoner's testimony is to say that Anne believes (the proposition) that what the prisoner said is true. Object belief, being thus reducible to propositional belief will not present us with a further and separate set of problems.

By "belief in," we mean those forms of belief which are expressed by sentences of the form "S believes in x," where "x" stands for a person or an institution, or a set of ideas. Thus Jennifer might believe in God, or in the Constitution, or in healthy eating, or in patriotism. Very often, believing in x is believing that x is important or beneficial in some way. But sometimes it means no more than believing that x exists. Thus if Wayne believes in ghosts, he will believe that ghosts exist, but may well not believe that they are important or beneficial. But as with object belief, "belief in" will not present us with a separate set of problems, since "belief in" also reduces to propositional belief, as illustrated above. So in what follows, we will be exclusively concerned with propositional belief.

(ii) The psychological state of believing p must be distinguished from what one believes

But propositional belief itself contains two elements which we need to comment on separately. Sometimes the term is used to refer to a psychological state, to my *believing* something; sometimes it is used to refer to a *propositional content*, to *what it is* that I believe. Beliefs in the first sense are states that occur in people's minds; they occur at particular times; they can enter into causal relations with other things in the world (such as the environment, the believer's behavior, his other mental states, etc.). But believings cannot themselves be true or false, they cannot imply or be implied by any propositions. By contrast, beliefs in the propositional sense can be true or false, and can stand in implication relations. But they do not occur in people's minds, nor can they enter into causal relations with other things in the world. In the first sense, you and I cannot have the same belief. When you believe that tigers have stripes and I believe that tigers have stripes, there are two beliefs (believings) because there are two people. But in the second sense, you and I *can* have the same belief— not just exactly similar beliefs, but the very same belief. *What* you believe (e.g., that tigers have stripes) is one and the same thing as what I believe.

(iii) One may be unconscious of what one believes

What, then, are beliefs in the psychological sense, that is to say, in the "believings" sense? We have seen already that they are states that have a certain content (namely, the proposition at which they are directed), and they may be unconscious, in at least three respects. First, it is clear that at any given time, you are not conscious of most of your beliefs. You no doubt believe that London is the capital of Britain. But you are not constantly rehearsing this thought in your consciousness. It is a belief which you know that you have, which you can bring to consciousness when it is needed. But for most of the time, it is not needed, and you are not conscious of it.

Secondly, there are beliefs that you have that you are not conscious of, in the stronger sense that you have *never* consciously entertained them. For example, you almost certainly believe that the world contains more than ninety-nine ants, but almost certainly, you have never consciously entertained that thought. It is a belief which you will have acquired in the course of acquiring other information, perhaps consciously, about ants, but it is not (we would bet) a belief which you have ever consciously entertained. It is nonetheless one of the many beliefs which you hold; you could certainly bring it to mind if the occasion required it, and if someone were to tell you explicitly "The world contains more than ninety-nine ants," you would not regard her as increasing your stock of information, but only as repeating something which you have already accepted.

Thirdly, and more controversially, we will take it that a person may hold beliefs not only which she has never consciously entertained, but also which she would fail to recognize as hers, or even disavow, if they were brought to her attention. It is not easy to give convincing examples of beliefs like these (especially examples which everyone would recognize and avow!) but characteristically they would be beliefs that had a great and perhaps unpleasant emotional significance for the person concerned, like a belief that your father hated you.

It follows from what we have just said that it is possible to believe that p without knowing that you believe it, and without even believing that you believe it. Equally it is possible to think that you believe that p when in reality you do not. This is not to deny that people are often good judges in general of what their own beliefs are, but it *is* to deny that they are infallible judges in this matter.

From what we have said so far, it might be thought that we are saying that there are two kinds of belief (in the "believing" sense), conscious and unconscious. But this would be a misunderstanding. Although we can become conscious of many of our beliefs, consciousness is not an essential part of any of them. When we become conscious of one of them, the belief itself does not change. All that changes is our cognitive attitude toward the belief. Here is an analogy: most people know what their own name is—they can, for example, consciously call it to mind if they want to. But having a particular name has no essential connection with knowing what that name is—it is simply that in most normal humans above a certain age, having a name and knowing what it is go together. But it is quite possible for a person to have a name and not to know what it is: she might suffer from amnesia, or she might be a child too young to grasp what naming is, for example. Similarly, there is no essential connection between having a belief and knowing that one has it—it is simply that in most normal human beings for at least a large number of their beliefs, having a belief and knowing that we have it go together.

That there are unconscious beliefs will be important to what follows. For once we allow that there are unconscious beliefs, it is very difficult to deny that there can be unconscious inferences (there could hardly be an inference which we were conscious of, when we were not conscious of the beliefs from and to which it was an inference). So the mere fact that we are not aware of going through a reasoning process, and are not aware of the beliefs that are thereby generated, is not a conclusive reason for saying that such reasoning has not occurred, or such beliefs are not ours.

There is very much more that could be said about the nature of belief (about how beliefs are to be individuated, for example, and about how they connect with our behavior). But let us turn now from the "belief" side of justified belief to the issue of justification.

4.3 Connections between "Belief" and "Justification"

(i) Why we should *prefer* justified beliefs

It will be clear first of all that the justification which is relevant here is what we earlier called epistemic (cf. 2.4 [iv]). What we are concerned with is belief that is reasonable, well-founded, or supported by the evidence; and it is worth reflecting for a moment on why we should prefer beliefs which are like this. After all, as we noted previously, gaining evidence to support our beliefs, or to make them reasonable or justified, is often expensive in terms of time and energy. So what is the point of doing it? Why should we prefer justified to unjustified beliefs? Why not simply believe the first thing that comes into our minds, or the thing that we find most reassuring or comfortable, or the thing that most people in our peer group believe? Those are ways, after all, in which some people do form their beliefs. What is wrong with such ways?

One answer to this question lies in the relations between belief, truth, and evidence. In general, we want our beliefs to be true. Sometimes this is because we are interested in truth for its own sake; sometimes it is because we want the actions which are guided by our beliefs to be appropriate to the world around us. If I am thirsty, and plan to drink some water, it matters to me whether my belief that the liquid in front of me is water or not. *Truth,* then, is certainly a property which we very often want our beliefs to have. But why justification?

The reason lies in the fact that we do not have a God-like access to the truth. If we were God, perhaps we would be able to "see directly" (in some sense of that phrase) what the truth is. It might be the case, for example, that for God merely to think that something is true, *makes* it true. Suppose that if God thinks that there is a cat on the mat, that makes it true that there is a cat on the mat. If this were so, then clearly it would be impossible for any of God's beliefs to be false. God could know from the mere fact that he believed a proposition p, that it followed that p was true. In that case, God would have no need of any evidence for the truth of p. Its truth would follow from the mere fact that he believed it.

But we do not in general have this sort of direct access to the truth. For enormously many of the things we believe and whose truth matters to us, the truth of what we believe does not follow from the mere fact that we believe it. We can in general gain access to the truth only by relying on indirect signs of it—in other words, by relying on evidence or the fact that we have a justification. So it turns out that anyone who wants her beliefs to be true (as we have suggested most of us do) ought to prefer justified beliefs to unjustified beliefs. An interest in the truth carries in its train an interest in justification.

We said above very cautiously that we do not "in general" have direct access to the truth, because there certainly are *some* propositions which are such that their truth follows from the mere fact that we believe them. Relatively uncontentious examples might be "I exist" and "I have at least one belief." As we shall see in due course, some philosophers have argued that the class of such propositions is very large, perhaps encompassing all first-person, present tense propositions about one's current mental state. We shall later argue that such a view is mistaken. But even if it were correct, it is clear that there are many propositions whose truth matters to us, and to which we do not stand in this God-like relation.

(ii) Beliefs must be sensitive to evidence

In this defense of the need for an epistemic justification for our beliefs, we said that "anyone who wants her beliefs to be true ought to prefer justified beliefs." This seems to leave it open that someone who felt indifferent about the truth of her beliefs could be similarly indifferent about whether any of her beliefs was justified. But there are some grounds for thinking that the connection between belief and justification must be closer than that. It is plausible to argue that beliefs must be *evidence-sensitive*. Part of what makes something a *belief* that p is that it displays *some* tendency to change in the light of relevant evidence. To be a belief that p, it must show some tendency to weaken or disappear in the light of massive evidence that p is false, and some tendency to be reinforced in the light of massive evidence that p is true. A state that displayed *no* tendency to be strengthened or weakened in the light of evidence supporting or undermining it might be a *hope* that p, or a *fear* that p, but could not be a belief that p. This is not to deny that unjustified belief is (unhappily!) possible. Beliefs can be held on the basis of inadequate, or even no, evidence, and they can be persisted in even in the face of some counterevidence. Wishful thinking is certainly possible. But what we are claiming is that our inner states could not be *totally* insensitive to the occurrence of evidence for or against the relevant proposition, and yet still count as genuine beliefs in the truth of that proposition.

This gives us, then, two reasons for linking belief and justification very closely. In the first place, justification is needed because it is a means to truth, and in general we want our beliefs to be true, sometimes for practical reasons and sometimes for the sake of truth itself. Secondly, part of what makes something a belief at all is that it is a state which is responsive to the presence or absence of justification.

(iii) Classifying the links between belief and justification

What, then, might a justification for a given belief consist in? There are many possible answers to this central question, and many ways of classifying them. We will consider the theories in terms of two main principles of classification: first, whether they give a primary role to normative concepts or not; and secondly, whether they hold that inference is necessary for justification or not. Combining these two independent classifications yields four categories of theory:

1. normative and inferential
2. normative and non-inferential
3. non-normative and inferential
4. non-normative and non-inferential

We will consider the normative/non-normative contrast in section 4.4, and then in sections 4.5 and 4.6 we will look at the inferential/non-inferential contrast.

4.4 Normative versus Non-normative Theories of Justified Belief

(i) A normative theory explains justification in terms of what we *ought* to believe

By a normative theory, we mean a theory which explains justification by reference to some normative concepts such as *good* evidence, or what one *ought* to believe. Goldman, for example, says:

> I regard epistemology as an evaluative, or normative, field, not a purely descriptive one. (Goldman, 1986, 3)

and when he comes to explain what justification is, he explains it in terms of what "right" systems of rules "permit" us to believe. Kornblith introduces the notion of "epistemic responsibility" and goes on:

> Sometimes when we ask whether an agent's belief is *justified* what we mean to ask is whether the belief is the product of *epistemically responsible action,* i.e., the product of action an epistemically responsible agent might have taken.

And then a little later, he remarks:

> Questions of justification are thus questions about the ethics of belief. (Kornblith, 1983, 34)

A similar notion of responsibility is invoked by Bonjour, who tells us:

> To accept a belief in the absence of [a good] . . . reason is to neglect the pursuit of truth; such acceptance is, one might say, *epistemically irresponsible.* My contention here is that the idea of avoiding such irresponsibility, of being epistemically responsible in one's believings, is the core of the notion of epistemic justification. (Bonjour, 1985, 8)

A final example is provided by Pollock, who writes:

> What are we asking when we ask whether a belief is justified? What we want to know is whether it is all right to believe it. Justification is a matter of "epistemic permissibility." It is this normative character of epistemic justification that I want to emphasise. That epistemic justification is a normative notion is not a novel observation. The language of epistemic justification is explicitly normative, and a recurrent theme has been that justification is connected with "the ethics of belief." (Pollock, 1986, 124)

Exactly how this commitment to a normative concept of epistemology is worked out varies from writer to writer, but it is easy to say in general terms how the connection is meant to go. The thought is that we *ought* to believe what we have evidence for, at least provided that it is *good* evidence, and no contrary evidence is *better.* If we do form our beliefs as we ought to, then we are epistemically *virtuous,* we are beyond epistemic *reproach* or *blame,* and can be *praised* as reasonable. If we do not form our belief as we ought to, then we go *wrong*, not in the sense of believing what is false, but in the sense of being epistemically *culpable* and perhaps *negligent*.

The guiding thought is that there is a strong parallel between forming beliefs on the one hand, and ordinary behavior on the other. Just as morality supplies us with normative principles permitting, prohibiting, and praising certain kinds of behavior, and a set of epithets for those who keep or break these principles; so too (it is thought) there is a parallel set of principles governing our epistemological conduct, and to which we need to refer in order to explicate the concept of justification.

(ii) A "non-normative" theory explains justification in terms of what is *probably true*

A non-normative approach, by contrast, would not place this heavy emphasis on the role of normative and evaluative concepts in explaining what justification is, but would instead stress the link between justification and truth that we mentioned earlier. A justified belief is one which someone in search of the truth has a reason to prefer. But we know that justification does not guarantee truth: it is possible to be epistemically justified in believing something which then turns out to be false. So justification has got to be something that links with the truth although it does not guarantee it. This suggests that this at least is a necessary condition for a justified belief: a justified belief is one which is at least more probably true than not. As will emerge in due course, a number of further questions lurk in this claim: what is meant here by "probably"? how can we tell whether a given belief is probably true? if probability is relative to evidence, as many people suppose, must the believer herself have the evidence (and if so, what does "having" here mean?)?

These are all legitimate questions, but even without answering them, we can get a sense of the division of emphasis between normative and non-normative theories.

(iii) The appeal of the normative approach—and the dilemma it poses

There is no doubt that in terms of this contrast between types of theory of justification, the normative approach has considerable appeal. It is a fact, which the philosopher needs either to explain or explain away, that normative terms do occur very frequently in epistemological description and assessment. And it is also true that it is possible for a person consciously to try to add to and revise her corpus of beliefs by reflectively following particular rules of belief formation, just as she might consciously try to guide her behavior by reflectively following moral rules.

There are also, however, some reasons for feeling dissatisfied with the normative approach. It faces a dilemma. The first horn is that the normative concepts are eventually defined in non-normative terms. For example, the concept of justification might be defined in terms of what you are permitted to believe by the best evidence you have, and then those two normative concepts defined in terms of the concept of probable truth. But if the normative terms do thus ultimately disappear, then given that what we want to know is what justification ultimately consists in, there is no point in focusing principally on derivative normative concepts.

The other horn of the dilemma is to accept that the normative terms are indefinable non-normatively. And the objection to that is that they then remain simply mysterious. One wants an explanation of *why* it is permissible, obligatory, or forbidden to hold a belief in various circumstances, and this means that we must dig to a deeper level than the normative alone.

Notice that given the way we have characterized the contrast between the two types of theories, a non-normative theory is not debarred from including normative conceptions. But in doing so, it will always assign to them a derivative role. They will be defined in terms of the non-normative concepts, and it is the latter which will supply the real heart of the theory.

4.5 Inferential Theories of Justified Belief

A different way of classifying theories of justification is according to the role they assign to inference. On some accounts all cases of justification involve inference, and on other accounts inference would be only one among a number of different ways in which a belief might be justified. Let us see first how an account stressing the role of inference might go.

(i) The form of a theory which explains justified belief in terms of inference

Suppose that I have a justified belief that Bucharest is the capital of Romania. What could give me an epistemic justification for such a belief? One natural answer that at once suggests itself is that I hold various other beliefs, which I take to be good grounds for thinking that Bucharest is the capital and from which I have inferred that Bucharest is the capital. I might believe, for example, that the *New York Times* has referred to Bucharest as the capital, and that the *Times* is a reliable source of information on such matters. Generalizing from this, we might be led to suppose that we might analyze "*S* has a justified belief that *p*" as the conjunction of two claims:

(i) *S* has some further beliefs *q*, *r*, etc.
(ii) *S* has inferred *p* from *q*, *r*, etc.

But a little reflection suggests that such an account is too simplistic. Suppose that I have indeed inferred *p* from *q*, *r*, etc. But *q*, *r*, etc. do not in fact support *p*. I have engaged in faulty reasoning. Surely then I have not really justified my original belief that *p*. I will not have produced any evidence that makes the truth of my belief more likely, and in that sense I will not really have justified my belief. This suggests that we need to add at least one further condition, namely

(iii) S's inference from q, r, etc. to p must be a justified inference

Condition (iii) at once raises the question of what makes a form of inference justified, which we will address later when we discuss the nature of deduction, induction, and inference in general. But for the moment let us simply take the notion of justified inference for granted and ask if our three conditions give us at least the outlines of a satisfactory account of justified belief.

It seems that by themselves, they do not. Imagine the following case. I believe that Pythagoras's theorem is true (that the square of the hypotenuse of a right-angled triangle equals in area the sum of the squares of the other two sides). You ask what justification I have for my belief, so I quote you the penultimate line in Pythagoras's proof, from which this conclusion follows, and say that I believe that penultimate line is true, and I have inferred the theorem from that line. In such a case, the three conditions which we have so far mentioned are met: I believe the theorem, I have inferred it from the penultimate line which I believe to be true, and the penultimate line does indeed imply the truth of the theorem, so my inference does meet the three conditions specified so far. So this ought straightforwardly to be a case of justified belief. But now suppose that my belief in the truth of the penultimate line of the proof is itself one for which I have no justification. Perhaps, for example, I have not understood the earlier stages in the proof, but have simply accepted without proof the penultimate step, and seen that it did imply the conclusion. Surely then my belief in the conclusion itself would not be a justified belief. It seems, in other words, that in order for me to have a justified belief that p, the further beliefs from which I infer p must themselves also be justified beliefs. If this is so, then we need to add a fourth condition to our account, namely

(iv) S's beliefs that q, r, etc. are themselves justified beliefs

This gives us the form of a typical account of justification in terms of inference, and such an account may well seem promising. It looks, for example, as if the link which we wanted between justification and truth could be secured if we could provide an account of justified rules of inference which would show them to be if not truth-preserving, at least probability-conferring. But the account will obviously not do as it stands. For if what we are trying to elucidate is the concept of justified belief, we would obviously have made little progress if our elucidation itself invoked the idea of justified belief. It is rather as if in elucidating what a *plok* is we had said that a plok is something that must be descended from another plok. To understand the phrase "descended from a plok," we would already need to know what a plok was; and if we already knew what a plok was, we wouldn't need the explanation. Similarly, it seems, we throw no light on what a justified belief is by being told that it is something that is inferred from another justified belief. This is clearly a problem which such an account of justification would have to address, and as we shall see when we consider the structure of epistemic justification, it is a problem for which supporters of this type of theory believe they have a solution.

(ii) Justified belief may be based on inferences and beliefs which are unconscious

Within the general family of theories which construe justification in these terms (i.e., as involving the inference of the justified belief from some further belief which one holds), a number of varieties can be distinguished. One theory holds that for there to be justification, the beliefs and inferences involved must be conscious. This is what Nathan has called "assurance."

> You evidentially assure yourself that *p* only if you consciously affirm a proposition which you consciously affirm to be evidence for *p*. (Nathan, 1980, 16)

This strong requirement creates a problem about the justification of perceptual beliefs, for example, which characteristically are not *consciously* inferred from anything. When I look at my desk and acquire the belief that there is a book resting on it, I do not consciously do any inferring—at the conscious level, the belief simply occurs to me immediately. But it is not only perceptual beliefs which create a problem for this view. Consider again the belief that the world contains more than ninety-nine ants. We are surely justified in believing this, even if we have never before consciously entertained it, nor consciously inferred it from anything else. But acceptance of the "conscious inference" view of justification would have the implication that our belief that the world contains more than ninety-nine ants was not justified and that indeed we have very many fewer justified beliefs than we thought. The only sort of justified belief which this account really fits is the kind that is acquired by a fairly thoughtful and articulate person who is consciously trying to reason her way to a conclusion. Philosophers have always had a soft spot for such reflective reasoning. But it is surely clear that even if all of us do it some of the time, none of us does it all the time, and for none of us is it the only way of acquiring justified beliefs.

A less demanding conception than Nathan's would invoke the idea of a "reconstructible" inference. According to such a view, a person need not either consciously or unconsciously have inferred *q* from *p*, but if challenged as to what her justification was for accepting *q*, she would produce her belief that *p*. Unlike the first interpretation of the inference involved in justification, this position does not require the believer to have *done* anything in order to have a justified belief. All it requires is that she should have the *ability* to do something if challenged (and of course the challenge might come from herself: she might ask herself what justification she has for accepting *q*). This certainly copes satisfactorily with some of the examples which we were considering above (e.g., the belief about the ninety-nine ants), but it still runs foul of perceptual beliefs. An unreflective person (perhaps a child of five?) can surely have a justified belief that there is a book on the table in front of her without being able to articulate all the beliefs she has which collectively form her justification. This is an account which still betrays the philosophical predilection for intellectualizing the concept of justified belief.

We could perhaps envisage a weakened version of this position which would require not that one should oneself be able to reconstruct the inferences but that one should at least be able to recognize them if they were reconstructed from one's stock of beliefs by someone else. One might call this "acknowledgeable" inference, but it seems too permissive a condition. It might be that I have sufficient perspicacity to recognize a justification if someone else constructs one for me from my antecedently held beliefs, even though my belief in q had nothing to do with the fact that such a justification was so constructible.

We might also consider weakening the Nathan conception in a slightly different direction, by allowing that the inference, as well as the premises on which it is based, may be unconscious. An author who takes this line is Harman, for example, who writes:

> Knowledge of the world is based on inference . . . If we are not conscious of the inference, then there is unconscious inference . . . If we were not aware of the premises, then we can make inferences without being aware of the premises of those inferences. (Harman, 1973, 20–21)

This is certainly an improvement on the positions we have outlined above. It clearly fits in very well with the conception of belief which we were outlining in section 1 of this chapter when we stressed the fact that beliefs are not conscious states, and that it was possible to have a particular belief without either knowing or believing that you do. Given this conception of beliefs as unconscious states with a certain propositional content, it is natural to allow that there can be unconscious transitions between these states, where the transitions made are a function of the content of the beliefs involved. This surely is what unconscious inference is. It copes well with the "ninety-nine ants" belief, and may be able to cope also with cases of perceptual belief.

If, therefore, we favor an inferential conception of justification, it seems that Harman's account is the most promising. But rather than seek to develop it further at this point, let us turn to non-inferential accounts of justification to see if they might prove more illuminating.

4.6 A Non-inferential Theory of Justification: Reliabilism

What would an account of justification in non-inferential terms look like? We now consider two such accounts, one in terms of the reliability of a method and the other in causal terms. We have already implicitly come across both of these when we were discussing the concept of knowledge. Although we did not there present them as accounts of justification, they are sometimes so presented by their defenders. Let us briefly consider how each might be deployed as a theory of justification, beginning with reliabilism.

(i) A belief is justified if and only if it is produced by a reliable method

According to the reliabilist theory of *knowledge*, what made a true belief a case of knowledge was that it had been produced by a reliable method of belief acquisition. According to the reliabilist theory of *justification*, what makes a belief justified is that it has been produced by a reliable method. Goldman asks:

> . . . which species of belief-forming (or belief-sustaining) processes are intuitively justification-conferring? They include standard perceptual processes, remembering, good reasoning, and introspection. What these processes seem to have in common is *reliability:* the beliefs they produce are generally reliable. (Goldman, 1979, 9–10)

This suggests to us both what it is that makes a belief justified (that it has been produced by a reliable method) and what methods are reliable. Notice that on Goldman's conception, a belief arrived at by inference can certainly be justified, but that when it is, the fact that it has been arrived at by inference is not really the crucial point. The crucial point is that it has been arrived at by a reliable method.

(ii) Strengths and weaknesses of reliabilist theories of justified belief

A reliabilist account of justification certainly looks more promising than most of the inferential theories which we have considered previously in at least three respects. First, it is well positioned to accommodate the link between justification and truth which we have insisted on. For the reliability of a process must be its reliability as a process which yields *true* beliefs (obviously a process that could be relied upon to yield false beliefs would be of no interest to us here!). Further, if justification is linked as we have suggested with the probability of truth, the connection with the idea of reliability seems even closer. For one way of measuring the reliability of a method might be in terms of the probability of it yielding true beliefs. If, for example, we could know that 90 percent of the beliefs produced by a particular process were true, then, in the absence of any other information, we could say of any given belief produced by that process that it was probably true and hence justified. Thirdly, the reliabilist account is surely right in thinking that in order to have justified beliefs, we do not *have* to perform any conscious activity (such as carrying out a process of inference): many and perhaps most of our justified beliefs come to us willy nilly.

Further, the reliabilist account of justification is not open to all the objections which we raised to the reliabilist account of knowledge. The issue, for example, of whether the method needs to be infallible or merely successful in general is no longer a problem. We can agree that different methods will vary along a spectrum in terms of reliability, just as justification itself does, although knowledge does not. We thus do not have to find any sharp dividing line on that spectrum on one side of which the reliability is enough to give justification and on the other side not.

But in spite of these merits, the reliabilist account of justification does face some of the difficulties which made us reject the reliabilist theory of knowledge. There is first the issue of whether in assessing the reliability of a method, we need to look only at its actual success rate; or whether we also have to compute what its hypothetical success rate would have been in counterfactual circumstances—and how the relevant set of counterfactual circumstances is to be specified. Secondly, there is the problem that a method might be reliable in relation to one type of belief and unreliable in relation to another. What principled way is there of relativizing the reliability of the method to a particular class of beliefs? Thirdly, the problem remains of how methods themselves are to be individuated from each other, something which we obviously have to be able to do if we are to calculate the success rate of any particular method.

To raise these objections is not to say that they are unanswerable. Clearly we do have a rough and ready grasp of the answers required. We do rightly make judgments to the effect that looking up someone in a phone book is a more reliable way of finding out their phone number than is consulting the output of a random number generator, for example. We can see that the issue of whether looking at a particular clock to discover the time is a reliable method must depend in part on what beliefs would have been acquired if the clock had been looked at at times when it was in fact unobserved. The problem with the reliabilist account is that it does not go beyond these rough and ready judgments to a set of clear general principles covering the problematic cases. So for the purposes of the kind of theoretical understanding which epistemology seeks, it is deficient.

4.7 A Second Non-inferential Theory: A Causal Theory of Justified Belief

Just as we can distinguish a reliabilist account of knowledge and of justification, so too can we distinguish causal accounts of knowledge and of justification. The causal account of knowledge claimed that what made a true belief a case of knowledge was the causal connections of the belief; the causal account of justification maintains that what makes a belief justified is in part its causal relations. Let us consider in a little more detail how this might go.

(i) A belief is justified if it is appropriately caused by a confirming belief

Suppose that I believe that the population is increasing annually (let us call this belief q), and I also hold some further belief (let us call it p) which confirms q (e.g., that this is what is revealed by the relevant government statistics). This by itself is clearly insufficient to justify my belief that q. For it might be that my belief that q is completely uninfluenced by my belief that p, that I would believe q whether or not I believed p. Clearly, if I am to have a justified belief that q, there has got to be some linkage between p and q. It must be that I believe that q *because* (in some sense of that word) I also believe that p. Inferential theories of justification try to secure this linkage and interpret this "because" by requiring that in such a case, q should have been *inferred* from p. But this is not the only way in which the linkage could be secured.

According to the causal theory of justification, the linkage is secured by requiring that the belief that p should *cause* the belief that q. Of course this causation *might* take the form of a conscious inference, but it does not have to. There might be causal links of a non-inferential kind between belief states, and hence the causal theory might allow as justified, beliefs which an inferential theory would have to disallow. It will be helpful here to recall the distinction made earlier (4.2 [ii]) between the psychological and the propositional sense of "belief," for what the causal theory of justification does is to make different claims about each of those two elements in the concept of belief. It is in the psychological sense of belief that there must be a causal connection, and it is in the propositional sense that there must be a confirmation relation. So, if S has a justified belief that p, then:

(i) S has a belief whose propositional content is p
(ii) S has a belief whose propositional content is q
(iii) the belief state in (i) causes the belief state in (ii)
(iv) the proposition in (i) confirms the proposition in (ii)

Notice several things about this conception. First, although the account speaks simply of *the* belief that p and *the* belief that q, it can readily allow that p and perhaps q are compound propositions. Our justification for believing something usually consists in many other beliefs, not in just one, and the causal account as presented is not denying that this is so. Those many other beliefs can be represented in the scheme by p.

Secondly, the account seems to converge on the least demanding sort of inferential account of justification, for example of the kind defended by Harman. Harman does not tell us exactly what he means by "inference."

> The only way to discover when a person makes inferences is to discover what assumptions about inference are needed to account for his knowledge. (Harman, 1973, 20)

But if that is so, perhaps there is no more than a terminological difference between

(i) S inferred (consciously or unconsciously) q from p and
(ii) S's belief that p caused his belief that q

(ii) Strengths and weaknesses of a causal theory of justified belief

Let us consider first how it fares in relation to the two problems which we mentioned for the causal theory of knowledge: the problem about how mathematical knowledge would be possible, and the problem of deviant causal chains (see 3.2 [ii] and [iii]). With the first of these, the problem seems to be a little less serious for the causal account of justification for the following reason. The causal relation invoked in the case of knowledge required that one's true beliefs about numbers should be somehow causally connected with *numbers themselves;* and, given the conception of numbers as timeless abstract objects, this seemed impossible. But the causal relation invoked in the case of the causal theory of justification requires that one's justified beliefs about numbers should be causally connected to one's other *beliefs,* not to what the beliefs are about. Given that beliefs (in the sense of believings) are events that occur in time, it seems at least possible that some of one's beliefs about numbers could be caused by other beliefs which one has. So the causal account of justification seems less exposed than the causal analysis of knowledge. But it may be that the only way to meet this objection wholly satisfactorily is to abandon the conception of numbers as abstract objects. To explore this fully is impossible here, but hints of what it involves can be gleaned from the second half of the book, especially Chapters 7, 8, and 11.

The second problem with the causal analysis of knowledge was that of deviant causal chains, and this is a problem which retains as much (and as little) force when applied to justified belief as it did in the case of knowledge. We have already said that we do not judge it to be a major objection, and so will say no more here.

But does the account have any positive merits? First, it shares with the reliabilist conception the merit of not overintellectualizing justified belief: it does not require the believer either to have done some relevant conscious reasoning or to be able to do such reasoning, in order to acquire a justified belief. Secondly (although not everyone would see this as a merit), it offers an entirely naturalistic account of justified belief. It does not invoke any normative notions (such as what a person *ought* to believe, or what is *good* evidence), notions which can be as puzzling as what they are invoked to elucidate. Instead, the causal account analyzes justification in terms of the natural relation of causation between the psychological states of belief, and the logical relation of confirmation between the propositional content of those states.

It is clear, however, that the account as it stands is at best incomplete. For example, and most obviously, it relies on the idea that one proposition can *confirm* another. But that at once raises the question of how and under what circumstances the confirmation relation holds. This is a very large and surprisingly complicated topic, and we will have something to say about it in Chapter 10. It also relies on the idea of causation, which is another concept that has turned out to be surprisingly controversial in philosophy. Under what conditions is it true to say that one event or state of affairs is the cause of another, and, more specifically, when can it be said that one *belief* causes another? Here, we shall not offer any detailed and explicit account of what causation is, but simply rely on the reader's intuitive grasp of the concept.

These are two respects in which the account utilizes concepts which themselves require further elucidation. But thirdly, the conditions mentioned for justified belief are surely themselves not sufficient. Suppose that S's belief that *q* is wild prejudice, but that the content of *q* does indeed confirm the content of the belief that *p*. Sam might believe, for example, that all women are featherbrained, and holding this belief might cause him to believe that no woman can be a competent mathematician. Here the first proposition believed does confirm the second, and Sam's belief in the second is caused by his belief in the first. But we would hardly say on this basis that Sam has a justified belief that no woman can be a competent mathematician. What we need is the thought that the causing belief must itself be justified if what it causes is to count as justified. But then it seems that we are threatened with an infinite regress. For if justified belief is explained partly in terms of causation by a second justified belief, that justified belief must itself have been caused by a third justified belief, which in turn will have been caused by a fourth, and so on. It looks as if we are facing a causal version of the infinite regress problem which we saw earlier (in 4.5 [i]) attaches to an explanation of justification in terms of inference. It is at this point that questions about the nature of justified belief merge into questions about the overall structure of our belief system, and it is these questions which will occupy us in Chapters 5 to 8.

Exercises

1. Without rereading the chapter, explain the distinction between believing something, and the propositional content of what you believe. Do this in half a page, then assess your answer for accuracy, clarity, and completeness against section 4.1 (ii).
2. Suppose no evidence or argument is capable of shaking Mike's belief in God's existence. Does that mean that he does not have such a belief? (cf. 4.2 [ii])
3. If it makes you *happy* to believe some proposition, why should you care whether it is true? Answer this question with examples of your own in no more than a page. When you have done this, critique your answer in light of sections 4.2 and 4.3.

4. Without rereading the chapter, explain the pros and cons of a reliabilist theory of justified belief in only one page. Then assess your answer for accuracy, clarity, and completeness against section 4.5.
5. Suppose that you have an unconscious belief that women are superior to men. Does it make sense to suppose that such a belief, of which you are quite unaware, could cause other beliefs? (Quite hard.)
6. What are the important differences between a causal theory of knowledge and a causal theory of justified belief? (Hard.)

CHAPTER 5

Foundationalism about Empirical Beliefs

5.1 The Infinite Regress Argument

It is agreed on all sides that things which we know and believe do not form a mere heap, as it were, of discrete items which exist in isolation from each other. Our beliefs form a complicated structure. Some of my beliefs are dependent on others. Mary's belief that her neighbor is having a bonfire is dependent on her belief that it is smoke which she can see rising over the garden fence. Normally (we will later claim "always"), any given belief is related to many other beliefs. The detective's belief that Morgan is the murderer is based on her beliefs that Morgan had an opportunity to kill, that he had a motive, that his supposed alibi can be shown to be suspect, that the murder weapon was found in his room, and so on. Further there is a great variety of relations which can hold between our beliefs. If we are thinking of our beliefs as psychological states, they can be related in a variety of causal ways. If we are thinking of the propositional contents of our belief states, they can be related in a wide variety of logical ways (implication, equivalence, inconsistency, etc.). So it is uncontroversial to say that our corpus of beliefs has *some* structure. The debate is about *what* structure it has.

Before we address that question, two preliminary points need to be noticed. First, the issue we want to address is not about the structure of our *total* corpus of beliefs, but only about that subset which consists of our justified beliefs. Secondly, although for the purposes of exposition we have separated the question of what makes a given belief justified from the question of what structure the totality of our justified beliefs has, we need to bear in mind that the two issues are very closely linked.

To see why this is so, recall what we were saying earlier about inferential theories of justification. We considered then the suggestion that "*S* has a justified belief that *p*" might be analyzed as

(i) S has some further beliefs q, r, etc.
(ii) S has inferred p from q, r, etc.
(iii) S's inference from q, r, etc. to p is a justified inference
(iv) S's beliefs that q, r, etc. are themselves justified beliefs

We pointed out that this could not be a complete or satisfactory account of justification as it stood, because it explained the justification of one belief partly
in terms of the justification of other beliefs, and hence did not give a general
answer to the question of what justified belief is. As an explanation of what
justified belief is, the account is circular.

Indeed, even if we overlooked this circularity, it seems that the view would
also be faced with an infinite regress. For we would be saying that in order to
have a justified belief in one thing, we would have to have a justified belief in
a second; and in order to have a justified belief in a second, we would need
to have a justified belief in a third; and so on infinitely. We would thus be
unable to have a single justified belief unless we had infinitely many justified
beliefs.

A similar problem about circularity and regress seems to threaten an
account of justification in causal terms, as noted in the last section of Chapter
4. If the justification of a belief consists in part in its being caused by another
justified belief, then that justified belief must itself have been caused by a third,
and so on. So if we are trying to explicate the concept of justified belief, we
are going round in a circle, invoking in our explanation the very concept that
we are trying to explain. And if we were trying to acquire a justified belief,
we would be faced with an infinite regress; to acquire one presupposes that
we already have a second, which in turn presupposes that we already have a
third, and so on.

What we have here is what is sometimes called the "regress argument"
about justification, and the argument marks a very important parting of the
ways for two radically different accounts of the structure of our justified
beliefs. According to foundationalism, the threats of circularity and of infinite
regress can both be met by recognizing that our corpus of justified beliefs is
like a building, with foundations on which rest higher and higher levels of
knowledge and justified belief; if the threats can be met, then (so many foundationalists would want to claim) the inferential view of justification deserves
further consideration. According to the other view, coherentism, it is impossible to find any such foundational beliefs, and we have to recognize that our
corpus of justified beliefs has more the structure of a net or a web or a wigwam, than of a building (we will explain these analogies in Chapter 7).

How, then, according to foundationalism, might the regress of justification
be stopped? To answer this question, recall exactly how the regress began. It
began because we assumed that justification requires the believer to have a
further justified belief. But suppose that even if this is true of some justified
beliefs, there are types of justification which do not require the believer to have

any further beliefs at all, and hence *a fortiori* do not require him to have any further *justified* beliefs. Clearly the regress would then be halted; and this is precisely the line that in their different ways rationalism and empiricism have taken. We will look first at foundationalism in connection with our empirical beliefs and then in connection with our a priori beliefs. But before we look at either sort of foundationalism, we need to sharpen this contrast between the a priori and the empirical.

5.2 The Distinction between A Priori and Empirical Belief

It is customary to define "a priori" as "nonempirical"—so what exactly does "empirical" mean? Hitherto, we have treated "empirical" as meaning "justified only by appeal to experience." The term "experience" here covers all the sensory impressions associated with the five senses. It covers what the internal senses, such as pain and kinesthesia, tell us. It covers anything we come to know by introspection. So beliefs about both the external world and about your own mind will count as empirical.

What about what we might call second-hand beliefs? If you tell me that Mount Fuji has erupted again, or I read of it in a paper, although I have no personal experience of it, does that count as empirical? Yes, it does, because in order to acquire the belief myself, I do have to use my own senses. I have to listen with my ears or look with my eyes in order to acquire the information second hand. The fact that I did not see or hear the eruption myself does not matter. I am still having to rely on my own experience of what you or the newspaper tell me, in order to acquire my belief. So that belief is an empirical one.

Thirdly, anything that I infer from what is known or believed empirically will itself count as empirical (provided that I could not have come to know the fact nonempirically as well). If I am a detective investigating a homicide, my senses might tell me that Slansky's fingerprints were on the murder weapon. If I infer from this that Slansky is the murderer, this too would count as an empirical belief, even though I had no personal experience of Slansky committing the murder, nor has anyone told me about it, nor have I read about it.

We can now define by contrast the class of nonempirical or a priori propositions. They will be propositions which can be known or justifiably believed on some basis other than experience, in the wide sense of that term indicated previously. It might be thought that, so defined, there could be no a priori propositions. For, it might be said, in order even to know the meaning of the words used to express a proposition, we have to rely on experience. We have to have people tell us what the words mean, or we have to look them up in dictionaries, or we have to listen to see how they are used and try to work out their meaning from that. And in all these cases, we will be relying on experience. So even to know something as trivial as "Sisters are female" we have to have whatever experience is necessary for us to come to know the meanings of "sister" and "female."

In replying to this objection, we could try to contest the claim that in order to formulate certain thoughts to ourselves, we must use words from a public language which we have learned empirically. But it will be simpler here to grant the objection and to change our definition of "a priori" slightly.

> A proposition is a priori if and only if it is a proposition which can be known or justifiably believed without having to rely on any experience beyond that necessary for coming to know the meanings of the words used to express the proposition in question.

Three further points need to be noted in connection with the empirical/a priori contrast. First, because of the way we have defined these terms, not all propositions that are in fact known or believed on the basis of experience will count as empirical. Suppose, for example, that you work out in your head the answer to some complicated mathematical calculation, and then you tell me the answer. My knowledge is then acquired by experience, my experience of hearing what you tell me. But *what* I come to know will not count as empirical knowledge, because it is not something which is knowable or rationally believable *only* by experience. I *could have* worked it for myself a priori, just as you did yourself. So what I come to know is an a priori proposition, although I come to know it by experience. By contrast, it cannot be the case that I come to know or rationally believe an empirical proposition by a priori means. For an empirical proposition is defined as one knowable or justifiably believable *only* on the basis of experience.

Secondly, although it follows from the way in which we have explained the terms that no proposition can be both empirical and a priori, it does not follow that every proposition must be one or the other. Suppose that there is some proposition, p, such that it is impossible in principle for us ever to know or justifiably believe that p is true or that it is false. It then cannot count as empirical (because it is not knowable or rationally believable on the basis of experience), nor as a priori (because it is not knowable or rationally believable *without* having to rely on experience). Whether there are such propositions is a disputed question, and we are not taking sides on that issue. All we are doing is pointing out that our definition leaves open the possibility of propositions whose truth value is in principle inaccessible to us.

Thirdly, it is worth emphasizing that the empirical/a priori distinction is an epistemological distinction. It is a distinction between propositions on the basis of how we can justify our belief in them. It is not a classification of the propositions in terms of their intrinsic logical features—in particular, it is not a classification of them in terms of whether they are necessary or contingent. This is a distinction with which the empirical/a priori distinction is often confused. For the moment, all that we need to notice is that there are two separate distinctions here, not one distinction with two different labels.

With that clarification of the distinction, let us return to foundationalism about empirical beliefs.

5.3 The Foundations of Empirical Belief: Experience

How might a foundationalist try to stop the regress in the case of empirical beliefs? What foundationalists have appealed to as a regress-stopper for empirical belief is *experience,* where experience is something which does not itself consist of beliefs (and hence not of justified beliefs) but which can nonetheless provide a justification for beliefs. It is thus cast in the role of something which can *provide* justification, but which does not itself *require* justification.

Drawing on these thoughts, we now have enough material (so the foundationalist will claim) to construct a rather more sophisticated account of justified belief than the naive one given in 5.1, an account which avoids the unwelcome consequences brought out by the regress argument. We need to distinguish between direct and indirect justification, in the following way:

1. S has a justified belief that p = S's belief that p is directly or indirectly justified
2. S's belief that p is directly justified = S has a justification for her belief that p, a justification which does not itself require any further justification, and which, in the case of empirical beliefs, consists in having an experience
3. S's belief that p is indirectly justified =
   (a) S believes that q
   (b) S has inferred p from q
   (c) S's belief that q is justified, directly or indirectly
   (d) S's inference from q is justified

This more sophisticated account enables the foundationalist to avoid the criticisms leveled at the naive account. There is no longer a circularity in the definition of justified belief; and it is no longer the case that all justified beliefs have to be derived from other justified beliefs (because some are justified directly), and hence the infinite regress is blocked.

(i) "Deep" and "shallow" foundationalism

But now we need to notice that there is an important division within the foundationalist camp on what "experience" means or what empirical foundational beliefs are about. There is a division between those whom we will call "shallow" foundationalists, and those whom we will call "deep" foundationalists. By a shallow foundationalist, we mean someone who maintains that the experience which blocks the regress of justification is on at least some occasions experience of the physical world. Suppose I believe that there is a red cup in front of me and that this belief is justified by experience. On the shallow foundationalist view, what justifies this belief is *my experience of a red cup,* of a real object in the physical world. So my foundational beliefs can be beliefs about the external world.

But the deep foundationalist offers us a different interpretation of the notion of experience, in which what we experience is never objects or events in the physical world but always objects or events in our own minds, *on the basis of which* we infer the occurrence of events in the physical world. She says that if I have a justified belief that there is a red cup before me, that is a belief which I must have inferred from a belief about my own private sense impressions, and that it is my belief about the occurrence of my own sense impressions which is the foundational belief. My experience is of my own sense impressions, not of the cup itself. My sense impressions justify the belief that I have sense impressions of a cup, and my belief that I have sense impressions of a cup is what justifies my belief that there is a cup in front of me. This point is sometimes put by saying that we have *direct* awareness of our own sense impressions but only *indirect* awareness of the external world. This way of speaking is a little misleading, in suggesting that what is at issue are two kinds of *awareness*. The point rather is that we have two kinds of justification, inferential (or indirect) and non-inferential (or direct).

We can summarize these points of contrast in the following way. According to the shallow foundationalist,

(a) Although justified beliefs about the physical world may sometimes be inferred, they do not have to be: sometimes they are justified merely by the occurrence of an experience.
(b) We do experience the physical world itself. Although experience *may* be just of our own sense impressions (e.g., if we are hallucinating), in general it is physical reality itself which we experience.

According to the deep foundationalist,

(c) Justified beliefs about the physical world are always inferred from other beliefs.
(d) We never experience the physical world itself (or we never experience it *directly*)—we experience only our own sense impressions which justify our belief that we are having these sense impressions, and that belief in turn is used to justify our belief about the physical world.

Historically, it has been the doctrine of deep foundations which has been the predominant one, and some version of it can be found in the writings of Descartes, Locke, Hume, Russell, and Moore, as well those of modern authors such as C. D. Broad, R. Carnap, A. J. Ayer, C. I. Lewis, and R. Chisholm. In what follows, we will focus primarily on deep foundationalism. Our ultimate conclusion will be that foundationalism as a whole is untenable. But it is worth bearing in mind that even if the many arguments which have been produced against deep foundationalism are cogent, foundationalism will still not have been undermined unless those arguments can be shown to apply to shallow foundationalism as well.

(ii) The deep foundationalist conception of experience

Let us start by trying to get clear what the deep foundationalist's conception of *experience* is. Imagine that you are looking at a white wall, and you have a hallucination of a large red circle painted on the wall. Since you are halluci-nating, there is no real red circle which exists in the external world and which you are perceiving. And yet surely, the deep foundationalist plausibly claims, when you are hallucinating the red circle, something is happening in your con-sciousness. It may be that part of what is happening is that you are acquiring a (false) belief to the effect that there really is a red circle painted on the white wall. But this, she will say, cannot be the heart of the matter. You might know, for example that you were hallucinating (you know that you have just taken a hallucinatory drug, other observers have just assured you that there is no red circle), so you do not acquire the false belief that there really is a red cir-cle. And yet even in the absence of the acquisition of a false belief, it could still seem visually to you just as if you were seeing a real red circle on the wall. Now, whatever is going on in your consciousness in such a situation, which is *not* a matter of the beliefs you are acquiring, is an example of what the deep foundationalist means by experience. In the case we have just described, you are having a visual experience of a red circle on a white background. The ter-minology can vary on this point. Some writers speak of having a sense impres-sion or a sense datum or a sensory state of a red circle, others speak of hav-ing an experience *as of* seeing a red circle, others again speak of having a red circle in one's visual field, and yet others of being visually aware of a red cir-cle. Some writers also speak in this connection of "inner" or "private" experi-ences, to emphasize the fact that these are experiences which occur solely in the mind, and do not require the existence of a corresponding external reality.

What we have illustrated in connection with the sense of sight is meant to apply to all the other sense modalities. Suppose that you have an auditory hal-lucination of a creaking door. There is no real creaking door which you are hearing, and (because you know that you are hallucinating) you have no belief that there is a real creaking door. But you are certainly undergoing some audi-tory experience. You are having an auditory impression or experience of a creaking door. In an analogous way, we may have tactual experiences, olfac-tory experiences, and gustatory experiences, even in the absence of any real objects which we are feeling or smelling or tasting.

That, then, gives us an initial characterization of what a deep foundation-alist has in mind when she speaks of experiences. But it would be a mistake to think that she believes experiences occur only in cases of hallucination. Some writers have thought that our dreams consist of experiences in this sense of the term, and that perhaps awareness of after-images is no more than the occurrence of sensory experiences. But much more important from our point of view is the deep foundationalist's thought that such experiences also occur in all cases of genuine perception, cases where we really see, feel, hear, taste, or smell something that actually exists. Consider the situation in which there is a red circle on a white wall, and I really see them both. Then, according to the deep foundationalist, my visual experience is *in itself* exactly the same as when I was having the hallucination. What differentiates the case of genuine perception from the case of hallucination is (at least) that in the former case but not in the latter, there is a real object corresponding to my visual impression. (Perhaps further conditions have to be met for genuine perception, such as that my visual impression is *caused by* the external object. But we need not explore that issue here.)

Where, then, do beliefs fit into this picture? The deep foundationalist will say that our foundational beliefs are beliefs about experience, in the sense of "experience" which we have just illustrated. Our beliefs about the external world are, to the extent that they are justified, inferred from beliefs about our experiences. So the normal case of perceiving the red circle consists of this:

(a) There is a red circle in front of me.
(b) I have a visual impression of a red circle, caused by the red circle in front of me.
(c) I have a belief of the form "I have a visual impression of a red circle." This would be a foundational belief that is justified solely by the occurrence of the experience it describes.
(d) From this foundational belief, I infer and thereby justify a higher-level belief to the effect that there is a red circle in front of me, that is, a real, red circle, not just a sense impression of one.

In the case of hallucination, this becomes

(e) I have a visual impression of a red circle.
(f) I have a belief of the form "I have a visual impression of a red circle."
(g) If I do not realize that I am having a hallucination, I will then infer from the belief in (f) the further (false) belief "There is a red circle in front of me." But if I do realize that I am having a hallucination, I will draw no further inference to the existence of red circles.

That presents us with a sketch of how the deep foundationalist views experience, and how she thinks it relates to sensory perception. But what reason do we have to accept this picture? In particular, what reason do we have to accept the assumption that there is something common to both a hallucination of X and a perception of X (and perhaps also to a dream of X)? After all, it has the strange-seeming implication that when we look at a cup and really see it, it is not the cup itself that we are visually aware of. It is only our visual impression of a cup that we are aware of, which gives rise to a belief that we are having a visual impression of a cup, from which in turn we infer that there is a cup before us. It is an account of experience and of perception that makes the real world more remote from us than it seems. Why should we accept it?

(iii) Arguments in support of this conception of experience

In support of her account of perception and experience, the deep foundation-alist can point to the fact that very often perception and hallucination are indistinguishable by the person concerned at the time they occur. Hallucinating a red circle on a white wall can be to the person concerned *exactly* like really perceiving a red circle on a white wall. That is indeed why hallucinations can often be mistaken for real perceptions. And does not that in turn imply that the state that the person is in, in such a pair of cases, is exactly the same? What differentiates perception from hallucination is not something going on *inside* the consciousness of the perceiver. It is what is outside the perceiver that makes the crucial difference, namely the existence of a real object for her to perceive. But if what makes the difference between perception and hallucination is outside the perceiver, that must mean that as regards what is inside the perceiver, hallucination and perception are the same: they both consist in the occurrence of an experience, in the deep foundationalist's favored sense of the term.

This conclusion can be reinforced by considering the way in which hallucination and perception can occur at the same time, merging into each other. Consider the case where I am really perceiving a plain white wall, but I am having a hallucination of a red circle on that white wall. Surely, the deep foundationalist will say, the kind of awareness that I have of something red and circular is exactly like the kind of awareness I have of a flat white expanse. It isn't that the first sort of awareness "feels" any different to me—the awareness of the red circle is just like the awareness of the white expanse. So the only way in which we can accommodate the fact that one is a case of perception and the other a case of hallucination is to agree that they are alike in that they both consist of the occurrence of a visual awareness (a visual experience or a visual sense impression) and differ only with respect to what is outside the person's consciousness, with respect to the existence (or not) of a real object corresponding to the sense impression.

This is not a *compelling* defense of the deep foundationalist's conception of experience, but it is a plausible one. If we accept it, what it means is that experience consists in the occurrence of a set of conscious states. Very often, these will be sense impressions (though we should note that since we may have such impressions even when we are hallucinating and perhaps when we are dreaming, they are impressions which do not require the use of the senses. Rather they are sense impressions in that they are *like* those which we normally expect our senses to give us.

There are two further complications that need to be added to this picture of the deep foundationalist's concept of experience. We have so far been focusing on the idea of *sense* experience, and it is certainly this which looms large in the deep foundationalist's picture. For it is by reference to sense experience that she hopes to be able to show that our beliefs about the external world can be justified. But as well as sense experiences, she recognizes some other kinds of mental state as playing potentially the same foundational role as that enjoyed by sense experiences. We have, for example, as well as the five familiar senses of vision, touch, hearing, smell, and taste, some "inner" senses such as the sense of pain, and our kinesthetic sense. These can give us sensations, although we do not normally take them as giving information about the world beyond our bodies. We also have other conscious states, states such as thoughts or wishes, which a deep foundationalist may acknowledge as being foundational. What is common to *all* these states, both the sense experiences and the "inner" sensations and the thoughts, is that they are conscious states accessible to introspection. According to foundationalism, a justified belief, in respect to each of these states, that we are in that state is justified solely by the occurrence of the state in question: it does not consist in inferring that belief from some other belief(s). It is therefore a belief which is capable of *direct* justification.

5.4 Objections to Empirical Foundationalism

Although a foundationalist account of justification has long seemed to many the only one with any plausibility, in recent years it has been heavily criticized. In relation to foundationalism as a theory about justified empirical beliefs, we shall consider four possible criticisms. The first three are directed at the deep foundationalist in particular, and the fourth at foundationalism in general.

(i) Deep foundationalism and self-knowledge

The first objection focuses on the notion of the self that the deep foundationalist is forced to adopt. The deep foundationalist maintains that all our knowledge and justified beliefs about the external world rest upon the sense impressions that we have. But we now have to ask what is covered by the phrase "the external world." Certainly it will cover cars and houses, mountains and pins, shoes and telephones. It will also cover other people's bodies, since the way that I know that there is another human body in front of me is the same as the way in which I know that there is a tree in front of me: by relying on my sense impressions. What about my own body—is that part of the external world? Presumably my hand, for example, must count as part of the external world—the way that I know that I have a hand is by relying on my sense impressions. What goes for my hand will also go for my arms and legs. For the same reason, my torso must be part of the external world. So we are already getting clear that the phrase "external world" does not mean "external to my skin." Is my brain part of the external world? By the same reasoning, it must be: it is by relying on my sense impressions (and inferences from them) that I can know that I have a brain. So the phrase "external world" means something like "external to my mind." Removing the spatial metaphor from this explanation, we can say that the meaning of saying "X exists as part of the external world" is " 'X exists' does not imply 'someone is aware of X.' "

Now let us pause and see what view of the self the deep foundationalist is implicitly adopting. She is supposing herself in a position to make judgments of the form "I now have an X-type sense impression" before she acquires any knowledge of the external world, since she thinks that all of her justified beliefs about the external world rest ultimately on her sense impressions. So what conception of herself does she have when (as she thinks) she is making judgments about herself (e.g., judgments about the sense impressions she is having) without making any judgments about external objects?

This is a large question. Because it belongs properly to the philosophy of mind rather than to epistemology, it is not one that we will consider in great detail. But we need to notice at least a little of the debate, since the deep foundationalist is giving hostages to fortune in this area. According to one view, it is a precondition of a person's being able to make judgments about herself that she should be able to pick out or identify within her experience some subject or owner of experiences, the person she is referring to by the term "I" when she says, for example, "I now have a red sense impression." Such identification is possible only because "I" refers to a being with a body. It is only by reference to the body that the denotation of terms like "I," "me," and "mine" can be tied down. So, according to this line of thought, someone who is in a position to make judgments of the form "*I* have a red sense impression" is presupposing a belief that they have a body, that is, presupposing something which is part of the external world. So the deep foundationalist's attempt to show how *all* of our justified beliefs about the external world rest on a more basic set of beliefs about sense impressions is a failure. Reference to the external world has to enter into those beliefs which were supposedly invoking only sense impressions. The external world enters as the "I," the owner of the sense impressions.

According to a second view of the matter, the belief that "I" can refer only to an object in the external world, such as a human being, is mistaken. The mere fact of consciousness is, on this view, sufficient for the making of judgments using "I." "I" means something like "*this* consciousness," where the "this" is accompanied by a kind of inner pointing. After all, it might be said, if I wake up in a hospital bed suffering from amnesia, the effects of anaesthesia, and total paralysis, I may be unable to sense my own body at all. I might be unable to move myself so that parts of my body would become visible to me; I may be unable to feel any internal kinaesthetic sensations. As regards my conscious states, it might be said, it would be for me just as if I had no body. And yet surely I could still have thoughts involving "I." I might think to myself "Who am I? Where am I? What has happened to me?" And if these thoughts are possible, then it seems that "I" thoughts do not require *any* kind of awareness of a body, and hence that this attack on deep foundationalism can be rebutted.

Whether this reply is indeed adequate may be questioned. But those tempted by deep foundationalism need to be aware that their implicit view of the nature of self-reference is a possible source of weakness.

(ii) Wittgenstein's anti-private language argument

Let us turn now to a second possible line of attack, deriving from Wittgenstein's attack on the possibility of a so-called private language. This is a highly contentious area, and there is little agreement among commentators about the details of the argument, or even what its starting and finishing points are. But it has been regarded by some as a very powerful line of objection to the foundationalist approach, and hence needs to be considered. Wittgenstein's text does not refer to foundationalism at all by name, nor does his discussion focus on sense impressions. So what we will consider is an adaptation of Wittgenstein's remarks, an argument that is true (as we hope) to the spirit rather than to the letter of Wittgenstein's text. For the sake of convenience, we will continue to speak of it as "Wittgenstein's" argument.

The general structure of the argument can be summed up in two propositions:

(A) The deep foundationalist is committed to the possibility of a private language (in a certain sense of that term).

(B) There could not be a private language, in the relevant sense.

If these two premises can be established, it will of course follow that

(C) Deep foundationalism is mistaken.

Let us consider (A) first. By a "private" language, Wittgenstein does not just mean a secret code in which, for example, someone might write a private diary. For it would always be possible for someone else to find the diary and to crack the code, thereby making it no longer private. By a private language, Wittgenstein means a language which is *by necessity* private, a language which it is not *possible* for anyone else to understand. How might there be such a language, and why is the deep foundationalist committed to its existence?

Consider the following two assumptions:

(i) The meaning of at least some terms describing sense impressions is partly determined by the sense impressions themselves, and

(ii) the only person who can have access to the nature of a sense impression is the person whose sense impression it is.

If these two assumptions were correct, it would follow that the language containing the terms in question would be private in Wittgenstein's sense (or at least that part of it containing those terms would be private). And the deep foundationalist must think of her own sense impression language as just such a language. Since she thinks that in the justification of her empirical beliefs, she has to start with her own sense impressions, there is nothing else that could give sense to the terms in which she describes her sense impressions than those impressions themselves. The very meaning of "red" for her would be at least partly determined by the seeming color of the sensations which she called "sensations of red." She could not explain the meaning of "red" by equating it with, for example, the color of blood, of sunsets, of cochineal, because blood, sunsets, and cochineal are all entities in the external world, and her knowledge of such entities and of their properties *presupposes* (in her view) that she already has knowledge of her own sense impressions. It is in terms of her prior knowledge of the nature of her sense impressions (including, e.g., the fact that some of them are red) that she is supposed *subsequently* to be able to justify her claims to know the color of external objects. So whatever meaning she attaches to "red" and to other terms describing her sense impressions must be determined by the nature of those sense impressions themselves.

Further, the deep foundationalist must think of her own sense impressions as inaccessible to other people. The most that they could know would be that confronted by blood, sunsets, and cochineal, she would use the term "red" in each case. But that tells them only that she gets a similar sense impression from the three kinds of object. It does not tell them what sort of sense impression it is. For all that they can tell, it may be that when confronted by objects of these three kinds, she has a sense impression which they would call a sense impression of blue, or even the sort of sense impression which in them is caused by sounds or smells. They can have no idea of what the nature of the sense impression is, as opposed to the sorts of objects which will cause it.

It seems, then, that the deep foundationalist is indeed committed to the existence of a private language. But why cannot she accept this fact with equanimity? This is where premise (B) comes in. Wittgenstein claims

(iii) that in any genuine language, there must be a distinction between the incorrect and incorrect uses of that language, and
(iv) that in the case of the supposed private language, no such distinction can be drawn.

In defense of the first claim, Wittgenstein urges that what gives a sentence the meaning it has is not some sort of experience or conscious mental state that the user has when she uses the sentence. Rather, the meaning of the sentence is determined by the *use* that is made of the sentence. If we oversimplify, we can say that meaning *is* use, where the use is governed by rules specifying what counts as a *correct* use. But where there is the possibility of *correct* use, there must also be the possibility of incorrect use or misuse. A rule which can be followed is also a rule which can be broken. Essential to the possibility of genuine language, therefore, is the distinction between correct and incorrect use of the terms comprising that language.

If that gives us a reason for accepting (iii), why should we also accept (iv)? Wittgenstein's thought here is that the "speaker" of a supposedly private language cannot distinguish between, on the one hand, "it seems to me to be so, but really it isn't," and on the other "it really is so." When we speak the ordinary language of external public objects, that is a distinction which we can draw. I know that things can appear to me to be so when really they are not so. I know, for example, that a straight stick will look bent when it is in water. I know that a blue object may appear brown in poor light. But if the deep foundationalist, confined as she supposes she must be initially, to the language of sense impressions, judges to herself that she has a red sense impression, what is the difference between it merely seeming to her that she has a red sense impression when really she does not, and it really being a red sense impression? Wittgenstein's claim is that in such a situation, there would be no difference, and he remarks

> . . . in the present case, I have no criterion of correctness. One would like to say: whatever is going to seem right to me is right. And that only means that here we cannot talk about "right." (Wittgenstein, 1963, sec. 258)

(iii) Deep foundationalism leads to skepticism about the external world

Let us turn now to a third objection which is sometimes leveled against foundationalism, especially against deep foundationalism. When we were looking at the arguments which lead to the conclusion that in sense perception, it is our own sense impressions that we are aware of, we noticed that if we are to gain knowledge of the external world from our sense impressions, it is because we rely on background knowledge which allows us to interpret the sense impressions correctly. If, for example, I am aware of a red patch occupying most of my visual field, and I thereby come to know that there is an apple held close in front of my face, it is because my background knowledge (about what apples look like when held close, about the likelihood of an apple being within sight, etc.) enables me to rule out all other interpretations of my sense impressions as improbable. But the background information that I am here relying on includes beliefs about the external world—beliefs about what objects look like under various conditions, how perspective affects their appearance, about the likelihood that they will be found in particular places at particular times, and so on. What justification do I have for all *these* beliefs? If the deep foundationalist is right, these other beliefs in turn must be based upon beliefs about sense impressions. But we have just seen that sense impressions do not *by themselves* yield justified beliefs about the external world. They yield justified beliefs about the external world *only* when combined with background information. So what we have to imagine is someone who starts with nothing but her sense impressions, and *from that basis alone* builds up a set of justified beliefs about the external world, beliefs which she can then invoke as background information, to be utilized when she interprets the further sense impressions that she gets. And of course if we are right in claiming that background information is *always* needed before sense impressions can give you any knowledge of the external world, it would follow at once that knowledge of the external world would be impossible. It could be achieved only by those who already had it. So for this reason, acceptance of deep foundationalism will lead to skepticism about the external world.

(iv) Experience, as such, cannot provide justifications

A fourth objection, and this time one that will apply to both deep and shallow foundationalism, focuses on the nature of justification. Hitherto, we have been supposing that what justifies you in holding a belief (if anything does) is another belief, where a belief is essentially the sort of thing that has a propositional content that can be true or false. If your belief that p is justified by your belief that q, this is to say in part that q *confirms* p, where what this in turn means is that the truth of q increases the likelihood that p is true. Justification, in other words, has been understood in terms of confirmation, and confirmation has been understood in terms of a relation holding between things (like beliefs) which can be true or false. What the foundationalist is implicitly proposing is a notion of justification that will not fit this account. If she is a deep foundationalist, she is supposing that my beliefs about external objects are justified by my beliefs about my sense impressions, and that my beliefs about my sense impressions are justified by the sense impressions themselves. But sense impressions cannot be true or false—they do not *say* anything, and hence do not say anything true or false. They just *are*. Because they cannot be true or false, they cannot stand in any confirmation relations to beliefs, and since we are interpreting justification in terms of confirmation it follows that sense impressions cannot act as justifiers of beliefs, not even as justifiers of beliefs about sense impressions.

Let us illustrate the point, this time focusing on shallow foundationalism. Suppose the detective believes that Morgan handled the gun. If she is to be justified in holding that belief, it is not enough simply that Morgan's fingerprints *are* on the gun; the detective must also *believe* that they are on the gun. If she believes that, then she may indeed have justification for believing that Morgan handled the gun. But the mere presence of fingerprints by themselves cannot act as a justification. They just *are* (as we said above that a person's sense impressions just are). Just as the sense impressions do not say anything, so too the fingerprints do not say anything, and hence do not say anything true or false, and hence do not imply anything, and hence cannot be used to justify the detective's belief. Of course, they could *come to be used* by the detective as justification for thinking that Morgan handled the gun, but only if she came to believe that the fingerprints were there. In that case, it would be her *belief* that the fingerprints were on the gun (not the fingerprints themselves) that justified the belief that Morgan handled the gun.

What this means is that the foundationalist is faced with a dilemma: either she must admit that states of affairs (either sense impressions or states of the external world) cannot play the fundamental justificatory role which she has assigned to them, or she must develop a quite different account of justification, one which makes it possible for there to be justificatory relations between beliefs and bits of the world.

5.5 Concluding Comment on Foundationalism about Empirical Beliefs

Each of the above arguments can be criticized—and those criticisms in turn attacked. So none of the arguments is by itself conclusive. But we believe that collectively they make foundationalism about empirical beliefs a good deal less attractive than it at first seemed. In spite of these problems which it faces, however, it might nonetheless be the best available theory. That is a question which cannot be settled until we have looked at its principal rival, coherentism, which we shall address in Chapter 7. But before we do so, we need to consider whether foundationalism fares any better with a priori beliefs than it does with empirical ones, and that is the question to which we turn in the next chapter.

Exercises

1. Without rereading the chapter explain the infinite regress argument for thinking that there must be foundational beliefs. Write no more than one page, and assess your answer for accuracy, clarity, and completeness against section 5.1.
2. Without rereading the chapter, explain the difference between a priori and empirical beliefs, illustrating your answer with two examples of each which are significantly different from those in the text. Also try to find two examples of beliefs which are difficult to place in either category, giving your reasons in each case. Write no more than a page and a half. Finally, share your answer with a fellow student and critique each other's reasoning.
3. Give yourself an after-image (look at a fairly bright source of light for a few seconds and then focus on a blank wall). Use this experience to help you explain the difference between deep and shallow foundationalism. Write no more than one page.
4. Close your eyes and concentrate only on the inner sensations which you are having. Imagine that all your information about yourself is of the kind to which you are attending now. Think what you would then know about yourself, and, using these reflections, explain why deep foundationalism leads to skepticism about one's knowledge of oneself. Exchange your answer with a fellow student, and assess each other's answers.

5. You notice one day that you have a sensation of a kind completely unlike any other which you have experienced. You wonder if the sensation will recur in the future and decide to watch out for it. How does Wittgenstein's anti-private language argument present difficulties for your project?
6. In the light of your previous answers, explain your current views on how experience can provide us with knowledge. Include your account of what problems remain to be answered. (Hard.)

CHAPTER 6

Foundationalism about
A Priori Beliefs

We have thus far looked at the account which the foundationalist provides of our justified empirical beliefs, and we have given some reasons for thinking that it is unsatisfactory. But even if the criticisms which we have voiced of it so far are correct, it might still be thought that at least in regard to our a priori beliefs, foundationalism is an adequate theory. So let us consider what the theory has to tell us about a priori beliefs and in particular how it responds to the regress argument of justification that we described in Chapter 5.

6.1 Self-evidence as the Foundation of A Priori Belief

Regarding a priori beliefs, the general principles of foundationalist theory are the same as with empirical beliefs. The foundationalist will claim that our justified a priori beliefs are justified either by being derived from something else, which in turn is justified by being derived from something else, and so on, or else they are basic beliefs and are justified non-inferentially. But instead of appealing to the notion of experience as the regress-stopper, for a priori beliefs, the foundationalist will appeal to the idea of *self-evidence*. We can thus complete the provisional foundationalist account of justification on page 74 as follows:

1. S has a justified belief that p = S's belief that p is directly or indirectly justified.
2. S's belief that p is directly justified = *either* S has an experience which justifies her belief that p, *or* p is self-evident for S.
3. S's belief that p is indirectly justified =
   (a) S believes that q.
   (b) S has derived p from q.
   (c) S's belief that q is justified, directly or indirectly.
   (d) S's derivation of p from q is justified.

What does the notion of self-evidence mean here, and indeed are there any beliefs which are self-evidently true? Something is self-evident in this sense if it can be seen to be true, by anyone who understands the propositional content of the belief, no matter what other information they might have. Both clauses of this explanation are important. There may well be things which are self-evident to an adult (such as $1 + 1 = 2$) which are not self-evident to a baby simply because the baby does not understand what is expressed by "$1 + 1 = 2$," and the fact that the *baby* does not find them self-evident does nothing to show that they are not self-evident in the sense being used here. Secondly, there are many things which we would ordinarily call "self-evident," because they are so obvious, but which will not count as self-evident in this sense. We might say, for example, that it is self-evident that humans need to breathe, that Eskimos are unlikely to buy ice, or desert people sand, and so on. But none of these obvious truths counts as self-evident in this sense, because all of them rely on other information that we have. Given what we know about human physiology, and about economics, it is obvious that people need to breathe, sleep, eat, and so on. But if we did not have that background information, it would be far from obvious that these claims were true.

Are there any self-evident propositions, so defined? We have mentioned one possible example ($1 + 1 = 2$), and there are many other candidates. Consider, for example, "All bachelors are unmarried." Of course this might not be self-evident to someone who did not know what a bachelor was or what being unmarried was—but then they would be someone who did not understand what the proposition was saying. If someone does understand what the proposition is saying, and hence knows what being a bachelor and unmarried are, then (so it seems) she needs no other information in order to be justified in accepting the proposition as true.

Writers in this tradition have not always used the language of self-evidence. Descartes and Leibniz spoke of "the natural light of reason" and of "intuition." Some writers such as Ewing speak of "seeing" (in a non-visual sense) that certain propositions are true. Empiricist writers have often invoked the thought that these self-evident truths are somehow true in virtue of language, or are true by definition. But what is common to all such writers is the idea that there is a nonempirical regress-stopper for our a priori beliefs.

There are several important features to note about the foundationalist conception of a priori knowledge. In the first place, the starting points are meant to be *self*-evident propositions: our justified acceptance of them does not require that we show them to follow from any other beliefs which are justified. Because they do not draw their support from any other beliefs, they cannot be undermined by any other beliefs. It is impossible to provide any evidence that they are false, since it is impossible both to understand what the belief is and also not to see that it is true.

Secondly, a precisely parallel status is supposed to attach to the rules of inference which tell us what we can deduce from what. It is not so much that they are self-evidently *true* as that they are self-evidently *reliable*, in the sense that anything which we deduce by their means from a true starting point must also be true. They are, as it is sometimes put, truth-preserving. We do not need to justify our acceptance of the rules of inference by appealing to anything beyond them, because their reliability is *self*-evident.

Thirdly, what justifies our acceptance of non-self-evident a priori beliefs is that they are deduced from the self-evident beliefs by means of the self-evidently reliable rules of inference. It thus follows (and this is an important point to which we shall return) that the direction of justification is entirely one way; the derivative beliefs are justified solely by reference to the self-evident ones, and the self-evident ones are not justified at all by the derivative ones.

In what follows, we will look in more detail at a foundationalist approach to the a priori in three main areas in which it seems to be especially plausible. These areas are geometry, number theory, and logic. Our final conclusion will be that in fact foundationalism about the a priori is mistaken, but it is important to see first why it can seem such a tempting account. (The reader may find it helpful to read the Logic Appendix, particularly 4.1, in conjunction with what follows.)

6.2 Foundationalism in Three A Priori Domains

(i) The axioms of Euclidean geometry look self-evident

Think for a moment of Pythagoras's theorem, which tells us that for any right-angled triangle, the square of the hypotenuse is equal to the sum of the squares of the other two sides. Suppose I claim that the theorem is true. How is my claim to be justified? If we assume that I am not simply relying on what someone else has told me, but have worked through the proof for myself, my belief must be justified by an appeal to other geometrical beliefs (for example, about the sum of the internal angles of a triangle), which in turn are justified by others . . . until we come to some basic geometrical beliefs which require no further justification. This is what a foundationalist would expect to find for Euclidean geometry. And on the face of it, this is just how Euclid does present his findings. The whole edifice of Euclidean geometry rests on certain basic claims or axioms which are not inferred from any further truths but are taken as foundational starting points from which everything else is inferred by valid logical principles.

Euclid divides his basic claims into two groups, called "common notions" and postulates. The common notions are logical principles with a quite general application, extending to many other areas besides geometry. They are:

(1) Things which are equal to the same thing are also equal to each other.
(2) If equals be added to equals, the wholes are equals.
(3) If equals be subtracted from equals, the remainders are equal.
(4) Things which coincide with one another are equal to one another.
(5) The whole is greater than the part.

The postulates are basic principles with a specifically geometrical content. They are:

(6) There is one and only one straight line joining any two points.
(7) A finite straight line may be extended indefinitely in a straight line.
(8) Given a point, a circle of any radius may be described about the point.
(9) All right angles are equal to each other.
(10) Given a straight line and a point not on that line, it is possible to draw one and only one line through the point parallel to the line. [This is not quite how Euclid himself expressed this axiom. It is instead something logically equivalent to the postulate which Euclid himself provided. It will become clear later why we have opted for this version of the axiom.]

Reducing our beliefs in a given area to a set of basic axioms, which are not themselves proved by reference to anything else, and a set of theorems, which are justified by being shown to follow rigorously from the axioms, is called an *axiomatization* of a domain. And it does seem that Euclidean geometry supplies one example of a highly complex domain, containing many very unobvious truths, which has been successfully axiomatized. For it does seem that the postulates and common notions on which Euclid relies have at least a good claim to be regarded as self-evident.

(ii) Deriving arithmetical beliefs from self-evident beginnings

The position with number theory (arithmetic) is similar to that which we have just noted for geometry. Here too the foundationalist will say that we must distinguish between a set of self-evident axioms, and the theorems about numbers which are derivable from them. There are in fact various ways in which arithmetic can be axiomatized. Since an axiomatization of arithmetic will be less familiar to many readers than the axiomatization of Euclidean geometry, we will show in a little more detail what it looks like. We shall follow the Italian mathematician Peano (1852–1932), because although his account is in some ways unsatisfactory, it will illustrate very conveniently the points we want to make. Peano takes three ideas as basic or primitive or undefined:

0,   number,   successor

In terms of these basic ideas, he advances five axioms:

Axiom 1:   0 is a number.

Axiom 2:   The successor of a number is a number.

Axiom 3:   No two numbers have the same successor.

Axiom 4:   0 is not the successor of any number.

Axiom 5:   Any property which belongs to 0, and also to the successor of every number which has the property, belongs to every number.

If we now use the expression "$S(n)$" to mean "the successor of the number n," we can define each of the natural numbers in this way:

Definition 1: 1 = $S(0)$ (i.e., 1 is the successor of 0)

Definition 2: 2 = $S[S(0)]$ (i.e., 2 is the successor of the successor of 0)

Definition 3: 3 = $S\{S[S(0)]\}$, etc.

Using these axioms and definitions we can now derive some very simple theorems of arithmetic. For example:

Theorem 1: 1 is a number (by Axiom 1 and def. 1).

Theorem 2: 1 and 2 are different numbers (by Axiom 3 and defs. 2 and 3).

Suppose that we add to our list of definitions a definition of "+." This is given by two formulas which tell us how we are allowed to transform expressions using "+" into other expressions which do not use "+." The two formulas are given by:

Definition 4: (A) $m + 0 = m$ (i.e., adding 0 to a number yields the same number)

             (B) $m + S(n) = S(m + n)$ (i.e., when you add m to the successor of n, you get the successor of adding m to n).

With this definition in place, we can now prove that $1 + 1 = 2$, as follows:

Theorem 3: $1 + 1 = 2$

$$1 + 1 = S(0) + S(0) \quad \text{(by def. 1)}$$
$$= S[S(0)] + 0 \quad \text{(by def. 4(B))}$$
$$= S[S(0)] \quad \text{(by def. 4(A))}$$
$$= 2 \quad \text{(by def. 2) Q.E.D.}$$

Of course the theorems we have proved above are wholly trivial ones. But the point of the exercise is to illustrate a *technique* rather than a set of results. What the foundationalist will claim is that we can start with self-evident axioms, and, proceeding by self-evidently reliable steps, we can prove any number of theorems. The very same techniques which are used to prove the obvious theorems which we have just illustrated can be used to prove the much more interesting results which number theory can yield. The distinction between what is a trivial theorem and what is an interesting one is a psychological rather than a logical or epistemological one. So if the axiomatization of arithmetic shows how both sorts of theorems fit into the structure of knowledge or justified belief in the same sort of way (i.e., being justified by being deduced from self-evident foundations) so much the better. The interesting theorems will then have the same security which attaches to the trivial ones. To achieve these more interesting results, we would need to add further definitions (e.g., of other arithmetical operations like multiplication, division, etc.)

but this presents no problem in principle. (Taking Definition 4 above as a model, readers may like to construct for themselves definitions of these other operations.)

Certainly when we look at the axioms and theorems of arithmetic, the foundationalist case does seem very strong. It *does* seem self-evident that, for example, the successor of a number must itself be a number, that no two numbers have the same successor, and so on. Even Axiom 5 seems self-evident, because although it may need some thought to see that it is true, once we understand what it is saying, we surely see that it, like the other axioms, has to be true. And when we look at the proofs of the theorems, it does seem that having once accepted the axioms, we *must* accept the theorems. They are derived from the axioms in a series of self-evidently reliable steps.

(iii) Are beliefs about logical truths based on self-evidence?

The position with logic is similar to that which we have seen with geometry and arithmetic. The domain can be axiomatized into a set of apparently self-evident axioms, and of theorems derived from those axioms by self-evidently reliable methods of inference. There are many axiomatizations of logic possible, but one of the most famous and historically important was that provided by Russell and Whitehead in their classic *Principia Mathematica.* Using p, q, etc., to stand for propositions, they proposed the following six axioms:

1. Anything implied by a true elementary proposition is true.
2. (p or p) implies p.
3. q implies (either p or q, or both).
4. (p or q) implies (q or p).
5. p or (q or r) implies q or (p or r).
6. If q implies r, then (p or q) implies (p or r).

The axioms are in fact expressed more formally than this, using logical symbols rather than English words like "and" or "implies." To avoid the symbolism, we have "translated" the Russell-Whitehead axioms into English. (For more on logical symbolism, see the Logic Appendix.) Although such translations do raise philosophical problems which will be referred to in Chapters 9 and 11, they are not relevant to the points which we are here making.

On the basis of these axioms Russell and Whitehead seek to deduce a number of theorems, just as we have seen Euclid and Peano do. Some of these theorems are obvious and trivial (e.g., "If the truth of p implies that p is false, then p is false"), and others are very unobvious (e.g., "(p and not-q) implies and is implied by the falsity of (p or not-q, or both)"). We will not provide the proofs here, as even with the simple theorems, the proofs can be cumbersome to produce without using a logical notation. The essential point here, as before, is to notice the plausibility of the foundationalist case. The axioms do appear to be self-evident, and if, as is generally agreed, the theorems follow them by self-evidently reliable inferences, our beliefs in the domain of logic appear to conform to the foundationalist account. (For further examples and discussion, see the Logic Appendix 5.1.)

It seems then that even if we grant that foundationalism has at the least very serious difficulties in accounting for our justified empirical beliefs, it does look very plausible when we turn to a priori beliefs. There, the organization of our beliefs into foundations and superstructure is not a philosophical postulation, but, in the form of axiomatization, is a reality. Mustn't we grant, therefore, that foundationalism should be accepted for at least some of our justified beliefs? It is to the assessment of this claim that we now turn.

6.3 Objections to A Priori Foundationalism

Following our division of the area in the last chapter, we shall divide our critical comments on foundationalism about the a priori into three, dealing first with Euclidean geometry, then with number theory, and finally with logic. We will argue first that contrary to first appearances, none of these domains is best accounted for by a foundationalist theory. Secondly, we will argue that no alternative foundations could be found which would satisfy the foundationalist's requirements. Finally, we shall argue that although the axiomatic way of organizing our beliefs in a given domain is of great importance and does increase the confidence we can place in what might have been relatively isolated beliefs, the epistemological status of axioms and theorems has been persistently misunderstood, especially in more recent times by foundationalists.

(i) Euclidean geometry reconsidered: alternative geometries

Let us start with Euclid's fifth axiom, the so-called axiom of parallels. For many centuries after Euclid, mathematicians thought that although the axiom was undoubtedly true, it might be *provably* true, and hence something that could appear as a theorem rather than as an axiom. But in fact, all attempts to prove it from the other axioms failed (and it can now be proved *not* to be provable from the other axioms). There are two developments in particular in the nineteenth century which we need to notice. First, a mathematician named Riemann substituted for Euclid's fifth axiom an alternative axiom which said

> Given a straight line and a point not on that line, *no* line can be drawn through the point parallel to the given line.

From that revised fifth axiom, together with slightly revised versions of the other four axioms, he then derived a consistent set of theorems which comprise a non-Euclidean geometry (it is sometimes called elliptic geometry). The theorems are often parallel (in a nongeometrical sense!) to the theorems of Euclid, but they are clearly different from Euclid's. For example, whereas in

Euclidean geometry, the internal angles of a triangle add up to two right angles, in Riemannian geometry, they always add up to more than two right angles, the sum approaching two right angles as the area of the triangle approaches 0, and approaching six right angles as the sum of the triangle approaches the maximum area for a triangle. For more details, see Table 1.

As an aid to imagining what elliptical geometry is like, imagine treating the surface of a sphere as a plane with the great circles of the sphere as straight lines. It will then be clear, for example, how the smaller the triangle is, the more nearly does it approach being a Euclidean triangle and hence having its internal angles equal to two right angles; how there is a largest possible area for a triangle; how no straight lines can be parallel to each other; and so on.

The second development came in the work of two mathematicians working independently, Lobachevsky and Bolyai. In place of Euclid's fifth axiom, they substituted the following:

> Given a straight line and a point not on that line, *more than* one straight line can be drawn through the point parallel to the given line.

They were then able to derive from that revised set of axioms a body of theorems which were non-Euclidean and non-Riemannian. This type of geometry is sometimes called hyperbolic geometry, and contains theorems which are analogous to, though different from, those of Euclid and of Riemann (see Table 1 for comparison of these geometries).

We have, then, three different geometries—and it is possible to produce yet others. Which one best fits the nature of space? What the nature of our space is, is an empirical question for the physicist to answer. But we (as non-physicists) can put forward a provisional answer as follows: our best current cosmological theories presuppose that space is *not* Euclidean. Current theories predict, for example, that if you measure large enough triangles (on an intergalactic scale) their internal angles do not total two right angles, and this is a prediction for which there is empirical confirmation. Current theories imply that the universe is finite but unbounded, and if it is finite, there cannot be any Euclidean straight lines (which, so Euclidean geometry tells us, can be extended to infinity). Current theories tell us that in every direction in which we look at the sky, objects are receding from us at a rate proportional to their distance from us, *and that this observation would hold true no matter from what celestial body it was made;* this is something which could not be true if space is Euclidean. In short, our space is described more accurately by an elliptical geometry than by a Euclidean one.

It is of course possible that scientific advances in the future will lead us once again to think that Euclid gives us the best account of the nature of space. But this seems unlikely. So the position we have is this: Euclid's axiom of parallels is not provable from other self-evident axioms and hence cannot be a theorem. It is false as a description of what our space is like, hence it is not true, and hence it is not self-evidently true. Since it is neither self-evident, nor

TABLE 1 Alternative Geometries

Euclidean	Lobachevskian	Riemannian
Given a line and point not on that line, there is exactly one line through the point parallel to the given line.	Given a line and a point not on that line, there is more than one line through the point parallel to the given line.	Given a line and a point not on that line, there are no lines through the point parallel to the given line.
The sum of the internal angles of a triangle equals two right angles.	The sum of the internal angles of a triangle is less than two right angles, but approaches two right angles as the area of the triangle approaches 0, and approaches 0 as the area of the triangle approaches the maximum area for a triangle.	The sum of the internal angles of a triangle is greater than two right angles, but approaches two right angles as the area of the triangle approaches 0, and approaches six right angles as the area of the triangle approaches the maximum area for a triangle.
The ratio of the circumference of a circle to its diameter is π.	The ratio of the circumference of a circle to its diameter is more than π; the ratio approaches π as the area of the circle approaches 0.	The ratio of the circumference of a circle to its diameter is less than π; the ratio approaches π as the area of the circle approaches 0.
There can be similar figures of different areas.	There cannot be similar figures of different areas.	There cannot be similar figures of different areas.
Straight lines are infinite.	Straight lines are infinite.	Straight lines are finite and they are all of the same length.

derivable from anything self-evident, it precisely does *not* fit the foundationalist conception of a justified a priori belief. Further, the elliptical geometry which seems closest to the truth relies on Riemann's fifth axiom quoted previously, and that axiom can hardly claim to be self-evident.

The foundationalist might object that this attack on her position is confused. For in arguing that Euclid's axiom of parallels is not self-evident, we have claimed that *as a matter of empirical fact* it is not true, whereas the foundationalist is assuming that it is a priori. It is after all the justification of our a priori beliefs with which we are concerned. This reply is fair enough as it stands, but it does not go far enough to save the foundationalist position. Euclid's axiom of parallels is not self-evident, as we have defined the term (cf. 6.1), because it can (now) be doubted by wholly competent mathematicians who fully understand what it is saying. Since the foundationalist claims that the foundations of our a priori justified beliefs must be self-evident, it would still follow that a belief in the truth of Euclidean geometry was never justified.

Notice it is not *we* who are saying that such a belief was never justified. The claim is rather that *a foundationalist* is committed to making such a claim.

(ii) The hypothetical interpretation of Euclidean geometry

There is one fall-back position which is sometimes adopted in response to the line of attack which we have just been sketching. It is sometimes said that we need to construe geometry hypothetically. We should construe it as saying, not:

> The axioms are true, and therefore the theorems are true.

but rather:

> *If* the axioms are true, the theorems are true (or: the theorems follow from the axioms).

This is indeed a possible interpretation of geometries such as Euclid's (though it is worth mentioning that for most of the 2200 or so years since Euclid was writing, it was the first and not the second way in which his writings were interpreted). But even if we were to adopt the second interpretation, it would be of no help to the foundationalist, for geometrical beliefs could still not be brought within the scope of her theory. On the traditional interpretation which we were attacking above, our geometrical beliefs have the form: the axioms are true, so the theorems are true. On the proposed hypothetical interpretation, we do not believe that either the axioms or the theorems are true. Our geometrical beliefs instead have the form: the axioms imply the theorems. So if the hypothetical interpretation is to help the foundationalist, she must display some further set of self-evident axioms (i.e., not Euclid's) from which it will follow that Euclid's axioms imply his theorems. The only plausible candidates for such axioms are those of logic itself. But we shall shortly argue that these are not self-evident either (6.3 [v]).

If Euclidean geometry fails to confirm the foundationalist conception of justification, why does that conception nevertheless initially seem so plausible, and what alternative account can we give of geometrical axiomatization? A full answer to this will have to wait until we have considered coherentism in Chapters 7 and 8 but we can indicate here some elements of the answer.

(iii) How axioms and theories really relate to each other

The first important point to remember (and this is a general truth about axiomatization) is that Euclid does not *start* with a set of axioms which he regards as acceptable because they are self-evident, and *then* discover that from those axioms he can derive the body of theorems which constitute Euclidean geometry. He starts by collecting a body of propositions which were widely accepted as being true, and which he wants to be able to include, *either* as axioms *or* as theorems, in his subsequent axiomatization. The division of these propositions into axioms and theorems is then a secondary stage in the process. In this secondary stage, how a proposition is classified does not depend on whether it is self-evident but on (a) whether it is needed in order to prove some of the other claims which Euclid wants to accept and on (b) whether it cannot itself be proved from anything else which he wants to accept. A proposition is thus accepted as an axiom because of what follows from it, and as a theorem because of what it follows from. Very roughly speaking, if you want to include a proposition and do not see how to prove it, then either you postulate some more axioms which *will* enable you to prove it, or you postulate the proposition itself as an axiom.

There is thus a play-off between axioms and theorems: with fewer axioms, you might have a cleaner, neater-looking system, and all the axioms might have some claim to be self-evident, but you may not be able to prove all the propositions which you really want to. With more axioms, you may be able to prove as theorems all the propositions that you want to, but the axiom set may then look very cluttered and may contain claims which really you feel should be provable. Those geometers who thought that Euclid's axiom of parallels was probably true were really saying that he got the axiom/theorem division wrong, not because the axiom was not self-evident, but because they thought he could have postulated fewer axioms without having to give up any of the propositions which he wanted to include in his system.

On this reading of axiomatization, the fact of self-evidence is irrelevant. If the axioms appealed are self-evident, well and good; that can be an added bonus. But that is not what makes a proposition an axiom. What makes it an axiom is that it is needed in order to prove some other propositions, and our justification for accepting the axioms as true is that they are needed in order to prove certain other propositions that we antecedently accept. The axiomatizer does not simply work "forward" from a set of axioms which she has accepted no matter what they lead to. Initially at any rate, she will work "backward" *to* the axioms from a knowledge of what she wants to derive from those axioms. Of course, once the axiomatic system is set up, with a small number of axioms which are fertile in yielding a wide range of theorems, the axiomatizer may accept other propositions *simply because* they follow from the axioms. But what then gives the axioms their security is their relation to the theorems that follow from them. They are accepted because they are seen to be the neatest and most convenient way of establishing the theorems.

(iv) Beliefs about numbers: Gödel's results

As we have discussed the case of Euclidean geometry at some length, we shall deal with number theory more briefly because many of the points carry across from one area to the other. As with geometry, many results of number theory were well known long before number theory was axiomatized, and the task of number theory axiomatizers was to *organize* preexisting bodies of knowledge into axioms and theorems, rather than to *progress* from self-evident axioms to previously unaccepted theorems.

However, the position for foundationalism in relation to number theory is in some ways more promising than it turned out to be for Euclidean geometry. With geometry, the axiom of parallels is both essential for the proof of many Euclidean theorems and yet not self-evident. With number theory, however, it is very hard to imagine anyone being able to understand the axioms which we presented in 6.2(ii) and yet remaining in doubt as to whether they were true. The axioms thus do seem to have an excellent claim to be regarded as self-evident. What, then, is the problem for the foundationalist about number theory?

Suppose that we could show that there were sentences about the addition and multiplication of whole numbers which we could understand and see to be true, and indeed could prove to be true to the satisfaction of competent mathematicians, but which *could not* be deduced from the axioms of number theory. This would present the foundationalist with a serious problem. There would be truths about the multiplication, division, and so on, of whole numbers which could not be justified in the way that the foundationalist requires. That this is in fact the position with number theory is what Gödel proved with his famous "incompleteness" theorem.

We shall not explain Gödel's amazing results in any detail, but it is worth taking a moment to convey the flavor of them. Imagine that we have organized our justified beliefs about elementary number theory in the axiomatic way, so that we have (a) axioms, (b) rules of proof, and (c) theorems. Gödel inventing a technique, subsequently known as Gödel numbering, which assigns unique numbers to all the axioms and theorems and translates the rules of proof into numerical relationships. By this ingenious device, he is able to translate sentence *about* the axiomatic theory (e.g., "Sentence S is provable from the axioms by a finite number of applications of the rules") into sentences *of* number theory (so that, e.g., Sentence S is provable from the axioms by a finite number of applications of the rules of the rules" gets translated into a sentence SN, about a finite sequence of numbers whose last number is the Gödel number of S, and whose preceding numbers include the Gödel numbers of the axioms, etc.). Gödel then shows that the sentence which says roughly "I am not provable from the axioms by a finite number of applications of the rules" is both *true* and *not provable* within the axiomatic theory. This is his famous "incompleteness" theorem.

But he also went further, and in a second theorem showed that one cannot escape this "incompleteness" in one's system by adding more axioms: either the incompleteness simply recurs in the extended system, or one adds axioms which make the system inconsistent. There is, astonishingly, no middle ground between incompleteness and inconsistency.

What Gödel's results show, then, is that any attempt to capture our justified beliefs about even so simple a theory as that concerned with the addition and multiplication of whole numbers is always bound to be incomplete, however many axioms we add. There will always be truths which we can see to be true but which cannot be proved from self-evident first principles.

(v) Self-evident logical truths? Problems with the law of the excluded middle

Logic, like geometry and like number theory, is another area in which the axiomatizer starts with a mass of propositions which she wants to include either as axioms or as theorems in her axiomatic system. Here too she will be working "backward" from possible theorems to see what she might derive them from, as often as working "forward" from already-accepted axioms to see what they imply. Here also, the question of what to accept as an axiom does not turn on whether it is self-evident or not, but on whether it contributes to an austere axiom set which nevertheless has rich implications.

But the situation is not just that the axiomatizer has a choice to make as to whether to treat something as an axiom or a theorem. Rather, there is a choice to be made between *incompatible* logics. We shall illustrate this point by reference to one of the so-called laws of logic, known as the law of the excluded middle. There are various ways in which it can be expressed, but we shall express it as:

For every proposition p, either p is true, or p is false.

This does not appear as an axiom in all axiomatizations of logic. Russell and Whitehead, for example, treat it as a theorem in *Principia Mathematica*, derivable from a combination of their axioms and earlier theorems. But in *The Problems of Philosophy*, Russell refers to it as one of a number of "self-evident logical principles" (Russell, 1912, 72), and certainly for the 2000 years or so before Russell was writing this would have been regarded as an unassailable truth. But in our own day, its universal truth has been questioned. We will mention two directions from which it has been challenged. First, the so-called intuitionistic mathematicians have doubted whether the principle is true when applied to infinite sets. Secondly, a number of philosophers such as W. V. Quine and H. Putnam have suggested some of the conceptual problems raised by quantum mechanics would be eased by abandoning the law of the excluded middle.

We do not need to decide whether the law should be abandoned either for infinite sets or for quantum mechanics. The striking aspect for our purposes is that competent practitioners should seriously consider abandoning the law. This in itself is strong evidence that even if it is true, it cannot be self-evident. But more importantly, the reason that they think of abandoning it is not that they have scrutinized it very closely (more closely than logicians for the past 2000 years!) and found that it is not self-evident after all. Rather, they are contemplating abandoning it because it yields results which, rightly or wrongly, they have come to think are unacceptable. From a foundationalist perspective, this is exactly the wrong reason for contemplating abandoning the law, but it is a reason which fits in perfectly with the claims which we were making above about the axiomatization of geometry. Axioms are to be accepted or rejected because of their *relations with* other propositions, not because of some intrinsic feature such as self-evidence.

6.4 The Failure of Foundationalism

We have now seen in some detail how and why the foundationalist's account of justified a priori belief is unsatisfactory. In geometry and logic the axioms are not self-evident, and in arithmetic not all justified beliefs can be derived from the axiom set, even when we allow every self-consistent extension of that set. This does not of course show that there is not some other area of justified belief in which foundationalism might be the best theory. But what we have done is to consider the three areas in which, prima facie, foundationalism is at its strongest. If it fails even in those areas, then we are justified in claiming that it will probably fail in all other areas too. Since we have already argued in Chapter 5 that foundationalism about empirical beliefs faces serious problems, we have now cleared the way for a consideration of an alternative account of justification. Hints about what shape such an alternative theory might take have already been given in what we said earlier about the axiomatization of a priori beliefs, and we turn to explore such a theory in more detail in the next chapter.

Exercises

1. Give your reasons for thinking that the following claims are or are not self-evident in the sense explained in 6.1.
   a. The only whole numbers which divide 37 without leaving a remainder are 1 and 37.
   b. Parallel lines never meet however far they are extended.
   c. Either a football stadium will be built on this park or it will not.
   d. If it is true that the first snakes had forked tongues and that every descendant of forked-tongued snakes has a forked tongue then all snakes have forked tongues.
   Discuss your answers with a fellow student and evaluate each other's reasoning.
2. Explain your reasons for thinking that Euclidean geometry is or is not true of space. How do your reasons challenge or support foundationalism with respect to the a priori? Write no more than one page and then compare your answer with 6.3 (i) and (ii).
3. If you have convinced yourself that "the only whole numbers which divide 37 without leaving a remainder are 1 and 37" would a proof of this from Peano's axioms make the result more certain? Answer in no more than one page.

4. **a.** Explain in your own words what an axiomatization of a branch of knowledge is.
   b. Without rereading the chapter, explain in your own words the significance for foundationalism of the fact that no axiomatization of arithmetic can capture all the truths of arithmetic (Gödel's incompleteness theorem). When you have done this, check your answer against 6.3 (iv) for clarity, accuracy, and completeness.

5. Use the explanation you gave in answer to 4(a), or an expanded version of it, to write your own evaluation of the case for and against foundationalism with respect to a priori knowledge. (Hard.)

CHAPTER 7

Coherence Theories of Justification Explained

In the last two chapters, we have been outlining the details of a foundational-ist approach to justification and looking at some of the objections that have been brought against it. We shall now turn to consider the main rival to foundationalism, namely coherence theories or coherentism.

7.1 The Wigwam, Web, and Crossword Metaphors

The foundations view utilizes the metaphor of a building, where the higher levels of justified belief rest on the lower levels, which in turn rest ultimately on the foundations. To illuminate the coherence position, a variety of metaphors is possible. One is to think of our set of beliefs as like a wigwam of sticks. Each stick is supported by other sticks in the bundle, and each stick in turn provides some support to all the other sticks. There is no one stick (a sort of foundational stick, as it were) on which all the other sticks lean for support. Every stick is supported in the same kind of way as every other stick: there is no asymmetry of support. A second metaphor, driving from Quine (1970), is to think of our justified beliefs as like the strands in a spider's web. The idea here is parallel to that in the image of the wigwam: the strands in the web form a mutually supporting web in which there is no basic or foundational strand on which all the others depend. Yet a third image is provided for coherentism by the idea of a crossword. This image is better than either of the first two, because it uses the notion of epistemic support, rather than the physical support which the wigwam and web metaphors rely on. In the image of the crossword, the answers in the crossword form the corpus of our beliefs, each individual answer that we fill in representing a single belief. When we get an answer that fits with an answer that we have already, that fact helps to confirm the correctness of the second answer. The first answer confirms the correctness of the second—not conclusively since there may be other answers which would also have fitted in with the first, but confirms to some degree. But it is equally true that the second answer helps to confirm the correctness of the first answer. There is no asymmetry here in terms of confirmation: the first answer confirms the second and *at the same time and in the same way*, the second confirms the first. Notice, too, that the more answers which we get that fit in with the answers which we already have, the better confirmed we regard *all* of the answers, both the original set and the later additions. Further, that there is no one set of answers which you *have* to get first, and which will then act as confirmers of all the other answers. *Any* of the answers might be the first one we get—there are no "foundational" answers. As we will remark later, there are some points at which the cross-word metaphor breaks down, but it is nevertheless a useful analogy to bear in mind.

7.2 Coherence and Foundationalism Contrasted

But how should coherentism be described in nonmetaphorical terms? This task is less easy than it was with foundationalism, for several reasons. First of all, the coherence theory of justification (which is what we shall here be concerned with) is sometimes confused with the coherence theory of truth, which is itself difficult to make plausible. Even writers who clearly distinguish between the two (such as Dancy) think that to make the coherence theory of justification plausible, it needs to be held in combination with the coherence theory of truth. But other writers, such as Lehrer, accept a coherence theory of justification and combine it with a noncoherence theory of truth. Secondly, foundationalism is a relatively old theory which has been repeatedly refined; whereas coherentism, although now perhaps the dominant orthodoxy, is a relative newcomer. Thirdly, until recently, those writers who supported coherentism were not in the philosophical mainstream. The mainstream was occupied for a number of decades in this century by empiricists of some kind, who have usually favored some version of foundationalism, whereas those earlier writers (such as Blandshard and Ewing) who favored a coherentist approach were idealists. Finally, coherentism does *seem* to be open to objections which are both easy to understand and fatal, whereas the objections to foundationalism are not so easy to see and are more difficult to assess.

(i) Three points of contrast

Let us start by summarizing the foundationalist position in three theses, so that we can sharpen the sense of where the disagreement with coherentism lies.

1. Justified beliefs are justified *either* indirectly by being inferred from other justified beliefs, *or* directly, by appeal to (i) some kind of self-evidence (for a priori beliefs) or to (ii) experience (for empirical beliefs).

2. There is therefore a class of *basic* beliefs (foundational, etc.), namely, those which are justified, but not justified by being inferred from other beliefs. They are justified non-inferentially.
3. Justification is thus asymmetric: if your belief that p justifies your belief that q, then your belief that q cannot also justify your belief that p. In terms of the metaphor of foundations, the foundations can support the upper stories, but the upper stories cannot support the foundations.

The coherentist position can be contrasted with foundationalism in the following set of counterclaims:

4. *All* justified beliefs are justified inferentially, i.e., by inference from other beliefs: there is no "direct" justification of the kind envisaged by the foundationalist.
5. There are no basic or foundational beliefs (this follows at once from the denial of direct justification).
6. Justification is nonasymmetric: it *can* (though it does not *have to*) be the case that your belief that p justifies your belief that q, and your belief that q justifies your belief that p.

This gives us a largely negative characterization of what the coherentist says. But what, positively, does she think that justification is? She maintains that a belief is justified to the extent that it is a member of a coherent set of beliefs, being more justified if it is either a member of a larger set of coherent beliefs, or a member of a more coherent set, or both. But that immediately raises the question "What does 'coherence' mean here?"

7.3 What Does "Coherence" Mean? Consistency and Explanation

(i) Consistency

Two necessary conditions are usually put forward by modern coherentists, one in terms of consistency and the other in terms of explanation. The first says that a fully coherent set of beliefs must be logically self-consistent. If a set of beliefs contained both the belief that p and the belief that not-p, the set would not be self-consistent, and hence would not be fully coherent, and this would weaken the justification for accepting other members of the set.

(ii) Coherence and explanation

The second condition, in terms of explanation, is where the real heart of coherentism lies (see, e.g., Bonjour, 1985, 98; the same emphasis can be found in Harman, 1973). The idea is that a completely coherent set of beliefs would be a self-explanatory set—that is to say, there would be within the total set of beliefs some explanation for the truth of every belief taken individually. Of course, the idea of a completely coherent set is a heuristic fiction, like the idea of frictionless motion. It represents a hypothetical state which we will never reach, but by reference to which we can get a sense of movement away or toward it. So if my belief that p is justified, the truth of p would have to be such that it would explain the truth of some other beliefs I have, or would itself be explained by the truth of some of my other beliefs.

Let us illustrate this with an example. I wake in the night, think that I can hear a tapping noise, and wonder what it is. Has an intruder broken into the house? Is it the cat playing with something? Is it a bough tapping against the window? Am I just imagining that there is a sound? These and other possible hypotheses occur to me, and the one which I am justified in accepting is the one which best fits in with (coheres with) the rest of my web of belief. I decide, for example, that although an intruder might make *some* noises, they would be unlikely to be as regular as those noises I can hear. I thus bring to bear some background knowledge about intruders (about their desire not to be detected, their belief that the more noise they make, the more likely they are to be detected), and perhaps also some background knowledge about where I am sleeping (the house is very well secured, so an intruder could not have got in without making a great deal more noise than I am now hearing, this is not the sort of area where intruders are at all likely, etc.). So I discount the intruder hypothesis. It is still of course possible—it is not directly contradicted by anything else that I believe, and later events may suddenly make it very much more probable (e.g., if I hear whispering). But as things stand, it is not something for whose truth the other things I believe would provide a good explanation, nor is it something which provides a very good explanation for any of the other things that I believe. It does provide *an* explanation of the tapping noise that I can hear. But it is not a very good explanation, since the noise that I think I can hear is not quite the sort of noise which an intruder would be likely to make.

By contrast, the hypothesis that it is the cat does cohere with my other beliefs. I recall that the cat has a small plastic ball, suspended on a string, which it can knock with its paw, and that when it does so, the ball taps against the wall (so the "cat" hypothesis explains not just that there is a noise, but also what sort of noise it is). I know that although it is fairly dark, cats do have some powers of night vision, that playing with the suspended ball is the sort of thing this cat enjoys doing, and that the cat was shut in the room where the ball is suspended. So if the cat is playing with the ball, that would help to explain the noise that I can hear and would itself be partly explained by the other things which I already believe about the cat (its location, its capacities, its proclivities, etc.). I am justified in accepting the cat hypothesis because it coheres with the other members of my belief set.

There are several features about this example which are important from a coherentist point of view. First, the justification for accepting the cat hypothesis does not consist in deriving it directly or indirectly from some set of more basic beliefs which I have, a set which simply reports on my "experience" in some sense of that term. It consists in seeing how the hypothesis fits in with a wide range of other beliefs which I hold, some of them generalizations (about intruders and cats), some of them particular beliefs (about where *this* cat is, and what it likes doing). There is no privileged set of "basic" beliefs from which I seek to show that the hypothesis is derivable.

Secondly, these other beliefs in turn fit into a yet wider range of beliefs. For example, in assessing the "intruder" hypothesis, I call on a set of beliefs about what human intruders want (to break in unobserved), how they will probably seek to achieve this (by being as quiet as possible), what their physical capacities are (they would have to break a window or batter down a door to get in, etc.). And *that* set of beliefs will fit in with a yet wider set which I hold (about human nature, about the workings of the system of legal ownership, about the physical constitution of human bodies, and of doors and windows, etc.). At each stage in this process, I call on a wider and wider set of my beliefs, until in theory my total world view may be invoked.

Thirdly, the justification for accepting the cat hypothesis is not just in terms of what the hypothesis explains (the noise that I can hear)—it is also in terms of how my preexisting beliefs would help to explain the cat hypothesis. I antecedently hold beliefs (about cats in general, and about this cat in particular) which explain how it could come to be the case that the cat hypothesis is true.

Fourthly, notice that if I come to accept the cat hypothesis, that will (to a very tiny extent perhaps) help to confirm one of the beliefs which in turn has confirmed the cat hypothesis. One of my preexisting beliefs which helps to render credible the cat hypothesis is that cats can see in the dark (or more strictly, in very poor light). If I now come to believe that the noise is made by a cat playing in very poor light with a ball on a string, that will in turn confirm further (perhaps to a very small degree) my belief that cats can see in very poor light.

Fifthly, notice too how coherence is a matter of degree. The number and strength of the links between the cat hypothesis and my other beliefs can vary. (Consider for example how the cat hypothesis would be strengthened if I heard miaowing interspersed with the tapping, and weakened if instead I heard whispering.) And since we think that justification is something that admits of degrees, to this extent at least coherence is well shaped to be an explication of the idea of justification.

We have illustrated at some length how the explanatory strand in the notion of coherence is meant to work. Are there any other relations included in the idea of coherence? Certainly explanation is the relation which has received most emphasis from coherentists, but other relations should be mentioned as well. For sometimes when we add to our stock of beliefs, our justification for doing so has nothing to do with explanatory relations. Sometimes we are justified in adding to our stock of beliefs because the new belief is straightforwardly *implied* by what we already believe. If I believe that there are

100 women on a dance floor, and I am reliably informed that each woman has one and only one male dancing partner, no two women having the same partner, then I can at once infer that there are 100 men on the floor too. But that fact does not *explain* any of the beliefs which I already hold, nor is it explained by them. It is justified simply by being logically implied by those beliefs.

7.4 Coherence and Consistency: "Universalism" and "Particularism"

But now we need to ask the question "Given that for a belief p to be justified is for it to cohere with other beliefs, with which other beliefs *exactly* must it cohere?" Two answers, which we might label "universalism" and "particularism," are prima facie possible. According to the universalist, p must cohere with the totality of my corpus of beliefs. According to the particularist, p must cohere with some subset of my corpus of beliefs.

(i) Universalism

A clear statement of a universalist position is supplied by Harman, who writes that:

> According to the coherence theory, the assessment of a challenged belief is always holistic. Whether such a belief is justified depends on how well it fits together with *everything else one believes*. (Harman, 1986, italics added)

More to the same effect can be found in Harman, 1973; and other coherentists taking the same line include Lehrer, 1974 and 1990; and Bonjour, 1976 and 1985 (with a qualification which we note shortly).

In favor of the universalist position, we can consider the following. Suppose that my belief that p coheres to a certain degree with some small set of my beliefs (perhaps with only two or three others), but does not cohere with my total corpus of beliefs; whereas a rival belief q coheres to the same degree not just with a few of my beliefs but with the whole lot. Surely then I would be justified in believing q rather than p. For in constructing my total belief set, I do not want merely a collection of subsets each of which is internally coherent. I want one comprehensive set of beliefs which presents me with a unitary, consistent, and intelligible picture of the world. If I accept p^1 because it coheres with some subset of my beliefs, and then p^2 because it coheres with another subset of my beliefs, and p^3 because it coheres with yet a third subset, then I might in fact be increasing the *in*coherence of my total belief set—which on the coherentist account is exactly what I do not want to do.

But on the other hand, if the justification for accepting p lies in its relations with the totality of my other beliefs, do I actually have access to the totality of my other beliefs? What we have said previously about the way in which none of my beliefs need be *conscious* states implies that I do not. Many of my beliefs

I have never *consciously* entertained at all, and many (perhaps most) of those which I have consciously entertained at some time in the past, I cannot consciously recall now.

Further, Goldman (1986, 197) has argued that if it is a necessary condition of a coherent set of beliefs that they should be consistent, and if the relevant set of beliefs is one's total set of beliefs, then an inconsistency in *any* part of one's belief system would mean that none of one's beliefs was justified, even if it concerned a subject very remote from that which the contradictory beliefs were concerned with. Given that probably everyone has inconsistencies somewhere in their belief system, this would mean, says Goldman, that no one was justified in believing anything.

But in reply to the first difficulty for the universalist, one might ask why we should assume that in order to use a belief for justificatory purposes, we should need it to be conscious, either at the time it is being used, or at any earlier time. Surely we are in the relevant sense using it if it is playing a causal role in the creation and maintenance of other beliefs which we hold.

Equally, we can argue that Goldman's point is overstated. Once we allow that coherence can be a matter of degree, the way is open for us to argue that a contradiction in one part of our belief system does not have equally damaging effects on all our beliefs. If I mistakenly believe that the decimal expansion of pi starts 3.14172, and hence hold a self-contradictory belief, that need not mean that my belief that I am now seated at a desk lacks all justification. For even though (if coherentism is right) my belief about pi and my belief about what I am now doing are indirectly connected, the link may be so weak that the contradictoriness of the former has a virtually negligible effect on the justifiability of the latter.

(ii) Particularism

If it is thought that what justification requires is conscious access to the beliefs which figure in the justification, then particularism will seem a more attractive option than universalism. For with particularism at least there is some chance that one will be able to recall a finite number of beliefs in order to see how well the new belief coheres with them. But if what my new belief *p* needs to cohere with is only a subset of my beliefs, the question then arises of which subset it is, what the principle is by which the subset is picked out, and what the rationale is for that principle.

The particularist might reply that these are unfair questions. Which subset of my beliefs *p* needs to cohere with will depend on the content of *p*. The relevant set for a belief like "The book on the table is red" might well have a large overlap with the set for "The book on the table is rectangular," but will be very different from the relevant set for "The mating call of a dormouse is a high-pitched squeak." It is simply not possible to specify in general terms, the particularist may say, which is the relevant subset of beliefs.

Perhaps a middle way can be found between the particularist and universalist by agreeing with the particularist that of course it is only with *relevant* beliefs that *p* needs to cohere, but then maintaining with the universalist that in at least a great many cases, it is the totality of our beliefs that is relevant. Some indication of how a very large number of background beliefs might bear on the justification of even a simple belief was indicated in our example of the cat above. But to illustrate further how the totality of our beliefs can be relevant, consider the meta-beliefs which any more-or-less sophisticated believer will have about her own capacities. She may hold such beliefs as that she is a fairly reliable belief-acquirer. This belief about her own capacities has a role to play in the justification of the myriad humdrum beliefs she acquires each day, such as the belief that her telephone is now ringing. It is in part because she has this meta-belief that she is justified in thinking that if something appears to her to be so, then, other things being equal, that is a reason for thinking that it is so (although of course not a conclusive reason). But it is equally clear that that meta-belief about her own capacities plays a part in the justification of many other humdrum beliefs (such as her belief last week that it was raining), which appear to have no connection at all to her current belief about her telephone. Even if there is no direct connection between the beliefs that last week it was raining, and that the telephone is now ringing, they are indirectly linked by the existence of these meta-beliefs. In terms of the earlier metaphor of the web, one strand in the web may be connected to a "meta"-strand, and thereby to every other strand in the web.

7.5 Coherentism and the Rejection of the A Priori/Empirical Distinction

Our examples so far have focused on empirical beliefs. But (it may be asked) what account can be provided of our a priori beliefs? Coherentists differ on the question of whether coherentism can be extended to the a priori. Some, like Bonjour (1985, 193), insist that their coherentism applies only to empirical beliefs. Others, like Quine (passim) and Harman (1973), reject the distinction between the empirical and the a priori, and argue that a coherentist account applies to *all* our justified beliefs, including those which their opponents describe as a priori. In Chapter 6 we saw reason to reject the foundationalist account of a priori beliefs, so in this section we shall explore how coherentism can be applied with the domain of the a priori.

(i) Dualistic coherentism

We can distinguish here between two ways in which coherentism may be applied to the field of the a priori. First, it would be possible to maintain that there is a sharp distinction between empirical and a priori beliefs and that each of these two distinct areas of our intellectual life displayed the kind of structure postulated by a coherence theory. In other words, our justification for accepting either an empirical or an a priori belief lay in the way in which it cohered with other empirical or a priori beliefs. Let us call this dualistic coherentism.

Dualistic coherentism is a possible position for those who, like Bonjour, wish to maintain an a priori/empirical distinction and also to support coherentism. But it is not in fact a position which has ever been taken seriously. (Bonjour embraces coherentism for empirical beliefs, but is simply silent about the structure of our a priori beliefs.) The much more common position is the one deriving from Quine, which combines coherentism with a rejection of the a priori/empirical distinction; so in what follows, we will concentrate on this combination, to see how it can be articulated and defended.

(ii) The Quinean rejection of the a priori/empirical distinction

The Quinean line of argument starts in effect with the assumption that the only plausible candidates for being a priori propositions are those propositions which are, in some sense of the phrase, true in virtue of meaning or true by definition. Such claims are usually called "analytic" (and nonanalytic ones labeled "synthetic"). These analytic propositions include remarkably dull claims such as that brothers are male siblings and triangles have three sides; marginally more interesting claims, such as that $2 + 2 = 4$, or that the internal angles of a triangle total 180 degrees; and finally very unobvious and exciting claims from, for example, logic and mathematics, such as that there is no highest prime number or that every even number is the sum of two primes.

The starting point, then, of the Quinean line of argument is the thought that the only way of defending the claim that beliefs such as these are a priori is by showing that their truth value can be determined solely by reference to the meanings of the claims themselves, hence that no reliance on experience is necessary, and hence that they are a priori.

The attack on this assumption then argues that the notion of meaning is insufficiently precise to do the work here assigned to it. In particular, we have no defensible principles or theory which will allow us to distinguish between propositions which are true *solely* in virtue of meaning, and those which are true partly in virtue of what experience reveals. Sometimes the facts about experience are *so* deeply embedded in our total set of convictions, or seem *so* obviously true, that we think that it is word meanings alone which make them true. But then some revolution may occur in our thought, and we come to see that they were not independent of experience as we had thought. Some examples will make this idea clearer.

Think back to the situation in which it was regarded as obvious that the earth was flat—a giant plane of perhaps infinite extent. And with that background assumption, consider the proposition:

(A) Two bodies which are both falling downward cannot be moving in opposite directions.

It is easy to see how this could have seemed an a priori truth, and indeed one guaranteed by word meanings. Downward is by definition a direction of fall, it could have been argued, so two bodies both falling downward must be falling in the same direction and hence *cannot* be moving in opposite directions.

We now know why this reasoning is faulty. Once we accept that the earth is approximately spherical, we can see at once that two objects, if dropped on opposite sides of the earth not only can but *must* move toward one another, since they are both moving toward the center of the earth.

Could it be argued that the old reasoning was in fact correct, given what the flat-earthers meant by the word "down"? The claim would have to be that part of what they meant by "down" was a direction that was the same from all points of space, whereas what the round-earthers mean by "down" is "toward the center of the earth." So, on this line of thought, what the move from the flat earth view to the round earth view amounts to in part is change in the meaning of the word "down."

But (and this is in line with the Quinean attack) we have no good grounds for saying that the change from one view to the other is in part a change of meaning, rather than that no meanings have changed and that it is only our empirical beliefs that have changed. All we can defensibly say in such a situation is that scientific advances have led us to say things which before the advance we would have regarded as bizarre or perhaps unintelligible. But the fact that we would have taken that attitude before the change does not mean that our old beliefs were *really* a priori or true solely in virtue of meanings. It means only that before the change occurs, we cannot see any way in which claims like (A) could be false.

Here is a second example from our own day. It is perhaps still "obvious" to many of us that

(B) if two events A and B occur, then either A is before B or it is not.

In particular, we (many of us) think that it could in no way be true both that A was before B and that B was before A. But after Einstein, we come to realize that the position is not that simple. One of the things that Einstein's Special Theory of Relativity showed was that temporal sequence (and simultaneity) is relative to an observer and to the framework she is using. Relative to one observer, A might precede B, while relative to another, B might precede A. This does not mean that one observer's judgment is right and the other's wrong. It means that judgments of right and wrong in such matters are relative to a framework. We are all familiar with the fact that A can be to the left of B relative to one point of view and to the right of B relative to another point of view. Judgments of left and right include a tacit reference to a viewpoint and are relative to that viewpoint. Einstein showed that, *very* surprisingly, judgments of time have the same feature. He thus showed that our initial obvious and a priori "truth" (B) is not even true as it stands, any more than would be the parallel claim that given two objects A and B, A is to the left of B or it is not.

Our two previous examples have been drawn from cosmology and physics. Here is an example from biology. Consider the assertion

(C) If a woman gives birth to a child, she is its mother.

Until recently, this might have been regarded as an a priori truth, and one which was true solely in virtue of word meanings. Motherhood, it might have been said, is *defined* in terms of giving birth, so we can know that the proposition is true no matter what empirical discoveries are made. But as with our previous examples, we now know that the position is not so simple. It is possible for the egg of one woman to be fertilized *in vitro* by a sperm, and then implanted in the womb of a second woman who nine months later gives birth to a child. Is she then the mother of the child? We can of course distinguish between a genetic mother and a birth mother, and say that she is the latter but not the former, and that the woman who donated the egg is the former but not the latter. But what does this distinction do to our supposed a priori truth (C)? After all, when (C) seemed to be an a priori truth that was not because we were interpreting "mother" as "birth mother." The concept of "birth mother" as distinct from "genetic mother" was one which had not even been thought of.

What these three examples show is the way in which unforeseen scientific advances can radically change our acceptance of propositions which initially seemed immune to empirical findings. In each case, our willingness to regard the "a priori truth" differently is based on the fact that the new empirical information undermines some very general assumptions which lay behind the old a priori truth. Sometimes, the new information will bring in its train concepts which have no sense in the old picture. For example, the concept of the *center* of the earth, which is essential to explain downness in the "round earth" system has no sense if the earth is thought to be an indefinitely extended flat plane. Sometimes the new information shows that the old "truth" was true if taken in one way but not if taken in another, *where the very idea that there are two ways in which that truth might be understood becomes intelligible only in the light of the new empirical information.*

According to universal coherentism, the moral to be drawn from these historical examples is clear: we may each find within our own corpus of beliefs, some beliefs which seem to us to be a priori, to be beliefs which we are justified in accepting *no matter what* empirical findings science may come up with. But if we do take that attitude toward our beliefs, that shows only the limits of our imagination, not that our beliefs will hold true in the face of all increase in scientific knowledge.

(iii) Even mathematical and logical claims are open to revision

Someone opposed to universal coherentism might object to the argument above by distinguishing between the sort of common sense supposedly a priori beliefs which we have so far been discussing and the kind of propositions found in mathematics and logic. It may well be true, she might argue, that common sense beliefs which were once thought to be a priori can be undermined by surprising advances in empirical knowledge. But no such advances can undermine any truths of logic or mathematics. No empirical findings could throw doubt on the proposition $1 + 1 = 2$, or on indefinitely many other comparable propositions. So there *is* a domain of pure a priori propositions, so a Quinean universal coherentism is false.

It is true that it is much more difficult to find convincing examples of empirical findings altering our logical and mathematical beliefs. But Quine at least is quite clear that this is possible. In his "Two Dogmas" article (first published in 1951 and reprinted in his 1953), he tells us:

> . . . no statement is immune to revision. Revision even of the logical law of the excluded middle has been proposed as a means of simplifying quantum mechanics; and what difference is there in principle between such a shift and the shift whereby Kepler superseded Ptolemy, or Einstein Newton, or Darwin Aristotle? (Quine, 1953)

And a year after that article, the same thought was expressed:

> Mathematical and logical laws themselves are not immune to revision, if it is found that essential simplifications of our whole conceptual scheme will ensue. There have been suggestions, stimulated largely by quandaries of modern physics, that we revise the true/false dichotomy of modern physics in favour of some sort of tri- or n-chotomy. Logical laws are the most crucial and central statements of our conceptual scheme, and for this reason the most protected from revision by the force of conservatism; but, because again of their crucial position, they are the laws an apt revision of which might offer the most sweeping simplification of our whole system of knowledge. (Quine, 1952)

It would take us well beyond the scope this book (and beyond the competence of its authors!) to consider whether the theories of quantum mechanics would be improved by changing any of what we now accept as the laws of logic. However, we can easily see how we could have good reason to revise our belief in presently accepted laws of logic *if* we have good reason to interpret differently the logically key words (like "not," "all," "if . . . then . . . ," etc.) which occur in such laws. How this might be the case is explained in some detail in the Logic Appendix, section 6. We explained in 7.5(ii) above how new and completely unforeseeable discoveries might give us reason to revise old, apparently a priori, and certainly deeply entrenched ideas. In effect, section 6 of the Appendix shows how related considerations might give us reason to revise our beliefs in the domains of logical and mathematical truth.

7.6 Lehrer on Coherentism

So far, we have been describing in general terms what a coherentist position is like, drawing on ideas from a number of sources. But since one or two coherentists have explored in some detail the ways in which coherentism can be developed, and their explorations go well beyond anything we have said so far, we will briefly sketch one such account, in order to illustrate the way in which coherentists seek to make their accounts ever more sophisticated. We shall choose Lehrer as our coherentist, and will focus on the latest version of his theory (see Lehrer, 1990; and for earlier versions, cf. Lehrer, 1974, and Bender).

(i) The idea of an "acceptance system" for a person

Lehrer starts with the idea of what he calls an acceptance system for a person. This is a system of statements of the form "S accepts that p," which lists all that S does accept. An acceptance system is thus not the same as a person's total set of beliefs, in two respects: first, Lehrer thinks that his notion of an acceptance is narrower than the notion of belief. Acceptance, he tells us, is believing something "for the purpose of attaining truth," and he thinks that not all beliefs are aimed at truth (Lehrer, 1990, 11). Secondly, a person's total set of beliefs will consist of beliefs other than those of the form "S believes that p," and hence other than the statements listed in the person's acceptance system. For every belief that Mary holds, there will be a corresponding statement in her acceptance system saying that she holds that belief. But the statement in the acceptance system is not *what* she believes, but rather is a statement *that* she believes a certain proposition.

Lehrer now defines what it is for a person to be justified in accepting proposition p (what he calls personal justification) in the following way:

> S is personally justified in accepting that p at [time] t if and only if p coheres with the acceptance system of S at t. (Lehrer, 1990, 115)

He then raises the question of how we should understand the notion of coherence which he is here using, and suggests that it should be defined in terms of "comparative reasonableness": p coheres with S's acceptance if and only if it is more reasonable for S to accept p than for her to accept any competitor belief to p. A competitor belief is defined as something, such that c's truth makes p less reasonable for S than does c's falsity. (Notice that in this sense of "competitor," one can justifiably accept both a belief p and a number of competitor beliefs—it is simply that the truth of the competitor beliefs makes one *less* justified in accepting p than one would have been had they been false.)

This implies that

> S is personally justified in accepting that p at time t if and only if, given S's acceptance system, it is more reasonable for S to accept p than for S to accept any competitor to p.

(ii) Two objections concerning foundationalism and "competitor" beliefs

Lehrer then considers two possible objections to what he has claimed, each of which leads to further refinements in his theory. The first objection is a standard foundationalist objection. A belief that p (so the objection goes) cannot be shown to be justified *merely* by being shown to cohere with an acceptance system, since there is no reason to think that anything in that acceptance system is itself justified.

To meet this objection, Lehrer says that an acceptance system needs to attribute to a subject something that he calls principle (T), namely:

> Whatever I accept with the object of accepting something just in case it is true, I accept in a trustworthy manner. (Lehrer, 1990, 122)

This means that although the mere fact that someone accepts something does not imply that they are justified in accepting it, the fact that someone accepts something when their acceptance system attributes to them principle (T) *does* imply that they are justified in accepting what they do. Of course, this does not guarantee that their belief is true, nor that it may not be overthrown by evidence which they later acquire. All that it implies is that given that I find that I accept something, and I know of nothing to indicate that it is false, I am justified in accepting it, because I know (or accept) that I am the sort of being who by and large does not accept things unless they are true. As Lehrer puts it:

> The consequence of adding principle (T) to my acceptance system is that whatever I accept is more reasonable for me to accept than its denial. (op. cit., 122)

What Lehrer is suggesting could be expressed as a little piece of reasoning as follows:

1. I accept that p. (premise)
so 2. 1 is part of my acceptance system.
and 3. I have good reason to accept anything that is part of my acceptance system. (this is principle [T]) (premise)
so 4. I have good reason to accept that p.

Lehrer is not claiming that in order to be justified in accepting that p, I must have gone through this piece of reasoning. His claim rather is that if someone has principle (T) in their acceptance system, then for any belief that they hold, they are in the same position in terms of justification as someone who *has* gone through this reasoning.

Lehrer now considers a second objection to his account of personal justification. The objection is that there can be cases in which someone is personally justified in believing p even though p does not beat all competitor beliefs. Consider the two beliefs:

(i) I see a zebra.
(ii) People sometimes dream that they see zebras.

(ii) is a competitor to (i). But on a particular occasion, it may be that (i) does not beat (ii), even though I am justified in accepting (i). It may be, for example, that although I am sure of (ii), it is irrelevant on this occasion because I am sure that I am not now dreaming. My acceptance that I am not now dream-

ing is what Lehrer calls a "neutraliser" to (ii). He claims that for justified acceptance of p, competitors to p must be either beaten *or neutralized*, and he thus
ends up with the following definition of justification:

> S is personally justified in accepting that p if and only if everything that com-
> petes with p for S on the basis of the acceptance system of S at t is beaten or
> neutralised on the basis of the acceptance system of S at t. (op. cit., 126)

With this definition, we seem to have come a long way from the coherentism which we outlined in the earlier sections of this chapter. But we can notice
two key ideas which link the earlier and simpler versions of coherentism with
Lehrer's more sophisticated account. First, there is the idea that the justification of any belief (or acceptance) is relative to the whole corpus of one's beliefs
(to one's acceptance system). Both the simple and the complex forms of coherentism reject the foundationalist idea of justifying a belief by tracing its origins directly or indirectly to a set of foundational or basic beliefs. Secondly,
there is the idea that crucial to the justifiability of a person's beliefs are second
order beliefs which they have about the reliability of their belief-forming capacities. This is something which we referred to in section 7.4 (ii), and it is something which appears in Lehrer's account as his principle (T). At the end of the
next chapter, after we have considered some general objections to coherentism,
we will mention some problems specific to Lehrer's version of the doctrine.

Exercises

1. Without rereading this chapter, write no more than one page explaining
   coherentism using the crossword puzzle analogy. When you have done this
   check your answer against 7.1 and 7.2 and assess it for accuracy, clarity, and
   completeness.
2. Miss Marple is investigating the murder of Lord Montague's brother. As
   her investigation progresses she gains more and more evidence. After a
   week the evidence strongly suggests that either the butler did it or that his
   master, Lord Montague did. In not more than one page, and without rereading the chapter, describe the different ways in which a foundationalist and
   a coherentist would see the detective's situation. Having done this, read the
   chapter again and assess your answer for accuracy, clarity, and completeness.
3. Some Christians believe that they have good evidence that the universe was
   created in 4004 B.C. by God. Some scientists believe that they have good evidence that it was created millions of years ago. Can an acceptance of both
   these views be made coherent? (Hard.)
4. Quine maintained that there is no satisfactory way of deciding whether a
   sentence is true solely in virtue of the meanings of its terms. Explain Quine's
   position by showing how, when it was believed that the sun went round a
   stationary earth, the claim "When the sun rises, it moves" would have

seemed to be true by definition. Then show how, after we discovered that the earth goes round the sun, it can equally plausibly be seen as a false empirical claim.

5. Without rereading the chapter, explain in no more than one page, what the discussion about *in vitro* fertilization shows about the claim that "if a woman gives birth to a child she is its mother." When you have done this, reread 7.5(ii) and assess your answer for clarity, accuracy, and completeness.

CHAPTER 8

An Assessment of Coherentism

8.1 Four Objections to Coherentism

So far, we have been implicitly suggesting that coherentism is a more promising account of justification than foundationalism. But it does face some serious objections, and we will look at four of them.

(i) The "plurality" objection: conflicting but internally coherent stories

The first objection, sometimes called the plurality objection, goes like this: if what makes a belief justified is internal to the belief set (that is, it is a question of how well the belief coheres with other beliefs in the set), then there could be many incompatible belief sets which were equally coherent. By contrast (so the objection might continue) if what makes at least some beliefs justifiable is something external to the set of beliefs, such as a relation between the belief and our experiences or between the belief and the reality which it is about, then reference to reality could serve to weed out competing belief sets. But if neither experience nor reality can exercise this constraining function, which is what the coherentist claims, there is nothing to prevent the formation of whole series of self-enclosed coherent belief sets where we would have no rational ground for choosing between them. C. I. Lewis gave a striking formulation of this objection when he said that if the coherentist were right, our total corpus of beliefs "could provide no better assurance of anything in it than that which attaches to the contents of a well-written novel" (173).

Several writers have tried to add detail to this objection by showing how, given one coherent set of beliefs, we can mechanically construct a different set which will have the same degree of coherence but be lacking in justification altogether (see, e.g., Sosa, 1991, 76–77; and cf. Chisholm, 1989, 87–89).

(ii) Where is the link between coherence and *truth*?

This leads on to a second objection. It can be put by asking why we should suppose that beliefs which are "justified" in the coherentist sense are more likely to be true than beliefs which are not so justified. As we commented earlier, we are not interested in justification for its own sake. What we want is the truth, and given that the truth is not immediately and infallibly accessible to us, we need a method of acquiring beliefs, which, even if not guaranteeing the truth of the beliefs which we thereby acquire, is likely to bring us nearer to the truth than any other method we might use. The question then is "If we adopt beliefs which are justified as the coherentist defines the term, will we have adopted the best method of belief formation, given that our aim is to end up with the truth?" And the reason for thinking that the answer to this must be "no" is that, as the previous objection implied, coherentism seems to allow our total set of beliefs to float free from the constraints of reality and hence to float free from the goal of truth.

(iii) How can perception justify our beliefs?

Perhaps the commonest objection to coherentism is that it cannot give a satisfactory account of perceptual or observational or experiential beliefs (see, e.g., Pollock, 1986 and Moser, 1989). We may concede (the objection would go) that with some of our beliefs, the justification for holding them lies in their coherence with the rest of our corpus of beliefs. But with perceptual beliefs, our justification for holding them lies not in how they relate to other *beliefs*, but in how they relate to our perceptions, where a perception is not itself a belief, but something that can support or justify a belief. Typically, when I look at a red patch, we can distinguish three separate items: there is the red patch existing in the external world and in principle viewable by other observers; there is my experience of the red patch, which I alone have and am aware of; and there is my belief that there is a red patch in front of me. According to the objection, this third item, my belief, is justified, at least in part, by the occurrence of the experience, hence it is not justified solely by other beliefs, hence coherentism is mistaken.

Different writers express this objection in different ways. Moser, for example, says that the contents of one's perceptual experiences are part of one's total empirical evidence about the world. In denying these experiences any sort of justificatory role, the coherentist is denying that there is any necessary relation between the holding of justification relations between her beliefs and the conformity of her beliefs to the evidence which she has (Moser, 1989, 177). Pollock makes a similar point in connection not just with perception, but also with memory, which he thinks presents the coherentist with problems parallel to those raised by perception. (He claims that, for example, my belief that I had coffee for breakfast this morning may be justified in part by my seeming to remember it, just as my belief that there is a red patch in front of me may be justified in part by my seeming to see a red patch.)

Given the central importance of perception or observation in generating for us an accurate picture of the world, it would clearly be a major deficiency in coherentism if it could not provide an adequate account of how perception enters into the justification of our beliefs.

(iv) The law of noncontradiction is not revisable

Finally, let us consider an objection that arises if we are tempted by the universal coherentism which we mentioned in sections 7.4 and 7.5 (the idea, that is, that the justification for *all* our justified beliefs, including the supposedly a priori ones, resides in their mutual coherence). Quine and others have suggested that the justification for even the laws of logic lies in the way they cohere with other clearly empirical beliefs and hence that even the laws of logic might be given up as empirical science advances. Our fourth objection to coherentism argues that this is not a possible option for at least one law of logic, namely the law of noncontradiction. (This law tells us that a proposition and its negation cannot both be true—more briefly, not both p and also not-p.)

To see why this is so, suppose that at one time I acquire the belief that p, then at a later time I acquire the belief that not-p. I then reflect on my corpus of beliefs and notice that it contains

> (1) p

and also   (2) not-p.

I think to myself "There's a contradiction there, so I must give up (1) or (2)." But then a Quinean reminds me that the laws of logic are in principle revisable, so that I *might* solve my problem by giving up not (1) or (2), but rather my belief in the law of noncontradiction

> (3) not (p and also not-p).

But (so the objection goes), there are two insuperable problems with this coherentist suggestion. The first is that even if I give up my belief in (3), my beliefs (1) and (2) still contradict one another so that I do not seem to have made any progress by surrendering a belief in (3). It is not clear whether the Quinean at this point holds

   (a) that if I give up (3), then (1) and (2) no longer conflict, and so I am entitled to retain them both;

or   (b) that if I give up (3), then although (1) and (2) still contradict each other, it does not matter any more, since in giving up (3), I am no longer committed to the requirement of consistency.

But each of these options, according to the objection, turns out to be untenable. The problem with (a) is that no sense can be made of the idea that (1) and (2) do not conflict—what could a conflict of belief be, if even p and not-p do not conflict with one another? As for (b), the problem is that there is no *content* to the assertion that p, unless it excludes not-p. If you ask me "Is there a book on the table?," and I assert "Yes, there is a book on the table," what my reply must minimally exclude is the truth of "There is no book on the table." If it does not do this, then your original question remains unanswered. Indeed, *nothing* could be an answer to it, for *every possible* answer to it would leave completely open whether there was a book on the table or not. So whether the Quinean opts for (a) or (b), his suggestion is ultimately untenable.

There is a second compelling reason (the objector will continue) why the idea that I might resolve the conflict between (1) and (2) by abandoning (3) runs into problems. We have imagined the Quinean saying "You *can* retain (1) and (2)—all that you have to do is give up (3)." But now it seems that we can imagine an ultra-Quinean, who says (even more liberally than the Quinean) "You *can* retain your belief in (1) and (2) *and* (3). All that you have to give up (or not adopt) is any belief in

(4) not [(1) and (2) and (3)].

If you give up (or do not adopt) (4), there's no reason why you should not retain (1) and (2) and (3)."

But once we have imagined the ultra-Quinean, we can see lurking behind him the figure of the hyper-ultra-Quinean, who says to us "You *can* retain your belief in (1) and (2) and (3) *and* (4). All that you have to do is to give up (or not adopt) the belief that

(5) not [(1) and (2) and (3) and (4)]."

It is clear that an infinite regress has here begun (behind the hyper-ultra-Quinean looms the super-hyper-ultra-Quinean, and so on). It seems that once we start down this road, we can never be forced to give up *any* of our beliefs, no matter what an inconsistent mass they form. It is also clear that the problem does not start with the hyper-ultra-Quinean, nor with the ultra-Quinean. It starts with the Quinean, who countenances solving our initial problem (that we hold contradictory beliefs) by letting us give up the law of noncontradiction. So, the objector concludes, if the rot is to be stopped at all, it must be stopped at the first stage. We must recognize that our original problem cannot be solved by giving up (3). We must recognize that the law of noncontradiction is a nonoptional part of our future intellectual equipment and hence is something that *no* possible future empirical discoveries could give us reason to abandon.

8.2 Replies to These Objections

The first two of the above objections imply that coherence is not sufficient for justification; the second two imply that it is not necessary. Collectively, they present a serious challenge to the truth of coherentism. What can the coherentist say to meet these challenges?

(i) The "plurality" objection again

Let us consider first the plurality objection, namely, that there could be many coherent sets of beliefs. The coherentist can allow here that in one sense it is true but harmless, and that in another sense it would be damaging but it is false. It is true in this sense: there is always an element of slack in the formation of our beliefs. How we should add to or alter our corpus of beliefs is never uniquely determined by what happens to us or around us. As the detective gets more and more evidence about the murderer, for example, she might adopt the hypothesis that the murderer has characteristics X, Y, and Z. But the evidence which justifies her in thinking this would be equally compatible with the hypothesis that the murderer has none of these characteristics and is simply laying false clues to make the detective mistakenly think that he (the murderer) has those characteristics. An entertaining example from history of someone reasoning like that is provided by the nineteenth-century English theologian and biologist Gosse (1810–1888). As a devout believer, Gosse accepted the Creation story along with the then-conventional and widely accepted view that the events in the Garden of Eden occurred in 4004 B.C. As a practicing scientist, he was also well aware of the geological and fossil studies by Lyell and others which seemed to show that the earth had to be hundreds of thousands of years old at the very least, and perhaps millions of years old. How could this conflict be resolved? Gosse hit upon a brilliantly inventive, though in fact wholly erroneous, hypothesis. He realized that all the geological and fossil findings were equally compatible with two hypotheses: first, that the earth was millions of years old, or second that the earth had been created by God in 4004 B.C. complete with a "bogus" geological and fossil record that made it *look* in every way as if it was very much older. Because of the nature of Gosse's alternative hypothesis, no amount of further detailed geological and fossil investigations could have proved him wrong. For the more the evidence seemed to suggest that the earth was millions of years old, the more Gosse could reply "But that is exactly what you would expect if in fact it was made in 4004 B.C. by an omnipotent creator who wanted to make it appear as if it were millions of years old."

In this connection, we can also recall the tale related about Wittgenstein. Wittgenstein asked a friend "Why did people ever suppose that the sun goes round the earth, rather than the earth round the sun?" "Because," replied the friend, "it *looks* as if the sun goes round the earth." "So how would it have looked," Wittgenstein then asked, "if it had looked as if the earth went round the sun?"

These three examples illustrate what we mean when we say that there is element of slack in our belief formation. Which beliefs we change, and how we change them, in the light of new evidence is not wholly determined by the nature of that evidence, and in that sense the plurality objection is true, but undamaging.

But if the plurality objection is that there is never any justifiable way of choosing between rival sets of beliefs, that (as Lewis puts it) they are all no more worthy of acceptance than the contents of a well-written novel, this is simply false. There *is* a justification for our belief that there was a person called Arthur Conan Doyle and there was nobody called Sherlock Holmes. We get a much more coherent set of beliefs if we assume that there was a real person Conan Doyle who wrote stories about a fictional character called Sherlock Holmes, than if we assume they were both real people. Of course, you *could* construct a world view in which the second hypothesis was accepted—but it would have to be an enormously more complicated picture than is needed by the rival view that Holmes was a fictional character. It would have to hypothesize all sorts of things arbitrarily, such as errors in the registry of births and deaths, errors in contemporary newspaper reports, errors in past police records, errors in tenancy records, and so on. But in that sense, even the foundationalist has to admit that different pictures of reality can be constructed. So in relation to the plurality objection, it seems that the coherentist can maintain her position.

(ii) The link between coherence and truth again

What about the second objection, that there is no reason to think that beliefs which are justified in the coherentist manner are any more likely to be true than those which are not so justified? The coherentist will simply deny that this is so or at least deny that her theory is in any worse a position than any other in this respect. Certainly she has to rely on principles of inference to get her from one justified belief to another, and questions can legitimately be raised about the justification of these principles of inference. We shall be addressing those questions in the next two chapters. But the need to utilize principles of inference is not peculiar to the coherentist: the foundationalist must equally rely on such principles and is equally faced with the problem of how they are to be justified. In considering the problems faced by a priori foundationalism, we have already rejected the idea that any such principles of inference could be *self*-evident. So what evidence they have must arise from the way in which they relate to each other, and from the transitions among our beliefs which they permit. We commented earlier on the way in which, in constructing an axiomatic system, a logician or mathematician will choose certain propositions as axioms in part because of what will follow from them, not because those propositions are self-evident. In a parallel way, in choosing certain principles of inference, a coherentist will ask, not which principles are self-evident, but which principles fit well with those inferences which she antecedently thinks are good ones. This applies both to the principles used in logical and mathematical reasoning and to those used in everyday and scientific contexts. We will say more about this below, when we consider the fourth objection.

(iii) How perceptions justify beliefs on the coherentist view

Let us consider thirdly what the coherentist can say about the role of perception or experience. Suppose that I believe (falsely) that sawdust dissolves in water. How, according to coherentism, could I test this belief by experience? At the level of *action,* what I *do* is to put some sawdust in water and see that it fails to dissolve. At the level of *belief,* what happens is that my original belief (that sawdust dissolves in water) comes in conflict with a set of new beliefs which I acquire as a result of my observations—such beliefs as "Here is some water," "Here is some sawdust," "The sawdust has been mixed with the water," "The sawdust has remained undissolved," and so on. And if the question is raised of my justification for accepting those further beliefs, the coherentist can say, for example, that my belief that this is sawdust is justified by my further belief that this substance has been produced by the action of a saw on wood, my belief that this is water is justified by my further belief that it came from the faucet in my kitchen, and so on. At each point in the justification of a belief, even of an observational belief, a whole range of further beliefs may be invoked. And, as we have noted earlier, part of my justification for accepting some specific observational belief, such as "This substance is sawdust" may be my belief in my powers of more-or-less reliable perception. And part of the justification of *that* belief will be the comprehensive and detailed set of beliefs which constitutes my world picture, part of which will be a representation of myself as one item within it, equipped with certain powers, including the power successfully to identify sawdust.

So, the coherentist will claim, what her theory abandons is not the idea of a perceptual connection between our total corpus of beliefs and reality. What she rejects is *a particular conception* of that connection, the conception offered by the foundationalist. The foundationalist suggests that the connection is supplied by an intermediary between reality and our beliefs, an intermediary called "experience" or "sensory awareness," or "perception" which is not itself a belief but which may be caused by the external world and which can supply justification for beliefs. But this is what the coherentist rejects as unintelligible. Clearly, having a table in front of you when your eyes are open in good light cannot by itself justify your belief "Here is a table." You might, for example, not even have noticed that there was anything in front of you, let alone noticed that it was a table. There has to be more than the mere existence of the table.

Will an *experience* of the table do? That depends on what "experience of a table" means. If it means "experience caused by a table," then experience is not enough: you could have that experience without connecting it with tables at all. You could have an experience which is in fact caused by a table, and you wrongly think it to be caused by something else. So in that sense of "experience of a table," such an experience will not justify the belief that there is a table in front of you.

Suppose then, "experience of a table" means "experience which, whether or not it was caused by a table, has a table-like content." This seems to be what Moser has in mind when he speaks of "the subjective contents of one's perceptual experiences" (Moser, 1989, 177). The problem here is to know exactly what is meant by the "contents" of a perceptual experience. Hitherto, we have spoken of the (propositional) content of a belief, and have defined it as what is specified by the "that . . ." clause in sentences of the form "*S* believes that *p*." The contents of beliefs were thus thought of as propositions, as entities which could be true or false, and it was in virtue of having contents with truth values that beliefs could stand in implication relations, and hence in justification relations, to each other. *If* Moser's "subjective contents of perceptual experiences" were contents in this sense, then they could indeed stand in justification relations to beliefs—but this is because they would then be beliefs themselves. If, on the other hand, what Moser is referring to is contents in some other sense, two questions need to be asked:

(i) What is the sense of "content" in which perceptual experiences have contents?
(ii) What is supposed to be the relation between, for example, having a perceptual experience with the (nonpropositional) content of a red patch, and having a belief with the (propositional) content "There is a red patch"?

Without an answer to these two questions, the coherentist can fairly claim that the objection that is being raised against her is not clear enough for an answer to be either possible or necessary.

Pollock, in voicing substantially the same criticism, expresses it rather differently. He says:

> It is *the fact that* I am appeared to redly that justifies me in thinking there is something red before me. (Pollock, 1986, 90, Pollock's italics)

(By "I am appeared to redly," Pollock means roughly "I appear to be seeing something red." It is for technical reasons that he prefers the former expression.) This may sound very different from the Moser line, but at bottom, it is the same. For Pollock is saying that what justifies my belief "There is a red patch" is *the fact that* I have a visual experience of a red patch. It is not entirely clear what Pollock takes facts to be (whether, e.g., they have propositional contents in the way that beliefs do), but it is probably fair to represent him as saying that it is *my having a visual experience* which justifies my belief "There is a red patch." But the coherentist can then point out against Pollock that my having a visual experience is an event; it is something that happens; it is not something with (propositional) content, hence not something that can be true or false, and hence not something that can stand in justification relations.

Davidson summarizes this coherentist line of thought succinctly when he says:

What distinguishes a coherence theory is simply the claim that nothing can count as a reason for holding a belief except another belief . . . The relation between a sensation and a belief cannot be logical, since sensations are not beliefs or other propositional attitudes. What then is the relation? The answer is, I think, obvious: the relation is causal. Sensations cause some beliefs and in *this* sense are the basis or ground of those beliefs. But a causal explanation of a belief does not show how or why the belief is justified. (Davidson in Lepore, ed., 1986, 310, 311)

(iv) Not even pains are a special case

So far, we have been construing "experience" as specifically *perceptual* experience, as it is perception which is often thought to present a major problem for coherentism. But if we were to construe the concept of experience more widely, to include our awareness of, for example, aches, pains, tickles, it might be thought that we could create a different sort of difficulty for the coherentist. Suppose that we again grant the coherentist that with at least some beliefs about experience, the justifiability of those beliefs depends on their coherence with our total corpus of beliefs. Even so (the anti-coherentist may say) there are *some* beliefs about experience, where it is *the experience alone* that justifies me in accepting the belief that I am then having that experience. Suppose, for example, that I have the belief that I am now in pain. Surely, the objector may say, my belief is then justified wholly by my current experience and hence not justified at all by its coherence with my other beliefs. What can the coherentist say about such a case? Doesn't it provide a clear refutation of her account of justification?

In reply, the coherentist can concede first of all that beliefs about one's current pain state are very likely to be justified (indeed, very likely to be true), since she can have a general belief about what sort of a thing a pain is, and the relatively few ways in which a belief about one's current pain can go wrong. But, she will maintain, such beliefs *can* go wrong, in principle at least. For example, someone who believes that she is currently feeling a pain might be merely dreaming, or she might be a victim of posthypnotic suggestion. The point of making remarks such as these is of course not to suggest that really we are not justified in holding the beliefs we do about our pains or to induce any sort of skepticism. It is to show that even my belief that I am now in pain gains its justification not from the occurrence of some nonbelief experience, but from the coherence with which that belief fits into a framework of other beliefs. Suppose that I do now have the conviction that I have a throbbing pain in my left foot, and suppose that it does turn out that I am the subject of a posthypnotic suggestion that I will feel such a pain. Would that show that my belief was either false or unjustified? Not conclusively, the coherentist will agree, for it is possible that hypnotism can induce genuine pains, not just false beliefs that one has a pain, and it is possible that although hypnotism is quite unable to induce real pain, I coincidentally had a real pain immediately after being hypnotized into thinking that I would. But then confronted by these rival hypotheses, we would have to ask ourselves what the justification was for thinking that hypnotism could induce real pains and not just false pain beliefs, and what the likelihood was of a pain occurring purely coincidentally after hypnosis. Suppose that our best available theories about the nature of pain and the nature of hypnotism imply that hypnotism does not induce real pain. (Perhaps, much too crudely, hypnotism works only on one part of the brain, and pain perception occurs in another part of the brain.) This would not prove that I did not have a pain when I thought that I did, for it does not conclusively disprove the "coincidental pain" hypothesis mentioned above. But what it does strongly suggest is that the justifiability of even so "immediate" a belief as the belief that I am now in pain in fact resides in its relations to other beliefs in my corpus of beliefs—beliefs, for example, that I am not subject to posthypnotic suggestion, and so on, and that it *could* be the case that we get a more coherent overall picture of the world by retaining my beliefs (i) that hypnotism does not induce real pains, and (ii) that I have been subjected to a posthypnotic suggestion that I will feel pain, and abandoning even so obvious-seeming a belief as (iii) that I now feel pain.

(v) The law of noncontradiction is consistent with coherentism

Finally, what can be said about the objection to extending the thesis of coherentism to cover logical laws? It is not entirely clear what the coherentist ought to say in reply. One thing which she could point out is that even if we agree that the law of noncontradiction is (contra the Quinean) absolutely indispensable to our thought, the *way* in which this is shown is more in tune with a coherentist than with a foundationalist approach. The law is shown to play an indispensable role by being shown to *cohere* with certain fundamental practices and principles, such as assertion and denial, the opposition between truth and falsity. It is not shown to be indispensable by a close scrutiny of the law itself, by being illuminated by an inner "light of reason," apart from its relations with other beliefs in our total network. So even if the law (and perhaps some other logical laws too) is unlike the mass of our beliefs in being indispensable, it is not so obvious that the justification for accepting the laws cannot be fitted into a coherentist framework.

But secondly, and more boldly, the coherentist might deny that the objection raised by the Quinean stance *does* show that the law of noncontradiction is indispensable. What it shows is that we are completely unable to imagine how it might be false. But in that respect, we are in the same position that the flat-earthers were of section 7.5 (ii) who were unable to understand how two objects which were both moving downward could be moving in opposite directions. Obviously, to abandon the law of noncontradiction would involve a colossal revision of our thinking, and it is characteristic of such revisions that it can be very hard to envisage them in any detail outside the specific context in which they are seriously put forward by scientists for our acceptance. (Think again, e.g., of Einstein's claims that temporal concepts like duration, succession, and simultaneity have to be interpreted relationally.) So, the coherentist could argue, the objection raised by the previous section shows (a) how enmeshed the law of noncontradiction is with other fundamentals of our belief system, and (b) how very difficult it is to envisage the law being overthrown by future empirical findings. But it is compatible with both of these claims to assert that our justification for accepting the law is coherentist.

8.3 Two Questions about Lehrer's Coherentism

Finally, let us return to the more sophisticated version of coherentism presented to us by Lehrer. We will mention two areas in which doubts may be felt about the Lehrer version.

(i) What is meant by "comparative reasonableness"?

First, in explaining what he means by coherence, Lehrer invokes the notion of "comparative reasonableness." He says that a belief p coheres with S's acceptance system if and only if it is *more reasonable* for S to accept p than for her to accept any competitor belief on the basis of S's acceptance system. But it would surely be a mistake to take this notion of "being more reasonable than . . ." as basic and undefined. If one belief is more reasonable than another, there must be something about the two beliefs and the relevant acceptance system *in virtue of which* it is more reasonable to accept one belief rather than the other. Two beliefs could not stand in exactly the same relation to a given acceptance system apart from the fact that one was reasonable and the other was not. So any satisfactory account of coherence in terms of comparative reasonableness needs to tell us something more about comparative reasonableness. Without this extra information, Lehrer's system rests on a notion that is too rich and too obscure to be a satisfactory starting point for an explanation.

Lehrer himself is aware of this point. In Bender (1989), he says:

> I think it is possible to give an interesting account of this notion of reasonableness in terms of the comparative expected epistemic utility of accepting one thing rather than another, measured in terms of our epistemic objectives. (253)

But he then immediately deprives this observation of force by adding

> . . . no such account, including ones I have articulated, strike me as quite adequate to my purposes. Moreover, for the purposes of applying the theory, I think that the notion of comparative reasonableness is clearer and more useful than the notion of comparative epistemic expected utility. Judgments of comparative epistemic utility will, I think, be derived from judgments of comparative reasonableness rather than *vice versa*. (253)

But Lehrer seems confused here. If comparative reasonableness *is* a clearer notion than that of comparative epistemic expected utility, there is no *point* in trying to explain the former in terms of the latter—the direction of explanation would have to be the other way round. So we are left with the criticism voiced above, that Lehrer is resting his theory on a rich but unclear concept.

(ii) Is Lehrer's principle (T) too strong?

Secondly, we might feel some uneasiness about Lehrer's principle (T), which says that whatever I accept with the object of accepting something just in case it is true, I accept in a trustworthy manner. This is the principle which Lehrer invokes in order to meet the objection that we cannot justify one belief by reference to another unless the second one is justified too. Clearly, something like principle (T) will be accepted by any self-reflective believer, that is, someone who raises to themselves the question of how reliable their various belief-gathering capacities (perception, introspection, reasoning, etc.) are. The problem with Lehrer's principle (T) is that he makes it a precondition for *any* of a person's beliefs to be justified. This means that all those believers who have not reached a sufficiently reflective stage to think about their own capacities (all animals, all children, many adolescents, some adults?) cannot have any justified beliefs.

Further, there is something rather suspicious about simply adding principle (T) to a stock of beliefs. Consider a person S whose acceptance system includes p, q, r, etc. and principle (T). It will then follow that *no matter what p, q, r, etc., are*, S has more reason to accept them than to accept their negations. For the mere fact that she finds herself accepting something partly constitutes what it is to have a better reason for accepting than for rejecting a belief. And since principle (T) is one thing she accepts, the fact that she accepts (T) is by itself sufficient to give her a better reason for accepting (T) than for rejecting it. But principle (T) is now suspiciously close to being a foundational belief of the sort that coherentism rejects. For it is a justified belief whose justification does not consist in its relation to other beliefs. It is certainly the case, as we have mentioned before, that (some) believers do hold a set of beliefs about their own belief-gathering capacities, and the reliability of those capacities, perhaps their various degrees of reliability under different contingencies. But if those beliefs are to be justified, they cannot simply be added arbitrarily to some preexisting stock of beliefs. The right to hold those beliefs has to be won. It could be won, for example, by some Darwinian reflections on the fact that, in order to survive, a species must have reliable means of gathering information about (certain aspects of) its environment. It also could be won in a psychological laboratory which tested memory capacities for various kinds of items, or reasoning skills, or capacity to locate sounds accurately. But a belief like principle (T) could not be justified simply by adding it to a preexisting stock of beliefs, claiming that it then applied to itself, and was hence a justified belief, and hence conferred justification on all other beliefs in that belief stock.

Exercises

1. Suppose you have a coherent set of beliefs. Is it possible to mechanically construct from this initial set another set of beliefs which is equally coherent but which is completely unjustified? Answer in one page. (See Sosa, 76–77, and Chisholm, 1989, 87–89.)
2. Gosse (1810–1888) attempted to reconcile the belief that the earth was created in 4004 B.C. with the fossil evidence that it was millions of years old. How does this story show that the existence of many coherent belief systems does not undermine the coherentist account of justified belief? (Answer in less than one page).
3. How might we distinguish between a coherent set of beliefs which are true and a coherent set of beliefs which are no more true than the "contents of a well-written novel"? Compare your answer with 8.2 (i).
4. Can you imagine any circumstances in which a coherentist could believe both p and not-p without discrediting her coherentism?
5. Suppose that you have a toothache. Do you "know" this simply because you can feel the ache or are other considerations relevant? Answer in one page, then compare your answer with 8.2 (iii) and (iv).

CHAPTER 9

Problems with Identifying Deductive Inferences

9.1 How the Discussion of Inference and Argument Is Organized

In the last few chapters we have been considering the question of what structure our system of justified beliefs has, and how whether a given belief is justified can depend on the way it fits into this structure. We have touched briefly on the question of what makes the inferential moves from one belief to another legitimate moves (in connection with the foundationalist's treatment of the principles of logical inference). But we have said relatively little about inference in general. We must now remedy that omission.

Traditionally, arguments and inferences have been divided into two major categories, which are usually seen as mutually exclusive and exhaustive, namely deductive and inductive. In due course (in Chapter 11) we will suggest that this traditional division is no more defensible than the other old divisions between empirical and a priori, necessary and contingent, and analytic and synthetic. But as a first step to establishing this, we need to understand how the distinction is meant to be drawn, and this we consider in section 9.2. We will then focus on the problems that arise with this distinction, dealing with problems about deduction in the rest of this chapter and with problems about induction in the following chapter. Then in Chapter 11, we will consider how the traditional distinction might be transcended in the light of the coherentism propounded earlier in the book. So our first task is to understand how this distinction is meant to operate (whether we ultimately decide that it is defensible or not).

Notice that it will often be more idiomatic in what follows to speak of types of argument rather than types of inference. This does not represent a change of subject, since to every inference (from proposition A to proposition B) there corresponds an argument (A, therefore B), and vice versa. (Remember that "argument" as used in philosophy is a term of art which has a different connotation from "argument" in ordinary speech—see the Logic Appendix sections 1 and 2 for more on this.)

9.2 "Deductive" and "Inductive" Argument Defined and Contrasted

(i) Deductive argument defined

There are several ways of defining deductive arguments, or (synonymously) deductively valid arguments, some of them more technical than others. We will offer two nontechnical definitions which are meant to be coextensive (that is, if one of the definitions applies to any given argument, then so does the other, and vice versa). For a more technical definition, see the Logic Appendix, section 3.2.

A deductive argument is

(A) an argument in which the truth of the premises absolutely guarantees the truth of the conclusion.
(B) an argument in which it would be self-contradictory to assert the premises and yet deny the conclusion.

Notice a number of points about deductive arguments, so defined. First of all, the definitions are entirely nonepistemological. For an argument to be deductive, we do not have to know or believe that the premises are true or false. What makes the argument deductive is that, whether we realize it or not, a certain relation holds between the premises and conclusion.

Secondly, neither the premises nor the conclusion of an argument needs to be true for the argument to be deductive. What makes the argument deductive is *the relation between* premises and conclusion. It is thus possible for an argument to be deductive, even though it has false premises and a false conclusion (for example: all fish are mammals, and all mammals are vegetarians, so all fish are vegetarians). Equally, it is possible for an argument to have true premises and a true conclusion without being deductive (for example: Monique speaks French, and all French people speak French, so Monique is French).

Thirdly, deductive arguments cannot vary in strength: there is no such thing as a more, or less, strong deductive argument. That this is so will be clear from both the definitions. The first definition tells us that the premises *absolutely guarantee* the truth of the conclusion—and being an absolute guarantee is not something that admits of degrees. Equally, being self-contradictory does not come in degrees—a set of propositions is either self-contradictory or not. Hence being a deductive argument is an all-or-nothing matter.

Fourthly, and as a corollary of the third point, it is impossible to strengthen or weaken a deductive argument by adding further premises. If the argument is deductive, then the premises already supply an absolute guarantee of the truth of the conclusion, and there is nothing stronger than an absolute guarantee. And if the premises *do* provide such a guarantee as they stand, they are in and of themselves sufficient for the truth of the conclusion. We could say that they guarantee the truth of the conclusion, no matter *what* else is the case; hence, whatever else is the case, whatever other premises are added, the absolute guarantee still holds.

Fifthly, these informal explanations of the concept of a deductive argument can be no more precise than the terms in which they are defined. They appeal, for example, to the concepts of an *absolute guarantee* and of *self-contradiction*, and hence the explanations can be no more precise than these concepts themselves are. And in fact it turns out that these concepts are very difficult to pin down in an entirely satisfactory way. But the informal explanations are adequate to give a preliminary working grasp of how the distinction between the two kinds of argument is meant to go.

(ii) "PSC induction" defined

In parallel to the definitions offered above of deductive arguments, we can define an inductive argument as follows. An inductive argument is

(C) an argument in which the truth of the premises *supports* the truth of the conclusion, but does not absolutely guarantee it.
(D) an argument in which although the premises support the conclusion, it would not be self-contradictory to assert the premises and deny the conclusion.

Let us call arguments so defined PSC inductions (short for "Premise Supports Conclusion").

In parallel to the points made previously about deductive arguments, we can note the following: First, that definitions (C) and (D) are like (A) and (B) in being nonepistemological (because we construe "support" to be an objective relation which obtains between propositions whether we realize that it does or not). Secondly, that it is again the *relation between* premises and conclusion that determines whether an argument is inductive or not. But thirdly, inductive arguments *can* vary in strength. The relation of support is one which does admit of degrees. It can range from overwhelming support, through very strong, strong, and moderate, down through fair to weak support. Hence, fourthly, it *is* possible to strengthen or weaken an inductive argument by adding further premises. Finally, notice that on these definitions, inductive and deductive arguments will form mutually exclusive classes: no argument can be both deductive and inductive. This is because no argument can both give an absolute guarantee (definition [A]) and yet not give it (definition [C]); equally, it is because no argument can have premises and a conclusion which in combination *are* self-contradictory (definition [B]) and yet are *not* self-contradictory (definition [D]). If we restrict our attention to arguments in which the premises give *some* support to the conclusion (either an absolute guarantee or something less), then the classification will be exhaustive as well as exclusive: every argument will have to be either deductive or inductive.

(iii) Different degrees of "support"

We have said in characterizing PSC induction that the premises *support* the conclusion. But the notion of support can here be taken in two different ways. We might mean, "support in such a way as to make the conclusion more likely to be true than not." In other words, the truth of the premises pushes the probability of the conclusion over 50 percent (though we should not assume that it will always be possible to attach numerical values to the degree of support). Secondly, we might mean "support in such a way as to raise the credibility of the conclusion above what it was before, without necessarily by itself making it belief-worthy." Consider, as an example, a detective gathering information about the murder of Smith. She finds that Jones had a motive for murdering Smith. This certainly gives some support to the hypothesis that Jones was the murderer, but equally certainly it does not make it more likely than not that Jones was the murderer. The detective then discovers that Jones had the opportunity to murder Smith. As before, this supports the credibility of the hypothesis that Jones was the murderer without making it more likely than not. The same point applies when the detective finds that Jones was with Smith at the time of the murder, that Jones was seen by other people to be very flustered immediately after the murder, that Jones then tried to leave the country in secret, and so on. Each piece of evidence taken separately, increases by a small amount the probability that Jones killed Smith and in that sense supports this conclusion. But only taken collectively do they support the conclusion in the sense of making it more likely than not. There is no generally recognized terminology to mark this distinction. So let us label the kind of support which makes the conclusion more probable than not "major support"; and the kind of support which merely raises the probability of the conclusion "minor support."

(iv) "OTU induction" defined

There is, however, a second way in which induction is commonly defined, and which we need to explain. Sometimes inductive arguments are defined not in terms of the *relation between* the premises and conclusion of the argument, but in terms of *what the premises and conclusion are about.* More specifically, they are defined as those arguments which have premises about what has been observed (or is being observed) and a conclusion about what has not been observed. They are defined as involving inference from the observed to the unobserved. Let us call these OTU inductions (short for "Observed To Unobserved").

An example of this kind of inference would be when the detective, having discovered that Jones was with Smith at the time of the murder, that he tried to leave the country in secret immediately after the murder, that his fingerprints were on the murder weapon, that he was being blackmailed by Smith, and so on, infers that Jones murdered Smith. Here, the premises record some matters discovered by observation, and the conclusion is about something which the detective did not observe. Sometimes OTU inferences move from premises about the observed past to a conclusion about the future (for example, I have seen my cat catch mice in the past, and I infer that she will do so again in the future); sometimes they move from premises about the observed past to a conclusion about the unobserved past (as in the detective example above); sometimes they move from something that I am observing here and now to something that is unobserved simply because it is spatially distant from me (for example, I hear distant explosions and infer that a battle is raging). What links all these apparently different kinds of argument is that they all involve OTU inference. In the next chapter, we will return to the topic of induction and discuss further the PSC and OTU conceptions. But having now mapped out the traditional conceptions of deduction and induction, we return to consider in more detail issues raised by deduction.

9.3 The Problem: Which Arguments and Inferential Principles Are Deductive?

We started then with a definition of deduction. But merely defining a term does not by itself tell you whether anything exists to which the term applies. I can define the term "unicorn," but that does not tell me whether there are any unicorns; I can define the phrase "highest prime number," but that does not tell me whether there is a highest prime number (there isn't!); and similarly, the fact that we have defined a type of argument, by itself leaves open whether there are any arguments which fit the definition. It *might* be the case that our definitions of "deductive argument" are like definitions of "unicorn": self-consistent, but with no application to anything in the real world. In fact, there has been widespread agreement that there are deductive arguments as we have defined them, and further, epistemologists have written as if there is no problem about *justifying* such a view. They have often written as if it is just obvious whether an argument is deductive or not and hence that the claim that an argument is deductive needs no justification, or that if it does need justifying, the justification is easy to give. Before we assess these responses, let us begin by getting clearer how the issue of justification arises.

Let us focus on arguments which rely on some principle of inference. The principle of inference is the principle you use in inferring the conclusion from the premises. For example, the argument

If Mary came, so did Jim.

Mary came.

So   Jim came too.

is naturally construed as relying on the principle, known as modus ponens, which says that if one thing implies a second, and the first is true, then so is the second. More simply and more abstractly, it tells us that if p is true, and p implies q, then q is true too (see the Logic Appendix, 4.1). Here is another argument illustrating a different principle of inference:

If Mary came, so did Jim.

Jim came.

So   Mary came.

This is naturally construed as relying on a principle known as "affirming the consequent," and usually regarded as a fallacy. This principle tells us that if p implies q, and q is true, then p is true too. We shall return to this example in a moment.

Other arguments will rely on more complicated inferential principles. For example, one of the two principles of inference known as De Morgan's laws (after the nineteenth-century English logician Augustus De Morgan, 1806–1871) tells us that the negation of the conjunction of two propositions implies (and is implied by) the disjunction of the negation of each of them. (If it is not the case that both p and q are true, then either p is false, or q is false, or both are false—and vice versa). Another example of a more complicated inferential principle is the following: if most A's are B's and most B's are C's, then most A's are C's. (We shall return to this in a moment.) And when we consider the realm of mathematics, we find principles of inference which are yet more complicated; for example, there is the principle of mathematical induction which says that if 0 has a property P and the successor of a number which has the property P also has the property P, then every number has the property P. (Note that the principle called "mathematical induction" is always regarded as a deductive principle and is completely unrelated to PSC and OTU induction.)

Now if we are trying to identify some arguments as deductive (or to *justify* the claim that they are deductive), we know that they must be relying on principles of reasoning which are such that the truth of the premises absolutely guarantees the truth of the conclusion, and/or in which it would be self-contradictory to assert the premises and deny the conclusion (see 9.2 [i]). Let us call these principles "deductive principles," and say that something is a deductive principle if it passes either the "guarantee test" or the "self-contradictoriness test."

Our question now becomes how we can tell of any inferential principle whether it is a deductive principle or not, that is, how we can tell whether a given principle passes either of the two tests. It is, after all, quite possible for a principle of inference to be nondeductive. Consider the example we introduced above:

If Mary came, then so did Jim.

Jim came.

So   Mary came.

As we said, this argument is naturally construed as relying on a principle of reasoning which is normally regarded as fallacious. It is fairly easy to see in this case *why* it should be regarded as a nondeductive principle: it is nondeductive because it can take you from true premises to a false conclusion. It may be that although Jim came, Mary did not come (perhaps Jim came regardless of what Mary did). So it is possible for the conclusion to be false even though both the premises are true, and hence it fails our guarantee test.

Here is a piece of reasoning using one of the more complicated principles which we have just mentioned.

> Most people would rather eat burgers than spinach.
>
> Most people would rather eat spinach than snails.
>
> So   Most people would rather eat burgers than snails.

It is perhaps not quite so obvious whether this argument relies on a deductive principle or not. Remember that the test is not whether the premises and/or conclusion are true, but whether the premises absolutely guarantee the conclusion, whether it would be impossible both for the premises to be true and yet for the conclusion to be false. And of course it might be a principle of reasoning which is a good one in some sense, without being one which is a *deductive* principle. (In fact, it is not a deductive principle.) So if there can be principles of inference which are not *deductive* principles, by what test can we single out the deductive principles, and thereby single out deductive arguments? Unless we can identify deductive principles, we will not be able to tell which arguments are deductive and which are not. In the next two sections, we will look at two ways in which a defender of the traditional deductive/inductive distinction can try to identify deductive principles (and thus justify the claim that a given argument is deductive); and we will argue that from her point of view, neither is satisfactory.

9.4 A First Answer: Foundationalism and Self-evidence

One way in which the traditionalist might try to tackle this problem is to divide our putative deductive principles into two groups, the simple ones and the complex ones. If she could then show how the complex ones could be derived from the simpler ones, she would at least have reduced the size of her problem. For the problem would then arise only for a smaller number of principles, and only for the simplest principles, and we might think that that residual problem would in turn prove tractable. How might such a reductive approach go in detail?

One illustration of it can be found in the Logic Appendix, section 5.1, in which a derivation of the principle of the transitivity of implication from the principle of modus ponens is sketched. What this shows is that *if* we are justified in accepting modus ponens, *then* we would be justified in accepting the transitivity of implication. And the foundationalist might hope to show that in a similar fashion, all the more complex principles which we want to use in our deductive reasoning can be derived either from modus ponens or from other equally simple principles.

Unfortunately for this program, there are many complex principles of inference which seem to be deductive but which cannot be derived from simpler ones. For example, the principle of mathematical induction which we referred to in section 9.3 cannot be derived from simpler deductive principles, and there are many other examples from the domains of mathematics and set theory, such as the Axiom of Choice.

But even if we overlook this objection, the foundationalist would not have *justified* those complex principles which can be derived from simple ones, merely by showing that this derivation is possible, unless the simple ones themselves can be justified. So what will show that the simple ones like modus ponens are justified? What is it that assures us that if we rely only on modus ponens in moving from premises to conclusion, then the argument will be deductive?

One natural response at this point would be to exclaim "But it's just obvious!" Unfortunately, although this reply may be adequate in some practical contexts, it cannot be satisfactory here. As section 7.5 (ii) showed, the history of thought contains too many examples of claims that were judged as too "obvious" to need justification which yet turned out to be false. How can we be sure that a principle like modus ponens, however obvious it may seem to us now, will not suffer the same fate? We would surely like to have a rather more substantial assurance than is afforded by an appeal to obviousness, if this is at all possible.

After our critique of foundationalism about the a priori (Chapter 6), it should also be clear that any appeal to the idea of self-evidence (Descartes's "natural light of reason") will be no improvement on the appeal to what is obvious. So unless the traditional defender of deduction can produce some more convincing vindication of the supposedly simple principles of inference, she will have achieved relatively little by showing that the complex principles can be derived from the simple ones.

However, this is the point at which an appeal might be made to certain techniques employed by logicians, and we will explore one of these in the next section.

9.5 A Second Answer: Meaning and Appeal to Truth Tables

On this approach to identifying deductive principles, attention focuses on the meanings of the logically key words which occur in principles of reasoning. These are the logical constants, like "not," "and," "or," "if . . . then . . .," and so on. The basic idea of this approach is to spell out precisely what these key terms mean and then show that given those meanings, it is impossible for certain principles to take us from true premises to a false conclusion; and from this it would follow that such principles are deductive.

Let us illustrate this general strategy by considering modus ponens in particular. The key terms in modus ponens are the concepts *and* and *if . . . then.* . . . So the first step is to provide precise explanations of their meaning. This is done by providing a so-called truth table for them (see the Logic Appendix, 5.21). When we have done this, we can then construct a truth table for the inferential principle as a whole. The Logic Appendix shows how to do this for the inferential principle which says that if one thing is true, and either a second thing is true or the first thing is false, then the second thing is true (see Logic Appendix, 5.23). If we construct an analogous truth table for the principle we are currently focusing on, modus ponens, it will look like this:

p	q	$p \supset q$	$[p \cdot (p \supset q)] \supset q$	
T	T	T	T	T
T	F	F	F	T
F	T	T	F	T
F	F	T	F	T
(1)	(2)	(3)	(4)	(5)

What this shows us is that no matter what p and q are about, and no matter whether p is true or false, or q is true or false, if they are combined in the form "p and (p implies q)," we can be quite sure that it follows that q is true.

We seem, then, to have made real progress. We have moved well beyond the vague ideas of what is "obvious" and what is "self-evident." We have in the first place produced a proof which is mechanical, in the sense that at no point does it rely on the reader's own "judgment" or interpretation: every stage of the process is covered by a precise rule which determines what the next stage will be. Secondly, the procedure appears to deliver in each case a wholly determinate result. It seems that we will never complete the process and yet be left unsure whether the principle is a deductive one or not. If we end up with T's in our final column we know that the principle is deductive; if there is anything but T's, we know that the principle is not deductive. Further, it is clear that the same technique can be applied to a number of other inferential principles. All that we have to do is to construct a truth table for them, and see if we have T's in the final column. Why, then, should it be thought that there is any problem left about identifying which arguments are deductive and which are not? That is the question to which we turn in the next section.

9.6 The Appeal to Truth Tables: Some Objections and Replies

Even within the domain to which it purports to apply (namely propositional arguments) the appeal to truth tables can be challenged on three importantly different grounds. One of these appeals to the everyday usage of logical words, like "if . . . then . . ." The second appeals to results from formal logic. And the third appeals to sophisticated work in mathematics and physics in the twentieth century. We will deal mainly with the first of these objections (in 9.6 [i]), and comment only briefly on the others (in 9.6 [iii] and [iv]) as they depend on technical work beyond the scope of this book.

(i) The challenge from ordinary language: truth tables do not capture the meanings of logically key words

Let us agree that *if* the ordinary language in which we reason can be accurately captured by the truth table technique, then we have a foolproof way of identifying at least some deductive principles of inferences and hence of identifying at least some deductive arguments. The question is whether the truth tables do accurately capture the meaning of our ordinary terms like "and" and "or" and "if . . . then . . ." We will concentrate on the latter, for it is there that the difference between ordinary usage and the corresponding truth table is most glaring. Consider again the truth table for "if . . . then . . ."

p	q	$p \supset q$
T	T	T
T	F	F
F	T	T
F	F	T

Two implications of this truth table are at once apparent. First, whenever p is false (rows 3 and 4), the truth table tells us that "if p, then q" is true. In other words, a false proposition implies absolutely every proposition! Secondly, whenever q is true (rows 1 and 3), the truth table tells us that "if p, then q" is true. In other words, a true proposition is implied by absolutely every proposition! These very well known consequences of the truth table for "if . . . then . . ." are called the paradoxes of material implication. ("Material implication" is another name for the "horseshoe" symbol: "$p \supset q$" and "p materially implies q" are synonymous.) Some examples will illustrate what these paradoxes actually mean in practice. If we accepted the truth table definition of "if . . . then . . . ," we would have to accept as true such claims as the following: if Lincoln was the first U. S. president, then all dogs have three legs; if Lincoln was the first U. S. president, then all dogs have four legs (these illustrate the first paradox: a false proposition implies every proposition); if all water is poisonous, then the earth is roughly spherical; if rocks are inedible, then some fish are edible (these illustrate the second paradox: a true proposition is implied by every proposition).

The main reason we might want to reject these bizarre "if . . . then . . ." claims is that there is no connection in subject matter between the "if" clause and the "then" clause. Normally, when we say "if one thing, then another," we do so because we take it that there is *some* sort of connection between the two ideas which we are linking—that in some sense, the second thing *depends on* the first. This is vaguely put and could be elaborated in any number of different ways. But whatever the detailed conception we have of this idea of a connection of content between the "if" clause and the "then" clause, it is a feature which is central to our use of the "if . . . then . . ." locution, and it is something which is wholly missing from the truth table account of the meaning of "if . . . then . . ." For according to that account, when "if *p*, then *q*" is true, there need be no connection at all in subject matter between *p* and *q*. All that is needed to make "if *p*, then *q*" true is that either *p* is false or *q* is true.

Given that this is so, it would seem entirely reasonable to say that the truth table does not capture the meaning of "if . . . then . . ." and hence cannot be used as a foolproof test of the deductive status of any inferential principle (such as modus ponens) which uses "if . . . then . . ." Given the centrality of the "if . . . then . . ." idea in inference, this is a crippling blow for the traditionalist. Of course the failure of the truth table account of the meaning of "if . . . then . . ." does not show that the other truth table definitions (of "or," "not," and "and") fail. Further detailed argument would be needed to show in each individual case that the truth table account of these concepts was inadequate. It is indeed possible to produce such arguments, though the inadequacies are nothing like as large and startling as they are in the case of "if . . . then . . ." Is there, then, any way in which this attack on the truth table test of deductive validity can be met?

(ii) Two possible replies to the challenge from ordinary language

We shall mention two possible replies to this attack on the truth table test of deductive validity. The first, found in the work of Bertrand Russell, insists that we can use the truth tables to decide which principles are deductive because the test "works," in the sense that it never identifies a principle as deductive if the use of that principle would lead one from true premises to a false conclusion. Although the use of truth tables produces some strange results, for example the paradoxes which we have just discussed, it does not admit as a principle of deductive reasoning anything which can lead us from truth to falsity. However, the problem with this response is that it presupposes that we can already identify which arguments are deductive, independently of the truth table test, and thus it begs the question.

The second response, derived from the work of H. P. Grice, argues that the truth tables do indeed capture the meaning of the logically key words (and thus can be used to decide which principles are deductively valid), and seeks to explain away the paradoxical results noted previously. The Gricean approach invokes some very general principles governing all assertive discourse, principles which have a plausibility extending far beyond the present context. Although some elegant and sophisticated results can be obtained from this line of thought, the claim that the truth tables can help us to identify deductive principles is open to still further objections.

(iii) A second challenge: results from formal logic

Even if the challenge from ordinary language can be met (à la Grice), there is a further reason for doubting whether the appeal to truth tables can decide which principles are deductive. It is that this method works for only a very limited range of the principles of logic (those relating to propositional reasoning). There are many principles of inference for which neither this method nor any comparably mechanical one is available. This is shown to be true by Church's Theorem, to which we refer in the Logic Appendix, section 7. Interestingly, it is not easy to give examples of principles which are undecidable by the truth table or a similar mechanical test, because the theorem tells us only that there is no general procedure which will work for all logical principles. This means that there are many principles for which we know of no method which will decide whether they are deductively valid, and from this it at once follows that the truth table method is not sufficient.

It might be thought that one could combine the truth table procedure for deciding whether some principles of logic are deductive with the (foundationalist's) derivation of complex principles from simple ones and thereby provide a way of deciding for any principle of reasoning whether it was deductive. Again, for reasons similar to those given in the previous paragraph, this cannot be done: there are many, indeed infinitely many, principles of inference which cannot be reduced to the simple principles for which this technique (or any comparable one) does work.

(iv) A third challenge: recent work in mathematics and physics

We turn briefly now to the third main challenge to the truth table method for deciding which principles are deductive. In this case, the meanings which should be attached to the logical constants have been challenged, not on the basis of considerations about the way we ordinarily use the logical terms, nor because of results in formal logic, but because of problems which have arisen in math and physics in recent decades. We shall not go into these technical matters in any detail, but they are briefly explained in the Logic Appendix, section 6. The key point is that if the logical constants are given a different meaning from that assigned by the truth tables, this yields different decisions about which principles are deductive and which are not.

9.7 A Concluding Dilemma

To conclude, we should notice that on the traditional view of argument and inference, any attempt to justify identifying certain arguments or principles as deductive would itself have to be either a deductive argument or an inductive one. This may produce something of a dilemma. If we attempt to justify identifying certain principles as deductive by using deductive argument, we are in danger of producing circular arguments which beg the question. On the traditional view, it is hard to see how to escape this vicious circle unless there are some self-evident deductive principles which we can use to justify all the others—in other words, unless foundationalism is right. However, we have already argued that foundationalism is wrong (cf. Chapter 6).

However, there are difficulties with trying to justify identifying deductive principles by using inductive arguments, whether of the PSC or OTU variety. For it is one part of the traditional view that the conclusions of inductive arguments can never be more than probable. The probability might indeed be high in some cases—that would depend upon the particular argument—but the conclusion could never be more than probable. Deductive principles, by contrast, have traditionally been regarded as certain, from which it would follow that they need more than an inductive argument to support them. How to escape from this dilemma is a problem which we happily leave for the traditionalist!

Exercises

1. Explain (in no more than one page and without rereading the chapter) *four* differences between deductive and inductive arguments, then check your answer against 9.2 for accuracy, clarity, and completeness.
2. You are told that a bag contains balls each of which is either red or white, and you are asked to remove balls one at a time from the bag. Every so often you are asked to predict what the color of the next ball will be. Consider each of the following cases and, if you can make any prediction at all, say (i) what your prediction is, (ii) what kind of inference is involved, and (iii) why you think your prediction is a good one:
   a. You know the bag contains no more than 50 balls and you have already picked out 10 at random and each was white.
   b. You do not know how many balls are in the bag, indeed the experimenter may be adding balls so that there is in effect an unlimited number. However, you have already picked out 10 and they were all red.
   c. You know that there are 100 balls in the bag and that 50 are red and 50 are white; you have just picked out 10 balls at random and each was white.

   Write no more than one and a half pages; then exchange answers with a fellow student and assess each other's reasoning.
3. Which kind of inference is involved in each of the following cases?
   a. Some people claim to have produced cold fusion, but other researchers have been unable to reproduce these results, so cold fusion is at best unproven.
   b. Schnitzer claims to have produced cold fusion, but anyone who makes such a claim is a charlatan, so Schnitzer is a charlatan.

    c. Many people are now confirming the results of researchers who first claimed to have produced cold fusion, so cold fusion will soon be a reality.

Exchange answers with a fellow student and assess each other's reasoning.

4. Assess the case for thinking that neither truth tables nor any similar procedure will enable us to decide which principles of inference are deductive and which are not.

5. What is the general case for thinking that it is difficult to decide when a principle of inference is deductive? (Hard.)

CHAPTER 10

The Traditional Problem of Induction

10.1 Different Ways of Stating "The Problem of Induction"

In section 9.2, we outlined two ways in which inductive inferences have traditionally been defined. The first was in terms of the relations between the premises and conclusion: the premises give support of a nondeductive kind to the conclusion. The second was in terms of the content of the premises and the conclusion: the premises were about what has been observed, and the conclusion about what has not been observed. The first we called PSC inductions (Premise Supports Conclusion), and the second OTU inductions (Observed To Unobserved). According to which definition we adopt, the traditional problem of induction will be raised in different ways. If we adopt the PSC definition, the problem becomes: how can we identify inductive arguments? If we adopt the OTU definition, the problem becomes: are any inductive arguments justifiable? Let us explain this further.

It might seem simply obvious on the PSC definition that there are inductive arguments. We ordinarily think that the detective investigating a crime is someone who gathers lots of pieces of evidence in order to support a conclusion about the guilty party, even though the evidence does not give a deductive guarantee of the truth of the conclusion. Again, if as I am handling some poisons, I think to myself

> This is arsenic. (premise)

So   If I were to eat four ounces of it in one sitting, it would
    kill me. (conclusion)

I have not reasoned deductively. But surely my premises do support (and hence support inductively) my conclusion.

Common sense, then, certainly suggests that there are PSC inductive arguments as we have defined them. But in fact it turns out to be very difficult to explain how this common sense view can be true, that is to say, to explain how it is possible for premises to *support* a conclusion, and yet do so in a non-deductive way. So if we are using the PSC concept of induction, the way to raise the problem of induction is to ask how we can identify inductive arguments, and if we can identify them, how it is possible for premises to yield nondeductive support for a conclusion.

If we adopt the OTU definition of induction, however, the claim that there are inductive arguments is uncontroversial. It is just a fact that people do infer conclusions about what they have not observed from premises about what they have observed. What is controversial about that is why, if at all, such arguments are rational or justifiable, that is to say, how the premises of such arguments can ever yield major support for their conclusions (see 9.2 [iii]). The position is summarized in Table 2.

It does not matter which definition we use, as long as we are clear which definition it is. Indeed, it is clear from what we have said so far that a single argument might turn out to be both PSC *and* OTU inductive. Of course, if that were so, what made it PSC inductive would be different from what made it OTU inductive. Just as an individual woman might be both a sister and a mother, but in virtue of different facts about her, so an individual argument might be both PSC and OTU inductive in virtue of different facts about it. But it is nonetheless important to be clear which definition of induction we are using, because the very thing which is obvious on one definition is what needs explaining and defending on the other, and vice versa. So if we were inadvertently to slip from one definition to another, we could become hopelessly confused about what was obvious, and hence could be taken for granted, and what was unobvious, and hence needed to be justified and explained. There are some technical reasons for thinking that the PSC

TABLE 2

	Type of Argument	
	PSC Inductive	OTU Inductive
Defined as	The truth of the premises supports the conclusion nondeductively.	The premises are about what has been observed, and the conclusion is about what has not been observed.
What is obvious	Accepting such arguments, if there are any, is rational.	There are such arguments.
What is not obvious	How we can identify such arguments, and how they are possible.	Why it is ever rational to accept such arguments.
Relations to deduction	By definition, cannot be deductive.	Its definition does not exclude the possibility of OTU deductive arguments.

definition is preferable, but a good deal of the literature adopts implicitly or explicitly the OTU definition, and in what follows, we will therefore do the same.

Notice that on neither definition of induction does inductive argument have any special connection with knowledge (or justified belief) about *the future*. This is worth mentioning because some authors suggest that the problem of induction is whether we can know that the future will be like the past. But this is a mistaken view of the problem. It is of course true that the future has not yet been observed, and it is also true that if we can gain knowledge or justified belief about the future, our evidence will come from what we have observed in the past and present. So arguments that have premises about past (and current) observations and conclusions about the future will certainly fit the OTU definition of induction. But precisely the same is true of arguments about the unobserved past. I believe not only that the sun will rise tomorrow, but also that the sun rose on the day before I was born, or that it rose on the day that Columbus sighted America, or that it rose 1 million years ago. My beliefs about those past sunrises which I did not observe are based on just the same evidence as my beliefs about the future sunrises which I have not yet observed. Certainly, on the OTU conception of induction, beliefs about the future may be inductively based and may yield particularly striking and easily grasped examples of the problem of induction. But from the logical point of view, it is because they are beliefs about the *unobserved*, not because they are beliefs about the *future*, that they are problematic.

We have, then, a problem about induction, expressible in two different ways:

(i) How can we identify PSC inductive arguments?
(ii) Why is it ever reasonable to accept any OTU inductive arguments?

If we were adopting the PSC definition, the problem we would be concerned with in this chapter would be parallel to the one we focused on in the last chapter, namely a problem of identifying certain principles of inference, principles which *by definition* it would be rational to use if we could find them. But as we will be using the OTU definition, our problem is rather one of justification: given that we can indeed identify OTU inductive arguments, what justifies us in accepting them?

10.2 When Is It Reasonable to Accept OTU Inductive Arguments?

(i) The appeal to probability

It might be thought that we can justify OTU inductive inferences by drawing a simple distinction between certainty and probability. Suppose we have an argument of the form:

(1) All observed A's have been B's.

So   (2) All A's are B's.

We can agree (so this line of thought goes) that our conclusion is not *certain*. So it would not be reasonable to accept the conclusion, if "accept" means "accept as certain." But it *is* reasonable if "accept" means "accept as probably true." For although we may not have observed every A, and therefore cannot say *for sure* that all A's are B's, we may have observed a great many A's, and that makes it reasonable to say that probably all A's are B's. Strictly speaking, the argument might continue, we should signal this fact by agreeing that the argument from (1) to (2) is not justified as it stands, and that what would be justified is the argument from (1) to

(2a) It is probable that all A's are B's.

But however attractive this move might initially seem, in fact it will not solve our problem. For suppose that all observed A's have been B's. Why does that make it *probable* as opposed to *certain* that all A's are B's? Of course, if we could somehow know that observed cases and unobserved cases would resemble each other, then indeed we could conclude that if all observed A's had been B's, it was probable that all A's were B's. But how could we know whether observed cases and unobserved cases would resemble each other? It is true that as a matter of common sense, we very often think that if we have observed lots of examples of something with a certain feature, then other examples of that same thing will also probably have that feature. But the problem is to show why this common sense assumption is justified. *Why* does the fact that lots of observed A's have been B's make it even probable that the next A will be a B? Asserting that it *is* a fact simply raises the problem anew, it does not solve it.

Notice that we are not here denying that the conclusions of OTU inductive arguments should be regarded as probable rather than as certain. That is not the issue which we have just been discussing. What we have just been arguing is that, as David Hume pointed out (Hume, 1739, 1748, 90), *even if* it is granted that the conclusions of inductive argument are never more than probable, that will not solve the problem of OTU induction.

(ii) An inductive justification

One natural thought which occurs to many people when they first start thinking about how induction could be justified is that its past success rate must count in its favor. Although by definition when I draw an OTU inference, I am not in a position to check the conclusion at the time, in many cases I can subsequently check whether my conclusion was true. I infer by induction that tomorrow will be rainy, tomorrow arrives, and sure enough I observe the rain falling. Sometimes, of course, the conclusion of an inductive inference turns out to be false even when the premises were true. But in general, so we might argue, when we check the conclusions of carefully carried out inductive inferences, they turn out to be correct. Since there is no reason to think that the method will cease to be reliable when we apply it to new cases, we are justified in thinking that the method will continue to be reliable in new cases.

This seems a neat solution to the problem, but it is not one which has attracted many supporters. It is not clear first of all how it could be established that *most* inductive arguments with true premises and whose conclusions we have subsequently been able to check by observation do have true conclusions. For it is not clear how to count the inductive inferences which people draw. But let us assume that this difficulty can be overcome. Secondly, we might wonder whether this defense of induction is presupposing an over-simple link between justification and truth. Does the mere fact that the conclusion of my inductive inference turns out to be true show that the inference was a justified one? Might it not have been true for reasons completely unconnected with the premises which in fact I was relying on? If so, it could hardly count as a justified inference.

But the principal problem with this defense is that it seems to be begging the question: it is assuming at the outset the very point which it is trying to prove. For the inference from the *observed* success of some OTU induction to the as-yet *unobserved* success of other OTU inductions is surely itself an OTU inductive inference. So it is an inference which we would be entitled to draw only if we had already established that reliance on OTU inductions was sometimes reasonable. We could express the point as follows: the supposed justification is

(a) OTU inferences have worked in observed cases.

So (b) OTU inferences will work in as-yet unobserved cases.

And the objection to it is that the inference from (a) to (b) is itself an OTU inference. So *if* OTU inferences are sometimes reasonable, then the inference from (a) to (b) may be sound. So in order to know whether the inference from (a) to (b) is sound, we need *antecedently* to know whether OTU inferences are sound. So we cannot use this supposed justification in order to prove that OTUs are sound.

Many writers from Hume onward have thought that this objection to an inductive justification of induction is conclusive (see, e.g., Achinstein in Swinburne, 1974). But other writers have argued that the objection is flawed. They point out that the inductive justification of induction does not beg the question in the common sense of that phrase, that is to say, it does not have as one of its *premises* the conclusion which it is trying to establish. Rather, it uses as its *principle of inference* the conclusion which it is trying to establish. However, supporters of the objection can admit this point and maintain that it does not undermine the objection, nor rescue the inductive justification of induction. For it is still the case that the truth of the conclusion has to be presupposed before one can have any reason to accept it: whether it is presupposed as a premise or presupposed as a rule of inference surely makes no difference.

What *is* true is that if one were to take a different view of justification from the one which we have so far been assuming, then the inductive justification might be defensible. We have been assuming that if you are justified in believing *p*, then (at least) you have some other belief *q* which supports *p*. Suppose that we had opted for a reliabilist conception of justification, of the sort discussed earlier (see 3.1, 4.6). This would claim that a belief is justified if it is produced by a reliable method. Given this conception of justification, we will be justified in believing the conclusion of an OTU argument, if OTU arguments constitute a reliable method of forming beliefs (whether or not we know they are a reliable method). In general, there is nothing circular about a method generating a belief in its own reliability. (For someone taking this line, see Van Cleve in French et al., and also Papineau, 1984.)

However, as we argued earlier, the reliabilist conception of justification seems unattractive, although the fact that it would allow a solution to the problem of induction is an important point in its favor.

10.3 Karl Popper's "Solution" to the Problem of Induction

(i) Exposition of Popper's solution

One writer who believes that he has provided a complete solution to the problem of induction is Karl Popper.

> I think that I have solved a major philosophical problem: the problem of induction [he boldly declares, before modestly adding that] . . . this solution has been extremely fruitful, and it has enabled me to solve a good number of other philosophical problems. (Popper, 1972, 1)

Popper was primarily concerned with the use of induction in science. But since his "solution," if correct, would apply in all inductive contexts, including those of ordinary life; and since Popper's writings have been extremely influential among nonphilosophers interested in induction, we will examine Popper's claim to see if it can be sustained. And in order to understand the solution, it will be helpful to backtrack a little, and consider how Popper thinks the problem of induction has arisen within a traditional understanding of the scientific enterprise.

On the traditional theory, the scientist is thought of as first of all observing the world around her, looking for regularities within her experience. These observations justify her in making some such statements as "All observed *A*'s have been *B*'s"—for example, that all observed swans have been white, or that all observed appearances of a new moon have been 24 days apart, or that all observed contact between litmus paper and acid turns the litmus paper red, and so on. She is then supposed to generalize these recorded observations by dropping out the word "observed," and claiming something of the form "All *A*'s are *B*'s" (or "Whenever *A*, *B*," etc.). These generalized statements then count as putative natural laws. The scientist proceeds to test them to see if they are genuine laws by looking for some confirming instances. If she finds an *A* that is not a *B*, she has disproved the supposed law. But if she finds more *A*'s that are *B*, she has confirmed the putative law; and the more instances of *A*'s that are *B*'s which she finds, the stronger the confirmation.

This process can be represented in three steps: (1) initial observation of a regularity; (2) generalizing from the regularity in order to advance a putative law; (3) making further observations which either confirm or refute the putative law. OTU induction thus enters into this account at two points: it is used first in inferring the generalizations from the initial observations, and secondly, if the subsequent observations are as predicted, treating them as confirming the generalization. Both the initial inference and the subsequent claim of confirmation are moving from premises about what has been observed to a conclusion about what has not been observed, and hence count as OTU induction.

Popper's solution to the problem of induction as it arises in this account of scientific method has the merit of boldness and simplicity. He denies that the scientist makes either of the two steps just identified as relying on induction. He denies, in other words, that the scientist ever does infer from observations to generalizations or putative laws, and he denies that the scientist ever does or could confirm her putative laws by subsequent observations. More generally, he denies that there are *any* good inductive arguments (in the OTU sense of induction); or (equivalently) that there are any inductive arguments at all (in the PSC sense of induction). The only good arguments are deductive ones. If an argument is nondeductive, it is not merely weaker than a deductive argument—it is an argument with no rational force. "Induction is a procedure which is logically invalid and rationally unjustifiable," he starkly declares (Popper, 1963, 45). How does Popper establish these sweeping claims?

He does so by arguing that *general* theories or hypotheses (or conjectures, to use one of his favored terms) are psychologically and logically prior to particular observations. We cannot, he says, simply wander about the world with an initially empty mind, letting regularities impinge on us. For *everything* is an instance of some regularity or other. If observation is to be possible at all, we must be selective. So right from the outset, we approach every situation with certain expectations, preconceptions, hypotheses. These will supply our criteria of relevance and hence will tell us what we are to observe. So we start with some preconceived hypothesis, such as that all swans are white, and this at once tells us what we are to observe (namely swans) among the indefinitely many possible objects of observation.

Furthermore, the scientist does not (in Popper's view) try to confirm her hypothesis: she tries to refute it (i.e., disprove it). In other words, she deliberately searches for swans which are *not* white. If she finds some nonwhite swans, her original hypothesis has been refuted and must be abandoned or amended. But if all she finds are more white swans, her findings do not *con-*

firm her hypothesis—they merely *fail to refute* it. So they do not justify us in saying that the theory is true, or probably true, or well confirmed. All that we are entitled to say is that the theory has so far withstood attempts to refute it. Popper rather confuses this point by saying that we have "corroborated" the hypothesis by failing to find any nonwhite swans. But it is clear that in speaking of a hypothesis as "corroborated," he means no more than "has withstood rigorous attempts to refute it." He does *not* mean that something which is corroborated has been supported by evidence or been shown to be probably true (Popper, 1972, 18).

This sounds like a neat solution to the problem of induction—but we will argue that on three grounds, Popper's account is unacceptable.

(ii) Three objections to Popper

First, suppose that Popper is right in saying that we approach every observation situation already armed with some theory or conjecture which we wish to test—say, that all swans are white. Students sometimes ask at this point "But where, on Popper's view, does this conjecture come from? Why should we be testing the hypothesis that all swans are white, rather than that they are red, or spotted, or striped? Surely, it is because we have *first* observed some white swans, and having noticed that they were all white, it *then* occurs to us that maybe all swans are white. And in arriving at that generalization, we are relying on induction."

But this first objection is one that Popper can meet. He is willing to allow that our observations may *cause* us to take seriously some hypotheses and to discount others. So seeing a lot of white swans and no nonwhite ones may cause us to entertain the hypothesis that all swans are white. What he insists on is that the observations do not *support* or *justify* the hypothesis. So he has an answer to the question of where conjectures come from. But he is nevertheless committed to the idea that there is no ultimate priority of observations over hypotheses or conjectures and hence accepts what he sees as an implication of this position, namely that some of our conjectures are innate (Popper, 1963, 47).

There is a second line of criticism which would again try to convict Popper of secretly relying on the induction which he has officially condemned. Recall Popper's suggestion that we test a hypothesis of the form "All *A*'s and *B*'s" not by looking for confirmation of it, which he thinks it would be impossible to find, but by looking for falsifying instances. We look for an *A* that is not a *B*. Suppose we find one. What we then naturally assume is not that the one we have found is the only counterexample to the hypothesis, but that it is a member of an indefinitely large class of counterexamples, and *that is why there is some point in looking for counterexamples*. Suppose my hypothesis is that water always boils at 100°C. I test this and find that sometimes it is false (for example, if the test is not at sea level). What I then assume is not that the sample of water I have tested is the only counterinstance to my general hypothesis, but rather that the sample is one of an indefinitely repeatable set of samples, each of which would be a counterinstance to the original conjecture. But in making this assumption, I am relying on an OTU induction. I assume that what I have observed in one case gives me some good reason to think that if I repeat the test keeping a certain (as yet unknown) set of variables constant, I will get the same result with future samples. But if, like Popper, I think that induction is "logically invalid and rationally unjustifiable," I will have no reason for thinking that the fact that my conjecture was falsified today gives me grounds for thinking that it will be falsified if tested in the same conditions tomorrow.

Of course Popper can reply, quite correctly, that if one's hypothesis is that *all* A's are B's, then a single A which is not a B is sufficient conclusively to refute one's initial hypothesis. It does not have to be the case that the non-B A which we find is a member of a large class of non-B A's. But the criticism of Popper we outlined can concede this point. What the criticism is saying is that although part of the interest in our finding a non-B A lies in the fact that it formally refutes the hypothesis that all A's are B's, another important part of the interest lies in the fact that it gives us (as we think) reason to believe that there will be *other* A's which we have not yet come across that will be non-B. In other words we are interested in a negative finding not just because it refutes our putative law, but also because it justifies an expectation about the future. But on Popper's account, this element of interest would be impossible. He can allow that our finding one A which is not B *causes* us to think that there may be other A's which are not B. But he is committed to denying that our finding can *justify* or *support* or *be evidence for* our belief.

The third and most important criticism which we will bring against Popper's position is that it leads to skepticism. The reason is implicit in what we have already said, namely, that Popper denies that observation can justify any beliefs about what we have not yet observed. To illustrate the point further, suppose that I am thinking of sitting down in a chair. Could I have any reason/justification/evidence for thinking that it will support my weight? Popper's answer must be "no." What I can have is at best a rigorously tested and so-far unfalsified theory (or set of theories) (e.g., about the rigidity of certain materials, their weight-bearing capacity, etc.) from which it will follow (with certain other assumptions, e.g., about my own weight, speed of descent when I sit down, etc.), that the chair will support me. But according to Popper I do not have any reason at all for thinking that the theory is true. So the theory cannot give me any reason at all for thinking that what follows from it is true. So I have no reason at all for thinking that the chair will support me. Popper of course does not have to deny that I do believe that the chair will support me, nor does he have to deny that there is an explanation of why I hold that belief. The central point of the criticism is that in his eyes there can be no *justification* for my belief, no grounds for thinking that it is probably true.

Given that huge areas of our total web of belief are going to share with the example of believing that the chair will support me, the crucial feature of being a belief which goes beyond what has currently been observed, it follows that in Popper's view, huge areas of our web of belief will consist of unjustified beliefs. So far from solving the problem of induction, Popper has simply embraced the most skeptical consequences that can be drawn from the problem. That Popper's position has these skeptical implications is partly hidden from the incautious reader (and perhaps from Popper himself) because he speaks in places in a way that sounds incompatible with skepticism. He tells us for example that

> . . . it is perfectly reasonable to *act* on the assumption that [the future will in many respects be like the past] and that well-tested laws will continue to hold. (Popper, 1963, 56, Popper's italics)

But he makes it clear that he distinguishes sharply between reasonable *belief* and reasonable *action*. He thinks that it is reasonable to act as if a theory were true, even when there is no reason to think that the theory itself is true. Thus if we have a well-corroborated theory (i.e., a theory which has withstood rigorous attempts to disprove it), it is reasonable to rely on it (e.g., when we decide to sit on a chair, use it to build bridges and space ships, test other theories, and so on). But none of the observations we make can give us any positive reasons for thinking that the theory is true.

10.4 Two New Versions of the Problem of Induction

(i) Goodman's Paradox: the predicate "grue"

We have been considering a number of possible responses to the traditional problem of induction and suggesting that none of them is really satisfactory. In this section and the next, we want to suggest that from the traditional point of view, the position is even worse than it may seem. Even if the problem of induction as we have posed it could be solved, there are yet further puzzles surrounding the idea of induction which we need to notice. The first of these, sometimes called Goodman's Paradox, or the new riddle of induction, will occupy us in this section. The second, sometimes called Hempel's Paradox, or the Paradox of Confirmation, will be presented in the next section.

We can approach Goodman's Paradox in this way: suppose that we have observed lots of emeralds and found them all to be green. We might then infer that (probably) all emeralds (i.e., both observed and unobserved ones) are green. This would be an example of what is called induction by simple enumeration, and the problem of OTU induction as we have thus far posed it is to explain why the premise (that all observed emeralds have been green) gives any support at all to the conclusion. Goodman's Paradox starts by assuming that we have somehow established that it is at least possible for this and similar inferences to be rational, and it then raises the question of how we should decide *which* inferences among these would actually be rational.

To show what lies behind this question, Goodman introduces a rather strange new predicate, called "grue." He defines "grue" as applying to everything which is *either* first examined before the year 2000, and is green, *or* which is not first examined before the year 2000, and is blue. (It is not essential to Goodman's discussion that the relevant time should be the year 2000. All that is essential is that it should be some time in the future.)

Since it is crucial to understanding Goodman's subsequent argument, let us pause for a moment on this definition. It is first of all a disjunctive definition—that is, in order to be grue, something has to satisfy one or other of the two conditions. There is nothing odd in disjunctive definitions as such. Think, for example, of the definition of a grandfather as someone who is *either* the father of one's father, *or* the father of one's mother. To be a grandfather, you have to satisfy one or other of the two conditions stated. Similarly, for something to be grue, it must satisfy one or other of the two stated conditions. There is, secondly, a further complexity in the definition of "grue," in that each of the disjuncts is a conjunction. (A disjunct is the "either" clause or the "or" clause in an "either . . . or . . ." proposition.) So if something is going to satisfy the first disjunct, it must *both* be first observed before the year 2000 *and also* be green. If it is going to satisfy the second disjunct, it must *both* be first observed after the year 2000 *and also* be blue. Notice that something which is grue does not change color at the year 2000. If it is grue because it is first observed before 2000 and is green, it can stay green after 2000 and still be grue. And if something is grue because it *will* be first observed after 2000 and be blue, then it can also be blue before 2000.

Given this explanation of "grue," we can see that all the emeralds which we have ever observed are grue. All the emeralds which we have ever observed satisfy the first disjunct, for all of them have both been observed before the year 2000 and also been green. Goodman now invites us to compare two inductive arguments:

(A)   All observed emeralds have been green.

So   (Probably) all emeralds are green.

(B)   All observed emeralds have been grue.

So   (Probably) all emeralds are grue.

If (A) is a good argument, then it seems that (B) should be a good argument too. For (B) has exactly the same structure as (A), and appeals to exactly the same set of observations, namely all the observations we have so far made of the color of emeralds. But (and this is where the problem arises) we cannot accept both (A) and (B), since they have incompatible conclusions. It cannot be the case both that all emeralds are green and that all emeralds are grue.

To see that this is so, consider an emerald which is first examined *after* the year 2000. Argument (A) says that such an emerald will be green; but argument (B) says that such an emerald will be blue, for argument (B) says that such an emerald will be grue. But it cannot be grue in virtue of satisfying the first disjunct, for then it would have been first examined before 2000, and the emerald we are considering is not first examined until after 2000. So if it is grue, it must be grue in virtue of satisfying the second disjunct; and if it satisfies the second disjunct, then it will be first examined after 2000 and be *blue*. So (A) and (B) make different predictions about the color of emeralds which are first examined after 2000: (A) says that they will be green, and (B) says that they will be blue. So the rational person cannot accept both (A) and (B). So which one should she choose—or rather, since we might think it is obvious that she should choose (A), what justification can be given for choosing (A) rather than (B)?

It is clear that what we have here is not just a single odd case which raises no issues of principle. Goodman's predicate "grue" is simply one of an indefinitely large number of such predicates. For example, we can invent the predicate "grellow" to be defined as *"either* is first observed before 2000, and is green, *or* is not first observed before 2000 and is yellow." Given this definition, all observed emeralds have been grellow (since they were all first observed before 2000, and all of them were green). So the following argument

(C)   All observed emeralds have been grellow.

So   (Probably) all emeralds are grellow.

seems to have exactly the same strength as (A) and (B) above. And yet the conclusion of (C) is incompatible with the conclusion of both (A) and (B). For the conclusion of (C) implies that emeralds which are first observed after 2000 will be yellow. And after grellow, we can construct parallel definitions for "gred," for "grurple," and so on. And these definitions can be used to generate further incompatible generalizations—all emeralds are gred . . . are grurple, and so on.

Further, it is not just color predicates which can be "Goodmanized" in this way. Parallel to Goodman's predicate "grue" we could define an emeruby as follows: something is an emeruby if and only if *either* it was first examined before the year 2000 and was an emerald, *or* was not so examined and was a ruby. Given this definition, it is clear that all the gemstones which have been extracted from emerald mines have been not merely emeralds but also emerubies. So we might naively expect the mine to continue to produce emeralds. But why is this inference any more rational than the incompatible expectation that the mine will continue to produce emerubies?

So the rational person faces a problem. Even if she can somehow obtain an assurance that it is rational to base expectations about unobserved cases on knowledge of what observed cases have been like, and even if all the *A*'s she has observed have had a number of features *F, G, H*, etc., she still has a problem. Should she infer that all *A*'s are *F* (where this means that they cannot all be *G* or *H*)? Or that all *A*'s are *G* (where this means that they cannot all be *F* or *H*)? And how can she justify her choice?

A first reaction to Goodman's Paradox might be to dismiss it as no more than a clever trick, a wholly artificial problem which is set up by creating wholly unnatural predicates like "grue," "grellow," and so on. It is not a problem, it might be said, which arises with normal predicates like "green" and "blue," so all we need to do is to "de-invent" the problem-creating predicates, and the problem will go away.

But such a response is altogether too shallow. It is true that in our language, it is "green" and "blue" which are the normal, natural, nonartificial predicates, while "grue" and "grellow" strike us as strained or even absurd. But on the face of it, there could be a language (let us call it grue-speak) whose speakers differed from us in what they judged natural. Suppose there is a term "bleen" which is defined as "either is first observed before the year 2000 and is blue, or is not first observed before 2000 and is green." Given such a definition, we could define "green" and "blue" in the following way:

green = first observed before 2000 and grue, or not so examined and bleen

blue = first examined before 2000 and bleen, or not so examined and grue

To us, "green" and "blue" are natural, and "grue" and "bleen" are contrived and artificial. But to a grue-speaker, "grue" and "bleen" would be natural, and "blue" and "green" artificial.

Since it is easy in discussing Goodman's Paradox to become bogged down in the minutiae of the definitions of the artificial terms, and to lose sight of the issues which those terms are meant to indicate, we will restate in three stages exactly what the problem is which these contrived examples are illustrating.

(1) Given any body of data, there are indefinitely many ways in which we can describe the data.
(2) Corresponding to each way of describing the data, there will be different and incompatible ways of extrapolating from the data (i.e., different generalizations which we can draw, and hence different predictions and explanations which we will infer).
(3) Hence there is a problem: what is the rational choice procedure for selecting one mode of description, and hence one generalization, from this indefinitely large range of descriptions?

In the light of this general characterization, we can easily provide an example more realistic than grue, to illustrate the paradox. Suppose that someone (let us call her Ms. Straight) is plotting two variables, *x* and *y*, against each other, and recording the results on a graph. She obtains a series of readings which look like this:

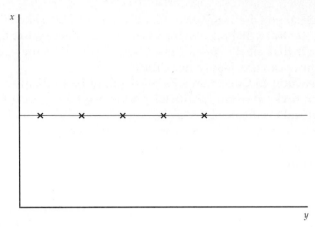

FIGURE 5 Ms. Straight.

That immediately suggests to her that the relationship between x and y is described by a straight line; and from this generalization, she derives predictions about as-yet unobserved cases. Her prediction obviously is that the value of x is constant through all increases in the value of y.

But someone else, Ms. Wavy, could interpret the readings differently. She could argue that the relationship between x and y is given by a wavy line, as in Figure 6. And from this wavy line, she would derive predictions about as-yet unobserved cases, predictions which were incompatible with those of Ms. Straight. She would predict, for example, that the value of x rose and fell as the value of y increased.

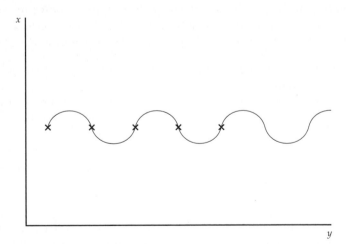

FIGURE 6 Ms. Wavy.

And someone else again, Ms. Loopy, could offer a different interpretation again. She could claim that the relationship between x and y is given by a loopy line, as in Figure 7. And from this loopy line, she would derive for the as-yet unobserved cases predictions which were incompatible with those of Ms. Straight and Ms. Wavy.

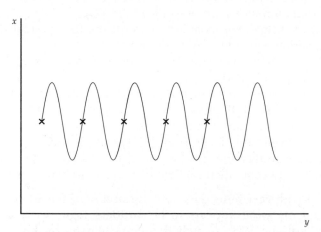

FIGURE 7 Ms. Loopy.

There could be yet other interpretations of the initial readings. In fact, given that there is an infinite number of possible lines that can be drawn through the finite number of points, there is an infinite number of possible interpretations. And each of these interpretations will generate different predictions for the as-yet unobserved cases of the *x-y* relationship, *even though they appeal for support to exactly the same evidence (the initial readings).*

The parallel with Goodman's Paradox should be clear. Each of the recorded readings on the graph is the equivalent of an observation of an emerald. Just as each point recorded on the graph is a straight-line-point, and also a wavy-line-point, and also a loopy-line-point, and a . . . (since each point falls on all these different lines); so each emerald that we observe is green, and also grue, and also grellow, and also gred. . . . And just as we can claim that all our *observed x-y* readings have been straight (or wavy, or loopy, or . . .) points, and hence that all as-yet *un*observed readings will fall on a straight (or wavy, or loopy, or . . .) line; so too we can say that as all observed emeralds have been green (or grue, etc.), so all as-yet unobserved emeralds will be green (or grue, etc.).

(ii) Hempel's Paradox: the paradox of confirmation

Goodman's Paradox warns us against a naive acceptance of induction by simple enumeration. Hempel's Paradox has the same effect. The paradox can be explained in the following way: take the two propositions

(a) All *A*'s are *B*.
(b) All non-*B*'s are non-*A*.

and consider the following argument:

     (1) (a) and (b) are logically equivalent. (premise)

     (2) Any X which is a Y confirms (to some degree) the proposition that all X's are Y's. (premise: the principle of induction by simple enumeration)

So (3) Any non-B which is a non-A, confirms (to some degree) the proposition that all non-B's are non-A's. (from [2])

     (4) What confirms a proposition, p, confirms to an equal degree every proposition equivalent to p. (premise)

So (5) Any non-B which is a non-A confirms (to some degree) that all A's are B. (from [1], [3], and [4])

So (6) Any non-black thing which is a non-raven confirms (to some degree) that all non-black things are non-ravens. (from [5])

So (7) Any non-black thing which is a non-raven confirms (to some degree) that all ravens are black. (from [1], [4] and [6])

So (8) A white handkerchief (i.e., a non-black thing which is a non-raven) confirms (to some degree) that all ravens are black. (from [7])

So starting with very innocuous-looking premises, namely (1), (2), and (4), and proceeding by what appears to be faultless logic, we arrive at a very bizarre-sounding conclusion, namely that you can gain some confirmation that all ravens are black by observing a white handkerchief.

As with Goodman's Paradox, the conclusion can seem so outrageous that one feels there must be some obvious blunder in the way the problem is set up. So let us review the steps in the argument to see that there is no elementary blunder. The first premise is (1), and this is usually regarded by all parties as an uncontroversial claim in all areas, both in this context and outside it. If the truth of (1) is not immediately apparent, it can be made so by the use of the following Venn diagrams.

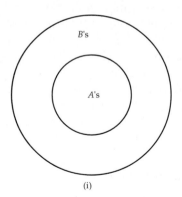
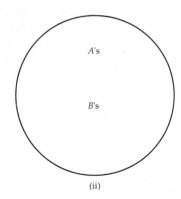

                    (i)   (ii)

If all A's are B's, then

either   (a) there are some B's which are not A's. (This is represented in [i].)
or   (b) there are no B's which are not A's. (This is represented in [ii].)

Whichever of these is the case, anything which falls outside the B circle (and hence is non-B) will also fall outside the A circle (and hence be non-A). So, if all A's are B's, then all non-B's are non-A's

FIGURE 8

The second premise comes in (2) and is the principle of induction by simple enumeration. Of course, finding a single *A* which is *B* may not confirm to a high degree the generalization that all *A*'s are *B*. But if we accept induction by simple enumeration (as perhaps common sense suggests that we should?), presumably finding a great many *A*'s which are *B* *does* confirm to a fairly high degree that all *A*'s are *B*. How high a degree of confirmation is achieved will depend on other factors (e.g., whether the observed *A*'s were from a biased sample). But from the viewpoint of common sense, it would be very strange to maintain that observing a great many *A*'s that were *B* ought to have no effect on one's attitude to the claim that all *A*'s are *B*. And if we allow that observing many *A*'s that are *B* ought to incline us to accept that "all *A*'s are *B*," then surely our observation of a single *A* which is *B* ought to have *some* effect, albeit a smaller one. So premise (2) does not seem to be very controversial either.

The remaining premise comes at (4). The underlying thought behind (4) is that whether a proposition is rationally acceptable depends on its *content*, on what it says is the case. So two propositions with exactly the same content ought to be rationally acceptable under exactly the same conditions. So they ought to be confirmed by exactly the same evidence and indeed confirmed to exactly the same degree by the same evidence. In other words, logical equivalence, which is what (1) maintains, implies confirmation equivalence, which is what (4) maintains.

A further indirect argument in favor of (4) comes from the fact that whether or not it is obvious that (a) and (b) have the same confirmation conditions, it is easily demonstrable that they have the same *dis*confirmation conditions. What would count as a disconfirming or refuting instance of the generalization "All non-*B*'s are non-*A*"? Surely a non-*B* which was *not* a non-*A*, in other words a non-*B* which was an *A*. And if we now ask what would be a disconfirming or refuting instance of the generalization "All *A*'s are *B*," the answer would surely be "An *A* which was not a *B*." But clearly an *A* which was a non-*B* would be the very same thing as a non-*B* which was an *A*. So (a) and (b) are equivalent for *dis*confirmation purposes. Given that, it would be very strange to say that they were not equivalent for confirmation purposes. For that would be saying that we would not know which hypothesis we were testing until we knew the result of the test. If the result goes one way (we find an *A* which is *B*), we have tested (and confirmed) the hypothesis that all *A*'s are *B*, but not the hypothesis that all non-*B*'s are non-*A*. If the result goes the other way (we find an *A* which is not a *B*), we have tested and (refuted) both the hypothesis that all *A*'s are *B* and the hypothesis that all non-*B*'s are non-*A*. To avoid this strange result, we have to accept that (a) and (b) are equivalent for confirmation purposes, and that is to accept (4).

If we were to reject (4), we would be saying that whether a given set of data confirmed a hypothesis depended not just on what the hypothesis was but also on how the hypothesis was expressed. Expressed one way, the data would support the hypothesis; but when the very same hypothesis was expressed differently, the data would not support it. Here is an analogy: it is as if evidence in favor of the proposition "Brutus killed Caesar" would not be evidence in favor of the equivalent proposition "Caesar was killed by Brutus," simply because of the different way in which the proposition is expressed, once in the active and once in the passive.

So the three premises which generate the paradox, (1), (2), and (4), look secure. Is there anything wrong with the inferences drawn from those three premises? (3) clearly follows from (2). It is simply a substitution instance of (2) (substituting "non-B" for "X," and "non-A" for "Y"), so there seems no room for criticism there. Again, it seems that (5) follows from (1), (3), and (4) in a noncontroversial way, simply drawing together the threads of what (1), (3), and (4) say. And (6) clearly follows (5) as a substitution instance again (substituting "raven" for "A" and "black" for "B"). (7) does no more than draw together what has already been said in (1), (4), and (6), and (8) transparently follows from (7) (provided that we make the surely safe assumption that a white handkerchief is neither black nor a raven!).

We thus arrive at the paradoxical-sounding conclusion that a white handkerchief confirms (to some degree) that all ravens are black. By parity of reasoning, a red shirt would confirm that all ravens are black, a blue sky would confirm that ravens are black, and so on. As with Goodman's Paradox, it is important not to become mired in the examples and overlook the principle which the examples are being used to illustrate. The real point is this: starting with very plausible and quite innocuous assumptions about the nature of inductive confirmation we seem forced to the conclusion that *almost everything* will count as confirming to some degree *almost every generalization.*

10.5 Summarizing the Problem of OTU Induction

This has been a long and difficult chapter, so let us now try to summarize what has been said. We first presented the traditional problem of induction, pointing out that it could be raised in two different ways according to how the term "induction" was defined. Secondly, taking the problem to be how we can justify *any* inferences which rely on OTU inductions, we looked at several possible responses to the traditional problem, some rather simplistic ones in 10.2, and one a little more sophisticated in 10.3. We then showed in 10.4 how even if we could establish in general that such inferences could be rational, there were further problems in determining *which* ones were rational. Goodman and Hempel show that if we accept induction by simple enumeration in a naive and straightforward way, then (a) we would be committed to accepting incompatible generalizations from our observations, and (b) almost anything that we observe will confirm almost any generalization that we care to formulate.

If we put together the conclusion of this chapter and the previous one, we find that *if* we accept the traditional division of arguments into deductive and inductive, there are major problems in showing that the inferential principles on which they rely are rationally defensible. What we will do in the next chapter is to suggest an alternative view of the inferential principles on which we all rely, a view which will enable us to throw new light on the problems which have occupied us in Chapters 9 and 10.

Exercises

1. Without rereading Chapters 9 or 10, explain the difference between PSC and OTU inductive arguments, giving examples of each which are different from those in the text. When you have done this, check your answer with the text for accuracy, clarity, and completeness.
2. Suppose someone argues that OTU inductive inference is justified because most such inferences which we have made in the past have turned out to be true. Without rereading the chapter, reconstruct the argument against this position. When you have done this compare your answer with 10.2(ii) and assess it for accuracy, clarity, and completeness.
3. Does the inductive evidence justify your belief that you will eventually die—or is this merely an unconfirmed hypothesis? Answer in one page.
4. "Induction is a procedure which is logically invalid and rationally unjustifiable." Does Popper establish these claims in your view? Answer in no more than a page and a half. When you have done this compare your answer with 10.3.
5. The media constantly bombards us with information about economic and financial trends—about unemployment, growth rates, government borrowing, and so on—and constantly makes predictions about future trends on the basis of that information. What does Goodman's Paradox tell us about the rationality of this process? (Hard.)

CHAPTER 11

A Continuum of Inferences

11.1 The Induction/Deduction Dichotomy Rejected

The traditional philosophical wisdom is that the inferences on which we rely in moving from one belief to another fall into two mutually exclusive classes, called deductive and inductive inferences. In the last two chapters we have seen how problems arise with this tradition; it is not easy to identify the principles of deductive inference, and it is not easy to justify OTU inductive inferences. In the case of deductive inferences, it has often been thought that the problem can be solved by appealing to formal logic—for instance, by invoking truth tables as a means of identifying deductive principles. We criticized this on three grounds. First, it would at best identify only a small number of the principles which are normally classified as deductive. Secondly, it is far from clear that truth tables do adequately capture the ordinary meanings of key logical terms, such as "if . . . then . . ." And thirdly, sophisticated work in mathematics and physics has thrown doubt on the logical ideas underlying the truth table account. In the case of induction, we saw that it was very unclear OTU induction could be justified. Goodman's and Hempel's Paradoxes warned us of the dangers of a naive approach to such inferences. Given that the old deductive/inductive dichotomy gives rise to such problems, let us see if we can find a better way of distinguishing good inferences from bad ones.

11.2 An Implication of Quine's Coherentism

In earlier chapters, we argued against the foundationalist conception of knowledge, in favor of a coherentist conception of rational belief. As part of this argument, we rejected the traditional cleavage between analytic and synthetic propositions, between necessary and contingent truths, and between a priori and empirical knowledge, in favor of a Quinean conception. All those earlier arguments have important implications for our conception of inference, and it is these implications which must now be developed.

If the traditional cleavage between analytic and synthetic (etc.) is to be rejected in favor of the Quinean ideas we expounded earlier, then we adopt a picture of our belief system on the model of the spider's web, where some propositions are more central to the system than others, and are less readily given up, whereas others are more peripheral. But now what are we to say about the inferential relations which exist between propositions in different parts of the web? They surely exhibit a similar variation, some being deeply embedded in our whole system of beliefs, and others being less so. The case for thinking so on a Quinean view of rational belief is very simple.

To any piece of reasoning, there exists a corresponding hypothetical statement of the form "If [the premises], then [the conclusion]," which we can call the principle of the argument. These principles can themselves be seen as propositions which may be believed or disbelieved. The principles of inference can thus be more or less deeply entrenched in the web of belief in the way that other believed propositions are. So they are best viewed as ranged on the same continuum rather than divided into the categories of deductive and inductive. Some of them are very close to the center of our web and are ones which we should be very reluctant to give up (they are very close to what the old tradition called "logical truths"). Others are more peripheral and are more readily given up (they are claims like "If Mary comes to the party, Joe won't," which might be based on the belief that each prefers to avoid the other).

Perhaps Quine himself recognizes this:

> The totality of our so-called knowledge or beliefs, from the most casual matters of geography and history to the profoundest laws of atomic physics or even of pure mathematics and logic, is a man-made fabric which impinges on experience only along the edges. . . . Reevaluations of some statements entail reevaluations of others, because of their logical interconnections—*the logical laws being in turn simply certain further statements of the system, certain further elements of the field.* Having reevaluated one statement we must reevaluate some others, which may be statements logically connected with the first *or may be statements of logical connections themselves.* (Quine, 1953, 42, italics added)

There seems no good reason to deny this picture once we have accepted the holistic metaphor of a "web of belief" and once we have recognized that any argument has its corresponding principle of inference. The implication is that Quinean arguments force us to recognize many different inferential relations, of differing degrees of strength, which should be studied in the contexts in which they occur, if we want a general understanding of the process of inference and what justifies different inferences.

Here is another metaphor which may be helpful in thinking about our inferential principles in a new way. Imagine a group of islands set very close to each other, each island connected to some its neighbors by different bridges. These bridges are of varying strengths and of a wide variety of designs. Some are made to an A-design, some to a B-design, some to a C-design, and so on. Certain traditional-minded travelers among the islands insist that there are only two designs for a safe bridge: there is the D-design and the I-design. Since the bridges in fact come in a variety of designs, these travelers go to great lengths to try to show that, contrary to appearances, every safe bridge can be seen as being *really* a D- or an I-bridge, even when it seems to be, for example, of an A-design or a B-design, and so on. In order to fit every safe bridge into one category or the other, they then have difficulty in formulating a specification of exactly what the D- and I-designs are. For each specification they come up with either includes some bridges which they want to exclude, or excludes some which they want to include. But other travelers who are not caught in the grip of the "D or I" dogma make judgments about which bridges are safe, and use these bridges without trying to see them all as fitting into either the D- or the I-design.

The application of the metaphor should be clear. The islands represent our individual beliefs; the bridges between them are our inferential principles; the insistence on the "D- or I-design" for all safe bridges is the traditional acceptance that every good inference is deductive or inductive. And just as in the island example, we should recognize that the safety of the bridges can vary continuously from the very safe to the very unsafe without any sharp divisions, so in the inferential case, we should recognize that inferences can be ranged on a continuum of strength, with no sharp divisions between the very strong and the very weak. (The analogy must not be pressed. As we urged, the inference from one belief to another rests on a principle which can itself be viewed as a further belief. But the bridge between one island and the next cannot be seen as an island. To paraphrase Donne, no bridge is an island unto itself!)

But, to return to our analogy, the obvious question is how we identify the safe bridges, and what makes them safe at all. Those who insisted that to be safe, every bridge had to be of D- or I-design were at least addressing this question. If we reject the "D or I" dichotomy, what is the alternative answer? How, in other words, can we identify reliable principles of inference? We will look at two ways in which that question can be answered, the first deriving from some reflections by Goodman, the second deriving ultimately from the ideas of the German philosopher Immanuel Kant (1724–1804).

11.3 Goodman and "Reflective Equilibrium" between Inferences and Principles

In his *Fact, Fiction and Forecast* (1955), Goodman argues that inference rules on the one hand, and judgments about particular inferences on the other are in continual interaction, each reinforcing or modifying the other so that they are brought into accord with each. To use a concept which we implicitly used earlier, the principles and judgments must be brought within "reflective equilibrium" with each other. This is the concept which underlies the discussion in 2.6 (iii). Because it is so central to Goodman's approach, we will give another illustration of the concept.

Suppose that we are considering some game and the rules that govern the game. What happens to the rules over time as the game is played again and again? Some of the rules seem entirely satisfactory and are never changed. But other rules turn out to be unsatisfactory. They may prove difficult to enforce, or may lead to what are thought of as unsatisfactory features of the games. Readers may like to supply their own examples here, but in soccer a good example is supplied by the "off-side" rule. An attacking player breaks this rule (roughly speaking) if there is no defending player between him and the goal-keeper when he is in a position to receive the ball. If this rule is challenged as unsatisfactory by those who play (or watch) the game, one of two things may happen. It may be generally agreed that it is still important to keep the rule, perhaps because no better alternative can be found. Alternatively, it may be decided to change the rule in order to improve the game. Of course, soccer games are played in accordance with the rules obtaining at the time. If we recognize a rule as a good one, we will insist on the rule and debar those practices which conflict with it. But equally, if we recognize a practice as a good one, we will insist on keeping the practice and we will amend the rules accordingly. Achieving this balance between rules and what happens in the course of play is a form of reflective equilibrium.

This does not imply that reflective equilibrium is some kind of ideal state which, once achieved, means that the game will never need to change again. Rather, it means that there is a *continual* tension between the rules by which the game is governed and what actually happens on the field of play. This requires continual review; sometimes we will insist on the rules being enforced, and sometimes we will change them to produce a better game. This is a dynamic process which maintains an equilibrium between opposing tendencies, just as opposing economic or physical forces are said to maintain *dynamic* equilibrium positions. (If two people are engaged in an arm wrestling contest, it may well be that despite the fact that they are both pushing with all their strength, their hands do not move. This is an example of dynamic equilibrium.)

Goodman's view is that there is a similar kind of interaction between the rules of inference which we accept and our actual inferential practices, and that this provides all the justification we can have of both the rules and actual inferences. He succinctly expresses the point like this:

> *A rule is amended if it yields an inference we are unwilling to accept; an inference is rejected if it violates a rule we are unwilling to amend.* The process of justification is the delicate one of making mutual adjustments between rules and accepted inferences; and in the agreement achieved lies the only justification needed for either. (Goodman, 1955, 64, emphasis in original)

So if our question is the one we raised at the end of the previous section (how can we identify reliable principles of inference?), the Goodman answer is that

they are those which do not license inferences which we reject and do not conflict with inferences which we accept. Let us illustrate the way that this works.
We find ourselves accepting such arguments as the following:

(A)   Patsy is hungry.

        If Patsy is hungry, she will get irritable.

So   Patsy will get irritable.

Here, we are convinced that *if* the premises are true, then the conclusion will
be true too. We have the same conviction with all arguments that are similar
to this in respect of their logical shape, and hence formulate a principle of inference like modus ponens, (p, and if p, then q) implies q. We then use that principle to justify our acceptance of other inferences like (A).

        Sometimes when we formulate a principle which we think adequately cap-
tures the inferences which we want to accept, we find that it also licenses inferences which we want to reject. For example, we might think that (B) is a fairly
good argument:

(B)   All observed ravens have been black.

So   All ravens are black.

If we ask ourselves what principle underlies this inference, a tempting reply
is that it relies on (C):

(C)   If all observed members of a class have had a certain feature, then all
         members of the class will have that feature.

But we then notice, as Goodman points out to us with his discussion of "grue"
and its cognates, that (C) would permit many inferences (infinitely many in
fact!) which we are convinced are poor inferences. So we do not in fact want
to accept (C)—we need to find some modification of it, (C*), which will both
permit the inferences which we want to accept and reject those which we want
to reject.

        What Goodman tells us, in the quotation cited, is that achieving this
balance between principles and inferences is "the only justification" which
we can ever find for our inferential principles. But now we might wonder
whether this justification *is* all that we can gain for our principles. For surely,
it is possible for there to be a reflective equilibrium between a poor inferential
principle and a poor set of inferences. For example, many people infer in
accordance with some version of the gambler's fallacy in playing games of
chance: the gambler's fallacy says that the likelihood of a 6 on the next
throw of the die increases as the sequence of non-6 throws lengthens. There
is good empirical evidence that the principle underlying their inferences
is in reflective equilibrium for these gamblers. For, when the principle is
carefully stated to them and they have a chance to think about it, they
accept both the principle and particular inferences which employ it (cf.
Stich, 1990, 83).

There must, then, be more to being a good principle of inference than existing in a state of reflective equilibrium with a set of practices. But where could this deeper justification of inferences lie?

11.4 Concepts and the Continuum of Associated Generalizations: A Kantian Turn

Part of the answer to that question must appeal to the concepts in terms of which we classify the world around us. For associated with each concept will be a range of more-or-less reliable generalizations. Associated with each concept, F, there will be a range of generalizations of the form "All (or most) F's are G," "All (or most) F's are H," and so on. Very often these generalizations will have qualifying clauses. They might say, for example, that all F's are G unless . . . , or provided that . . . , or only if. . . . The generalizations will often be *defeasible*, that is to say, they will not apply if any one of an indefinitely large range of circumstances holds. But what the existence of such generalizations implies is that if something is identified as an F, one is entitled to infer that it is almost certainly G, that it is probably H, that it might or might not be J, that it very probably is not K, that it will not be L unless it is also M, and so on. In other words, each concept for a kind of thing or a kind of stuff is associated with a set of generalizations, and these generalizations constitute principles of inference.

Let us illustrate this, taking "cat" as our F term. Suppose I identify something as a cat. What inferences can I draw? I will infer that it is *certainly* a mammal, that it *certainly* has a heart, and that it was *certainly* born from another cat. I will infer that it *very probably* has four legs, and weighs less than 10 pounds. I will infer that it is *quite likely* to enjoy fish, to purr and to miaow, and to have whiskers, and that it will *probably* be capable of bearing kittens, provided that it is female and has not been spayed. I will also draw a number of negative inferences. I will infer that it *certainly will not* eat wood, and that it would lose in a fight with an elephant, and that it could not swim the Atlantic Ocean. It is *unlikely* to answer to its name unless it has been taught to do so, and it is unlikely to survive if shut in a deep freeze overnight. And in saying these things, of course I am not drawing on any *specialized* knowledge of cats. Nearly everyone who uses the concept of a cat with any facility will be able to draw hundreds of humdrum inferences of this kind. And for hundreds of other concepts of kinds of thing and kinds of stuff, they will similarly be able to draw hundreds of inferences. The concept of a cat is the locus of intersection of these and dozens of similar generalizations. It is not the case that we *first* identify things as cats, and *then* seek to establish generalizations about them—generalizations which we can use to license inferences. Rather, to identify things as cats is *already* to be using some generalizations. In other words, what justifies the inferential principles we use is not just that they are in reflective equilibrium with our inferential practices. It is that they are implicit in the very concepts in terms of which we categorize the world. That is partly why, if we are going to use those concepts (of cat, gold, rain, etc.), we are entitled to rely to varying degrees on the associated generalizations.

It was characteristic of the traditional view of inference that for each of these generalizations associated with a term like "cat," either the generalization was true by definition of the term "cat," or it was established by observing many cats and extrapolating from one's observations (induction by simple enumeration). If the generalization fell into the first category, the inference was deductive; if it fell into the second category, it was inductive. (Recall the insistence of some island travelers that every safe bridge had to be either a D- or an I-design.) But we can now see that forcing all the generalizations into one or other of these categories is unjustified. The generalizations, like all our beliefs, are best seen as ranged on a continuum of entrenchment. Some of these generalizations are entrenched so weakly that we could easily give them up, without being tempted to say we were no longer talking about "cats" (for example, all cats have tails). Very often as our beliefs change, it is not so much that we give up altogether an inferential principle which is associated with a concept; rather, we regard it as less reliable than we had originally thought. We replace the belief "If it is a cat, then it certainly . . ." with "If it's a cat, then it very probably . . ." And that "very probably" might in time become weakened further to "probably" or even to "possibly."

By contrast with this process in which an inferential principle becomes weaker, there can be cases where the reverse occurs. An inferential principle may at first be relatively weak and hence license conclusions (about cats, in the example we are considering) which are no more than probable. However, it can gradually get enmeshed with so many other beliefs in our web that it becomes stronger and licenses inferences to conclusions which are nearly certain. In time, it might become so deeply entrenched that we would feel that if we gave it up, we would no longer be talking about *cats* at all. The belief that all cats have a specific genetic constitution might be such a belief. But (and this is where the view outlined here diverges from traditional conceptions) there is no sharp cutoff point separating one such generalization from the next; hence no sharp dividing line between principles traditionally called deductive and those called inductive; hence no sharp dividing line between deductive and inductive arguments.

11.5 The Role of Background Information in Inference

Of course it can sometimes be illuminating to group together some arguments which might seem to be different, and argue that they all have some underlying common features (such as formal features) which are more important than their differences. On the other hand, sometimes focusing on such similarities can direct our attention away from the relevant features, away from those features which make the inferences good ones or bad ones. But either way, whether such similarities can be identified is not a precondition of the arguments being rationally acceptable.

To illustrate this, consider the two following inferences:

(A) If Harry has swallowed a pound of arsenic, he will be dead. He is dead.

So   He swallowed a pound of arsenic.

(B) If the building burnt to the ground, there will be only a pile of ashes. There is only a pile of ashes.

So   The building burnt to the ground.

These two inferences have the same structure, namely:

(C) If one thing, then a second; the second, so the first.

And both of them would be classified as nondeductive by the old tradition. They would both have been classified as instances of the fallacy known as affirming the consequent. But surely the truth of the matter is that whereas the first is a weak argument, the second is a good argument. How is this to be explained?

The explanation lies in the fact that we implicitly take both of these arguments in a certain context. In relation to (A), we know that the great majority of people do not die of arsenic, and hence the mere fact that Harry is dead is not a good reason for thinking that he has taken arsenic. If he is dead, he is far more likely to have died of some cause other than ingesting a pound of arsenic. We can, however, easily imagine a different context in which the argument would rightly be regarded as a good one. Suppose Harry is a prisoner under sentence of death, and the prevailing mode of execution is for the prisoner to swallow a pound of arsenic. Given a number of other background assumptions (that prisoners are not usually murdered before their sentence can be carried out, that Harry did not have some medical condition which might have caused his death before his date of execution, etc.), then the inference in (A) would be a good one.

By contrast, we do take (B) as it stands to be a good argument. Here the relevant background assumptions are that it is very unlikely for a building to be replaced by a pile of ashes unless the building itself has burnt down. So from the presence of ashes, the inference to the burning of the building is sound. But again, we can imagine the argument set in a different context in which it would no longer be sound. Suppose that an insurance company does not pay out on buildings that simply collapse through poor workmanship, but it does pay out on buildings that are burnt down. We can imagine a large-scale fraud in which shanty buildings are simply bulldozed and cleared away, some ashes are then delivered to the site, and an insurance claim submitted for arson. If the insurance company fraud investigator were to rely on argument

(B) in *those* circumstances, he would rightly be deemed insufficiently critical. So the strength of (B), like that of (A), varies according to the context in which we are considering it.

There are two ways in which we might respond to this point about the relevance of background information. The first way would be to say that judgments about the strength of a given argument are always *relative*, in the sense that such judgments always take the form of saying that relative to one background, the argument is a good one, but relative to another, it is a bad one. But the argument could not be simply good or simply bad in itself. Just as Einstein discovered that temporal judgments are best viewed as relative (see Chapter 7.5 [ii]), so this would be saying that judgments of argument strength were relative. The claim would not be that they were subjective, in any sense of that ambiguous term. It would not be saying that how good an argument was depends on anyone's feelings or beliefs about how good it was. Rather, the strength of the argument would depend upon the background information in relation to which the argument was being considered.

The second way would be to say that what we have been calling "the argument" so far is really only a truncated version of the real argument, for the real argument ought to include as premises all those background beliefs which contribute to the strength of the argument. So if the strength of (B) presupposes further facts which the arguer is simply taking for granted as too obvious to need stating (such as that no insurance fraud of the kind described above is in operation), then that fact needs to be listed as one of the premises. The ground for this claim would be that those facts are being *used* by the arguer, and hence should be *stated* by the arguer when she sets out exactly what her argument is.

We can illustrate the difference between these views of the matter by referring to an example which we have used earlier (see 7.5 [ii]). Consider the argument

(D)   Susie is a mother.

So   Susie has given birth.

This is an argument that would until recently have been regarded as deductive. The justification for so thinking would have been that associated with the concept "mother" was the generalization "All mothers have given birth," and that this generalization was part of the very meaning of the term "mother." So it would be self-contradictory to say of someone that she was a mother but had not given birth. So (the traditional view would have said) you can classify the argument as deductive without needing *any* background information. And adding further information cannot lead you to qualify your original assessment of the argument as absolutely watertight.

We can now see how and why this approach to the argument is too simplistic. Let us overlook one assumption which must surely lie behind the belief that the argument is watertight, namely that Susie is a human. (If "Susie" were the name of a fish, then she might have offspring (and hence be a mother) even though her eggs are fertilized outside her body, and she never *gives birth* to anything.) And let us also overlook the fact that some people might regard having a child delivered by Caesarean section as not exactly "giving birth." What we pointed out in 7.5(ii) was that there is a perfectly intelligible sense of "mother" in which a woman can now be the mother of a child without having given birth. *In vitro* fertilization means that she can now be the genetic mother even though she does not give birth, in any accepted sense of "give birth."

We can thus see that background information *does* make a difference to our assessment of the argument. Adding to (D) the further premise "Susie is a birth mother, not just a genetic one" (not to mention such premises as "Susie is human," "Susie did not have a Caesarean," etc.) does strengthen the argument. Adding the negation of these premises would weaken the argument. And an argument which can be strengthened or weakened by adding further premises cannot, according to the traditional view, be a deductive one.

On the first view which we referred to previously, we would have to say that the strength of the original argument (D) was relative to a background. Against a historical background, it was a very good argument; against a modern technological background, it was good, but not absolutely watertight (good, because in the vast majority of cases still, the birth mother and the genetic mother are the same person). On the second view which we referred to, we would have to regard argument (D) as no more than a truncated version of the argument which we actually intended, the intended argument being the one which was specified by adding in as premises all the background information which the arguer is using in putting forward the argument.

Each of these two responses goes very much against prevailing orthodoxies about the nature of argument (though in this connection, note the universalist coherentism embraced by Harman et al., 1973, referred to in 7.4 [i]). The prevailing orthodoxy is that it *is* possible to consider at least some arguments in isolation from anything else and determine whether they are good or not. And this view can seem very plausible. Consider such an argument as:

(E)   All men are mortal.

       Socrates is a man.

So   Socrates is mortal.

Surely, it might be said, such an argument does not have to be relativized to any background beliefs to see that it is a good argument. Examining the argument in isolation from all other considerations, we can see that the premises supply *conclusive* support for the conclusion. And further, since there appears to be no relevant background which is being presupposed, this argument cannot be regarded as simply a truncated version of a fuller argument which would include the missing background material as further premises.

But this is where our discussion of principles of inference links with what we were saying earlier (7.5, 8.1 [iv], and 8.2 [v]) about a coherentist conception of the a priori. The principle underlying (E) is one that is *very* highly entrenched, and hence is one which it is very difficult to imagine us giving up. It has good claims to be regarded as one of the so-called laws of logic. (It is a version of what is sometimes called the Principle of Universal Instantiation, which says, to express the point nontechnically, that if all members of a class have a certain property, then any arbitrarily selected member of the class will have that property.) We would feel tempted to say, for example, that if we gave up the principle, we would have changed the meaning of some crucial term like "all." But, as we also saw earlier, what were regarded as the laws of logic (such as the law of the excluded middle) can be, and have been, challenged by new information and new ways of thinking (quantum mechanics, intuitionistic mathematics—see the Logic Appendix, section 6). We cannot here suggest how the principle of inference underlying (D) could be overthrown, or even be shown to be less than completely reliable. But precisely the same could have been said of the law of the excluded middle before the developments we referred to previously. In view of this fact, it would be rash indeed to assert that the inferential principle underlying (D) could not suffer the same fate.

11.6 The Relevance of These Ideas to "The Problem of Induction"

(i) The role of background information

Let us return to the issue discussed in the previous chapter, the so-called problem of induction. We can now see how it is quite possible for there to be PSC inductions, that is to say arguments in which the premises support the conclusion but do so nondeductively. Such arguments will be those in which the underlying principle of inference is a proposition which is well entrenched in our continuum of beliefs, but is not among our most highly entrenched beliefs. As an example, consider the following:

(F) Matt has just finished running a marathon in less than four hours.

So   Matt will be feeling tired.

Here the underlying inferential principle might be "Anyone who has just run a marathon in less than four hours is very likely to feel tired." And *that* inferential principle is one which we believe and which is fairly well embedded in our web of belief. It coheres well with the rest of what we believe, and that is why we are justified in believing it; and because we are justified in believing it, we are justified in drawing inferences like (F) which use it as a principle of inference. (We say this *might* be the principle, since the arguer might not want to accept a principle about how everyone would feel, but, e.g., only about how

Matt in particular would feel or about how Matt in particular on this specific occasion would feel.)

What can we say about induction when we understand this term in the OTU way? In some cases, noting that all observed members of a class have a certain feature will constitute good evidence that the next observed member of the class will have that feature or perhaps that all other members will. That will depend on what the class is and what the feature is. To illustrate this, let us consider again the case of ravens:

(G) The first observed raven was black.

So   All ravens are black. (probably)

On the old conception, this is a very weak argument, as it generalizes from a single case. But on our view, (G) can be quite a strong argument. Crucial to our belief that this is so is the fact that we are talking about *birds* and about their *color*. We know that ravens are a species of bird, and that the color markings of birds do not vary randomly. Indeed, many of the features of a given species of bird (its size, the shape of its wings, the length of its beak, the color of its plumage, etc.) are central to our concept of that species. This is where the background information to which we referred in section 7.5 comes into play. It is our background knowledge about birds in general that allows us to extract so much information from the observation of even a single raven, and it is what explains why an argument like (G) might be strong when used by one person and weaker when used by another. By contrast, if when I see my first raven, it has a ring around one leg, that is no evidence at all for thinking that all other ravens have a similar ring. For the property of having a ring round one's leg is not one of those properties which is constant among birds.

All this background information which we have about ravens is omitted if we construe the strength of (G) as depending on no more than the fact that it has this structure:

(H) The first observed *A* was *B*.

So   All *A*'s are *B*. (probably)

There are many arguments with this structure which are extremely bad ones. But that should not tempt us to think that (G) is a bad one too. (H) leaves out precisely the things which make (G) a reasonable inference (the background information which we have about birds and their coloration).

(ii) OTU inferences with limited background information

Consider, by contrast, a situation in which I try to deploy an argument with the structure of (H) where there is no background information for me to draw on. Situations like this are actually rather difficult to imagine, since in virtually every situation in real life, we have access to *some* background information which is relevant to the inferences which we would be entitled to draw.

But consider the following: you are in a psychological laboratory which, so you are told, is conducting tests on people's inferential and predictive habits. The test you are given is this: the experimenter offers you a bag with two balls in it. You have to take one ball out and on the basis of the color of the ball you have taken out, you have to guess the color of the remaining ball. You pick out a red ball. What should you guess is the color of the remaining ball?

It is difficult to see that you could have any grounds for *any* prediction about the color of the second ball. You have no grounds for thinking that it will be the same color; and no grounds for thinking that it will be different. Of course, even in this situation, you have *some* background information. You know that whatever the color combination is of the two balls, it has been determined by a deliberate human choice. The experimenter has decided on the color combination for a particular purpose. If you could work out what hypothesis she was trying to test in conducting the experiment, you might have some reason to think that the two balls would be of the same color or of different colors. But in the experiment as described, the color of the first is no guide at all to the color of the second.

Now imagine the experiment slightly changed. There are now 50 balls in the bag. You are allowed to pick out 10, and asked to predict the color of the remaining 40. The first 10 you pick out are all red ones, and on this basis you predict that the remaining 40 will also almost certainly be red. This is presumably a reasonable prediction, but what makes it reasonable is not just your observation of the 10 red balls. It is also some background assumptions you are making. You are assuming, for example, that it is not the case that the balls have been electronically treated so that all and only the red ones gravitate toward a human hand, and all and only the non-red ones are repelled by the presence of a human hand. If you came to know that this was the case, then your inference from the 10 observed balls to the remaining 40 would no longer be reasonable. So you are tacitly assuming that there is an equal chance of your picking each of the balls, or at least that if there is an unequal chance, that unequal chance has nothing to do with their color. Thus it is by reference to background information that we pick out the reliable inductive generalizations from the unreliable ones.

(iii) Why should we accept generalizations as background information?

This naturally raises for us the question of what justifies our acceptance of this background information, which, after all, often has the form of a generalization. We said above, for example, that we know that the coloration of birds depends on their internal physiology and does not vary randomly between members of the same species. This is a generalization which (so it might be thought) can be known only by OTU induction. And if we agree, as was suggested previously, that such induction yields support for a conclusion only in the presence of background information of a general kind, then we seem to be embarked on an infinite regress. The rationality of one inductive inference will presuppose that we have knowledge of, or reasonable belief in, some background generalization, and we could have knowledge of that background generalization only on the basis of a further inductive generalization whose rationality would presuppose yet further background generalizations, and so on. But (so the objection will go) at each stage we are presupposing that we have some background knowledge of generalizations. What we have not explained is how this process can ever get started.

There are two lines of reply to this objection, which perhaps eventually converge. The first line of reply would be to invoke the thought mentioned earlier in section 11.4. This claimed that associated with each of our concepts for kinds of objects and kinds of stuff, there is a range of generalizations which legitimate all sorts of inferences. Once we have identified something as a raven or a cat or as gold or water or bread, there is a range of inferences which we are forthwith entitled to draw, with varying degrees of certainty, according to how deeply entrenched the connection is between the concept in question and the associated generalizations. So it isn't the case that we first of all make lots of observations of individual things and kinds of stuff, and then have the further and separate task of arriving at generalizations about them. To identify them as being examples of ravens, cats, gold, and so on, is *already* to have accepted some generalizations which license further inferences.

The second line of reply to the challenge about where our background generalizations come from is to invoke once again a coherentist account of justified belief. The request to find a justification for all our general beliefs is really a disguised and misplaced form of foundationalism—or at least, it is in the form which this request here takes. For what is being presupposed is that the justification *must* take the form of finding a series of particular observational beliefs which serve as the premises from which our first generalizations are then derived. That this is being presupposed is clear from the way in which a justification that presupposes other general beliefs is held to be begging the question. Clearly the objection is assuming

(a) that there is a problem about the justification of our general beliefs,
(b) that the solution to this problem must not invoke any further general beliefs (on pain of begging the question),
(c) that there is no comparable problem about the justification of our observational beliefs,

presumably because it is thought

(d) that the justification of particular beliefs does not invoke any other beliefs (beliefs about whose justification questions would then arise) but is instead achieved "directly" by a confrontation with the world.

This simply amounts to an acceptance of traditional foundationalism in respect of empirical beliefs. But (so the reply goes) we need to take coherentism seriously. There is no question of our first having observational beliefs, then of our inferring our first general conclusion, then of going on to infer other generalizations with the help of the first, and so on. Rather, we start with both observations and generalizations. We start with a world picture as well as with observations about particular things. Sometimes we justify particular beliefs by reference to general ones, sometimes the other way round. But there is not a *one-way* dependence of the general on the particular. In terms of the metaphor of entrenchment, the distinction between strong and weak entrenchment does not correlate with that between observational and general beliefs. So the challenge to show how our general beliefs are to be justified, if that means tracing them back ultimately to inferences from generalization-free observations, is not one that needs to be met. It does not need to be met because that is not a precondition of our general beliefs being reasonable.

There are thus two lines of reply to the question "What justifies our acceptance of the generalizations which we use in inductive inferences?," and they converge on the thought that there is no priority of observation over generalization. The first line of reply maintains this on the ground that each concept that we use to describe what we observe comes already associated with a set of generalizations: to apply the concept to what we observe is to accept the legitimacy of a set of inferences. The second line of reply maintains it on the ground that a belief in the priority of observations over generalizations (inferential principles) is simply an expression of a discredited foundationalism.

Exercises

1. "... Quinean arguments force us to recognize different inferential relations of differing degrees of strength ..." Without rereading the chapter, explain the reasoning which leads to this conclusion in no more than one page. Assess your answer for accuracy, clarity, and completeness against 11.2.
2. Without rereading the chapter, explain the idea of reflective equilibrium providing your own illustrative examples. Write no more than a page and a half. Assess your answer for accuracy, clarity, and completeness against 11.3.
3. What generalizations of different kinds spring to mind when you think of the words "school teacher" (easier) or "pain" (harder). What inferential principles do these generalizations support and how reliable are they? Do not write more than one page.
4. "He's writhing on the ground clutching his stomach and moaning, so he must be in considerable pain." In no more than one page expand this description in two different ways, one which *strengthens* the inference and one which *weakens* it.
5. Look back at the answers you wrote to question 9.2 and revise your answers in the light of 11.6(ii), drawing particular attention to the assumptions you made in answering 9.2. Write no more than one page. Exchange your answers with a fellow student and assess each other's work for clarity and completeness.

CHAPTER 12

Quine and Naturalized Epistemology

12.1 Coherentism Is Often Thought to Imply Naturalized Epistemology

In the last few chapters, we have been broadly sympathetic to the coherentist position. Having argued in Chapters 5 and 6 that foundationalism was unsatisfactory, we suggested in Chapters 7 and 8 that coherentism seemed more promising, and this claim was extended and deepened in Chapters 9 and 11. But coherentism is often thought to imply that epistemology as traditionally conceived needs to be replaced by a revised or improved version, usually called naturalized epistemology (NE for short). Quine in particular has argued for this claim. So in this chapter, we will address the questions of what naturalized epistemology is, whether it is significantly different from traditional epistemology (or TE for short), whether it is indeed implied by coherentism, and what its merits and weaknesses are.

12.2 Three Initial Contrasts with Traditional Epistemology

The expression "naturalized epistemology" originates with Quine's article entitled "Epistemology Naturalised" (1969). He does not there offer any definition of what exactly he means, but it is clear that he intends to invoke the evidence of natural science in a way which is novel in epistemology. It will help us to see what is distinctive about naturalized epistemology if we briefly characterize some previous approaches.

One striking contrast with naturalized epistemology is what we might call *super*-naturalized epistemology, that is to say, an epistemology which explicitly invokes a supernatural being like God in its account of how human knowledge is possible. The seventeenth-century French philosopher René Descartes produced such an epistemology. He argued that it is only because there is a nondeceiving God that we have any ground for thinking that our perceptions of reality more-or-less match reality itself. It is God alone who ensures that my perceptions are, by and large, reliable guides to the nature of the world around me. So if there were no God, we could never know what reality was like. We might have beliefs about it, but we could never be justifiably certain of the truth of any of those beliefs. So one thing that NE is rejecting is an epistemology in which a supernatural being like God has any role to play.

Another strand in non-naturalized epistemology invokes evaluative ideas (*good* reason, *justified* belief, *right* to be sure, *legitimate* inference, etc.), and then insists that these values go beyond any facts which science can study. The idea that there is radical contrast between *moral* values and the world of science is a common one in much modern thought (which is not to say that it is a correct idea); and this version of non-naturalized epistemology posits a similar contrast between *epistemological* values and the world of science. After the scientist has established all the scientific facts of the case, there still remain (on this view) the further nonscientific questions about the values with which the epistemologist is concerned.

A third feature of non-naturalized epistemology, and one which has been very influential in the twentieth century is what we might call the "armchair" approach. This is used by those who think that epistemology properly relies only on a priori reflection, including (for example) the techniques of logical analysis which we illustrated in earlier chapters of the book. It is part and parcel of this approach that epistemology is completely insulated from the findings of science.

Given these contrasts with NE, we can expect any version of NE to reject epistemologies which either go beyond the realm of science (e.g., by appealing to a God-like being or to a set of science-transcendent values), or fail to utilize the findings of science. With those preliminary reflections, let us now turn to see in detail what Quine has to tell us about the relations between TE and NE.

12.3 The Quinean Project

TE, says Quine, was thoroughly foundationalist. "Epistemology is concerned with the foundations of science," he declares (1969, 69). But this search for foundations has been unsuccessful. In mathematics, it has failed, partly because of Gödel's results (see 6.3 [iv]), partly because the claims of set theory (to which at best math might be reducible) themselves lack the certainty which foundations of knowledge ought to possess. In the area of natural science, it has failed because there can be no watertight linkage of the kind the foundationalist sought between supposedly foundational beliefs about our sense experience and our scientific theories.

Given this inevitable failure, what if anything is left for the epistemologist to do? Quine's suggestion is that epistemology might somehow merge with psychology or at least with one branch of it. One of the tasks of psychology, Quine thinks, is to explain how we are able to construct our overall picture of the world on the basis of the sensory evidence that we have.

> [The] human subject is accorded a certain experimentally controlled input— certain patterns of irradiation in assorted frequencies, for instance—and in the fullness of time, the subject delivers as output a description of the three-dimensional external world and its history. (op. cit. 83)

It is the task of the psychologist to explore the relation between this "meager input" and the "torrential output." What processes must go on within us, for example, to transform the (broadly) two-dimensional stimulation of the retina into a belief in a three-dimensional world? What processes transform acoustical disturbance at my ears into a belief that you are wishing me a good day?

The project that Quine thus envisages appears to be a quest for *causal* explanations, in that the task of the psychologist is thought to be tracing the causal path from the input to the senses through the cognitive pathways, presumably in the brain, to the output, namely to the set of beliefs (or perhaps verbal expressions of those beliefs) which we have about the world at large.

It is to this causal task that Quine directs the modern epistemologist.

> Epistemology in its new setting . . . is contained in natural science, as a chapter of psychology. (ibid.)

In assigning epistemology this status, Quine is quite willing to allow that there are differences between the old and new conceptions of epistemology. The "conspicuous difference" which he mentions is that the old epistemology was meant to be carried on without utilizing any of the findings of natural science or psychology (because it was meant to be supplying the foundations for these areas of knowledge), whereas the new epistemology "can make free use of empirical psychology" (ibid.).

But, partly as a consequence of this difference, there are other differences between Quine's NE and TE, differences of a kind and scale which have led other philosophers to deny that NE can rightly claim to be *epistemology* at all. We will focus on three of them, concerned with the issues of skepticism, data, and epistemic norms. In section 12.3, we will outline the case for thinking that NE is very different from TE, so different as to make it misleading to call it epistemology at all. Then in section 12.4, we will mention other factors which qualify this initial assessment and give us a more rounded grasp of what NE amounts to.

12.4 Three Distinctive Features of Quine's Naturalized Epistemology

(i) NE assumes that there is an external world

One of the questions which TE tried to answer was "Can we know anything? Is knowledge possible at all?"—or, in a less sweeping way, "Can we know whether there is an external world and what it is like?" In answering this second question, it was always regarded as illegitimate to call on the resources of science—for example, to say that science has proved the existence and nature of many things in the external world. For our knowledge that science has done this presupposes that we have knowledge of the existence of scientists, laboratories, books recording scientific findings, and so on. And if the question is "Can we know *anything* about the existence of the external world?," we do not get an answer by *presupposing* that we know of the existence of *some* things in the external world, and using them as evidence for the existence of other things. For our initial question applied as much to the existence of scientists, laboratories, and books as to the existence of X-rays, viruses, and distant galaxies. Epistemology, then, had to start without any assumptions that there was an external world and show how that assumption could be justified.

Quine's NE appears not to operate under this constraint. The way in which Quine usually describes the epistemologist's task already presupposes that there is an external world. The epistemologist, like the psychologist, is to *start* with the assumption that there is an external world containing a person (in fact, lots of people) who receive various kinds of data, such as retinal radiation, and who produce a physical output in the form of behavior, both verbal and nonverbal. Given this starting point, the epistemologist then has to explain what processes intervene between the data which the person receives and the world view which she then acquires on the basis of those data. Speaking of the traditional epistemological concern with the relation between science and sense impressions, Quine writes:

> I approach it as an input-output relation within flesh-and-blood denizens of *an antecedently acknowledged external world,* a relation open to enquiry as a chapter of the science of that world. (Quine, 1990, 19, italics added)

What this implies is that the NEist simply does not address one of the questions which TE dealt with, and that would be *a* reason (though not yet a strong reason) for saying that NE is not really epistemology at all.

(ii) Physical stimulations, not conscious states, are the data of NE

A second difference between TE and NE focuses on Quine's conception of the data which the subject receives. In TE, the data were thought to be mental states of some kind. Descartes in his *cogito* takes "I think" to be something of which he can be certain, he assumes that some other beliefs about the contents of his own consciousness can be similarly certain, and that these other beliefs can form the foundation on which he can try to build an equally certain theory about the nature of the universe at large. In traditional empiricism, the data were usually construed as sense impressions, as modes of awareness or consciousness. In particular, the data were not thought to be physical stimulations—retinal irradiations, pressure waves at the ear drums, and so on. In part this was because, as we noted previously, the epistemologist was supposed to begin by being neutral on the question of the existence of such physical entities: that was something which had to be proved, not presupposed. In part, it was also because such physical events could not by themselves (i.e., in the absence of awareness of such events) count as evidence for any beliefs the subject might have. Having your retina stimulated might *cause* you to believe that there was a hamburger in front of you, but could not be your *justification* for thinking the hamburger was there, since ex hypothesi you would be unaware that your retina had been stimulated. Furthermore, the stimulation of your retina could not have any sort of content, such as a propositional content, which could stand in confirmation relations to anything else (see 5.4 [iv]).

The naturalized epistemologist precisely reverses this emphasis. Quine makes clear that when he speaks of data or input, he does not mean conscious states of any kind, but rather the physical interactions that take place between our physical sense organs, and the physical environment (see, e.g., Quine, 1990, 19). The significance of this difference will be clear in the light of the third difference between TE and NE, the role of norms, to which we now turn.

(iii) NE focuses on what causes our beliefs rather than on what justifies them

TE was concerned not primarily (or even at all) with asking why, as a matter of fact, we *do* believe the various things that we do, but rather with whether we were entitled or justified in believing them or in what would count as good evidence or justification for believing them—in other words, about the norms governing belief formation. Putting the contrast oversimply for emphasis, it was concerned with what we *ought* to believe, not with what we *do* believe. Thus, in considering the question of our belief in the reliability of inductive inferences, the relevant question was not "What causes us to think that induction is reliable?," but rather "What, if anything, would justify the belief that induction is reliable?" In connection with beliefs about the external world, the question was not "What causes us to believe in the existence of a mind-independent world of three spatial and one temporal dimensions, containing persisting objects?," but rather "What justifies this belief?"

The difference between these two kinds of question, one about the cause of our beliefs and the other about their justification, can be disguised by asking such questions as "Why do we believe that *p*?" Presumably most people who wonder whether their belief is rational, either decide that it is or else abandon the belief. So, if we assume that our belief that p is rational, the causes and the justification of the belief will coincide: it is the fact that we have good reasons for the belief that causes us to hold the belief. But the fact that the two questions *can* in some cases have a single answer should not blind us to the fact that there are indeed two questions here, one about cause and the other about justification and that TE was concerned with the second and not with the first.

By contrast, NE seems to be concerned with the first and not with the second. Two things in particular suggest this. First, as noted above, Quine construes the "data" on the basis of which people form their world picture not as states with a propositional content, such as beliefs, nor even as conscious states like awareness of sense impressions, but rather as physical events (irradiations of the retina, etc.). And it is quite clear that physical events like these could not themselves be the justification for anything. Secondly, and perhaps as a consequence of the first point, Quine hardly ever refers to the relation between our data and the theories we form on the basis of the data in justificatory terms. It is true that he refers to the data as "evidence," but he is strikingly unconcerned with the question of what *makes* data evidence, or good evidence, for one thing rather than another. Rather, his central concern is always with how we are to explain what causes a person to end up with the theories she does, given the data she starts with.

From this perspective, it seems that the new epistemologist will not be interested in the distinction which was of central importance to the old epistemologist, the distinction between justified and unjustified beliefs. For unjustified beliefs will be explicable in just the same way that justified beliefs are explicable: the new epistemologist will be looking for some cognitive mechanisms in the subject which take the data as input and yield the beliefs as output. Whether in addition the data *justify* the beliefs will be a further and independent question, which (apparently) the new epistemologist will not be concerned with. Thus it might be that the *very same* visual mechanisms are involved in generating (1) accurate perceptual beliefs in standard conditions, and (2) perceptual illusions in nonstandard conditions. So in this third respect it seems as if the contrast between the aims of TE and NE is so great as to make it positively misleading to regard NR as a continuation, even in revised form, of the old subject.

12.5 Three Reasons Why TE and Quine's NE Are Not Really So Different: Skepticism, Data, and Norms

We have seen, then, that there are at least three points of substantial difference between TE and NE as Quine conceives of it. But we now need to take account of some complicating factors which make the picture less clear-cut than we have so far suggested, and which make it much more intelligible why NE should be regarded as a kind of epistemology at all. Of course the real issue here is not what we *call* an area of study, but rather how significant its similarities and differences are with TE.

(i) Quine's response to skepticism about the external world

The first complication comes in relation to Quine's response to skepticism. For as well as saying that NE should simply sidestep the issue and presuppose the existence of the external world, he also appears to accept the traditional challenge of skepticism, and tries to meet it with more-or-less traditional philosophical arguments. He deploys (albeit rather fleetingly) two such antiskeptical arguments. First, he suggests that our belief that there is an external world of a fairly specific kind is justified in virtue of being the best explanation for our sensory data. This response to skepticism accepts the starting point of much traditional debate (that at least I know of the existence of my own private sense impressions and experiences). Given that I have these private experiences, there are various hypotheses which I might formulate about them. One would be, for example, that there is no external world of the kind accepted by common sense, and I am simply having a long, vivid, very detailed, and very coherent set of hallucinations. A variant of this theory would be that I am in the position of the victim of the mad scientist described in section 3.3(ii). A third hypothesis would be that my experiences are a more-or-less accurate reflection of the nature of a mind-independent world around me. According to the "inference to the best explanation" argument (the IBE argument for short), it is the third of these hypotheses which is the most plausible. It is the one which provides me with the best explanations of why I have had the experiences which I have had, and which provides me with the best predictions about the experiences which I will have. It is this that justifies my belief in the existence of the external world and which thus refutes skepticism. Thus we find Quine telling us:

> Physical objects are conceptually imported . . . as convenient intermediaries
> . . . comparable epistemologically to the gods of Homer. For my part, I do . . .
> believe in physical objects and not in Homer's gods . . . But in point of epistemological footing the physical objects and the gods differ only in degree and not in kind . . . The myth of physical objects is epistemologically superior to most in that it has proved more efficacious than other myths as a device for working a manageable structure into the flux of experience. (Quine, 1953, 44)

The second antiskeptical argument which we can find in Quine is that scepticism (about the external world at least) is *self*-refuting. For the skeptic, noting that some of our experiences are illusory, raises the possibility that in fact all of our experiences may be illusory, so that for all we know, nothing about the nature and existence of the world is how it appears to be to us. But,

Quine objects, the contrast between reality and illusion can be drawn only by someone who accepts that there is a real world with which illusions can be contrasted. If *per impossible*, everything were an illusion, there would be no sense to the idea that anything was illusory. As Quine puts it:

> The sceptics cited familiar illusions to show the fallibility of the senses; but this concept of illusion itself rested on natural science, since the quality of illusion consisted simply in deviation from external scientific reality. (Quine, 1974, 3)

We are not now concerned with assessing how strong either of these arguments against skepticism is. The point here is simply to see that in relation to one traditional epistemological problem, that of skepticism about the external world, Quine recommends two very different strategies, one of which simply sidesteps the traditional problem while the other confronts it head-on with some traditional philosophical replies. There is, of course, no incompatibility between these two lines of thought. The obvious and natural way to combine them would be this: first, Quine shows how the traditional problem can be solved (either by appealing to IBEs or by showing that skepticism is self-refuting). Secondly, he uses this antiskeptical conclusion to raise questions which presuppose that we do have a good deal of knowledge of what the contents of that world are like, questions in particular about the transformation which we each manage between our "meager input" and our "torrential output." So we can see good reasons in this area at least for thinking that NE has substantial overlap with TE, even though it raises questions which go beyond the latter.

(ii) The data of NE must be physical stimulations *and* conscious states

Secondly, in relation to the different conceptions of the data with which the NEist operates, we can now see that Quine must also be relying on two conceptions of data. Insofar as the NEist is playing the role of psychologist, she will be tracing a causal path from the neural stimulation through to the verbalized output of the human subject. In that investigation, the NEist can assume that for her subject, the neural stimulations count as "data." Whether the subject is *aware* of these data or not, they are the physical stimulations which the subject starts with (temporally) in arriving at a picture of the external world, and they count as data in at least that sense.

But Quine must also be utilizing another conception of data, and one that is much closer to the traditional conception. For when he says that we can meet the challenge of skepticism by relying on an inference to the best explanation, he must be assuming that we as subjects have cognitive access to the data which get explained by the hypothesis of the external world. And that means that he must think of the data as consisting of sense experiences or sense impressions in very much the traditional empiricist way.

(iii) Science can uncover norms

Finally, in relation to the issue of epistemic norms, there is again good reason to think that the differences between NE and TE are not as great as we might originally have thought. In response to the charge that naturalized epistemology abandons the concern with normative questions that characterizes the old epistemology, Quine says this:

> Naturalism not only consigns the question of reality to science; it does the same for normative epistemology. The normative is naturalised, not dropped . . . It is natural science that tells us that our information about the world comes only through impacts on our sensory surfaces. And it is conspicuously normative, counselling us to mistrust soothsayers and telepathists.
>
> For normative content of a more technical kind, we may look to mathematical statistics. These norms, again, are at the level of science itself. (Quine in Barrett and Gibson, eds., 1990, 229)

This response is interesting for several reasons. First, it makes clear that naturalized epistemology need not abandon questions about the norms of belief, questions about what we ought to believe as opposed to what we do believe. What it does is to locate the normative realm *within* the factual realm, and hence within the realm which can be legitimately investigated by science, at least if we construe the latter term fairly widely (e.g., to include mathematical statistics). There are various ways in which this accommodation of the normative within the factual might be accomplished. Suppose, for example, we took a reliabilist view of justified belief, of the kind which we considered in section 4.6 (and cf. also 3.1). We would then define a justified belief as one which had been generated by a reliable method, and we could then interpret the concept of reliable method in terms of the probability of it producing true beliefs. Since it is presumably a factual matter what methods produce which beliefs, and what the probability is that any given belief so produced is true, we would have explained the normative in terms of something which science could certainly investigate. The same sort of naturalistic approach could be achieved in terms of the account of justified belief which we actually favored (see 4.7). For we defined a justified belief roughly as one which was causally sustained by another belief, where the propositional content of the first made the propositional content of the second more likely to be true than false. Here again the normative question of what we ought to believe is interpreted in terms of causation and probability, concepts with which science is entirely at home.

But secondly, notice that on this conception of a naturalized epistemology, epistemology does *not* become (in Quine's words) "a chapter of psychology." If we assume that the psychologist is concerned with the question of how the input (sensory stimulation) is transformed into the output (our [perhaps verbalized] beliefs about the nature of the world), the question of which beliefs in the output are justified and which are unjustified is simply not relevant. What *is* true, as we have suggested above, is that the question can be answered while remaining within the realm not of psychology in particular but of science in general. It can be answered by appealing to facts which are not themselves explicitly normative, such as what causes what, what makes what more probable, and so on.

The issue is complicated by the fact that there are two theorizing activities in question here, one by the individual knower, the other by the psychologist. The individual knower is the person who confronts the world as we all do and tries to make sense of it. He takes as data his sense experiences, and in trying to make sense of them he produces as output a "theory" of the external world (roughly, what is believed by common sense). So his theory tries to explain and predict the sense impressions which he has had and will have. The psychologist, by contrast, takes as her data the fact that the individual knower, subject to a certain range of physical stimulations has produced a theory about those stimulations. Her data, in other words, are not sensory stimulations at all. They are transformations, that is to say the transforming processes by which the knowing subject moves from his private and fleeting sense experiences to a belief in a public and enduring world. And the theory which the psychologist comes up with is a theory about what those processes of transformation going on within the knowing subject are like.

It is of course true that in carrying out this task, the psychologist (like any good scientist) wants to produce a theory which she is justified in believing on the basis of the evidence she has (i.e., the stimulation/belief transformations in the knowing subject), and to that extent she must *use* the concept of justification. But although she uses it, she does not have to *theorize* about it. She does not have to ask what it is for a belief to be justified, nor does she have to have an account of how justification links with related concepts. Nor does she have to ask herself which of the beliefs held by the knowing subject are justified and which are not. From the point of *her* explanatory project, they are all on a par. So, insofar as the NEist comes up with a naturalized account of how we ought to form our beliefs (i.e., a naturalized account of *justified* belief), she will be going beyond the concerns of the psychologist. But, precisely because her account is a naturalistic one, she will be staying within the overall world picture given to us by science. She will be avoiding any science-transcendent norms of a kind which could threaten naturalism.

We can thus see that the stark contrast between TE and Quine's NE that emerged from section 12.4 needs to be very much qualified, and that when the qualifications are introduced, although some differences remain between NE and TE (e.g., in the different roles which they assign to psychological investigations), they have enough in common for it to be more than arbitrary mislabeling to call NE a form of epistemology.

12.6 A Different Route to Naturalized Epistemology

So far, we have considered only one route to naturalized epistemology taken by Quine. We saw that it turned essentially on the failure of foundationalism and hence on the impossibility of philosophy being able to provide any foundations for science. But there is a different route to naturalized epistemology, one that goes via the rejection of the old dichotomies of a priori and empirical, necessary and contingent, analytic and synthetic, logical and factual.

We saw in section 7.5(ii) that in place of these old dichotomies, Quine proposed that all our beliefs could be ranged on an entrenchment continuum. They range from the most highly entrenched to the most weakly entrenched, where degree of entrenchment measures the degree to which any particular belief is entwined with other beliefs. The crucial point here is that the beliefs differ only in *degree* and not in *kind*. This means that the old conception of the difference between philosophy and science has to be abandoned. This was the tradition which said that philosophy was entirely a priori and science entirely empirical; philosophy dealt with necessary propositions and science with contingent propositions; philosophy was concerned with logic and not with facts, science was concerned with facts and not with logic. Clearly this account of the philosophy/science contrast collapses if the distinctions in terms of which it is formulated are untenable.

In its place goes the thought that philosophy and science differ in degree but not in kind. Philosophy tends to be more abstract and theoretical, science more concrete and particular. But these contrasts, crude at best, are only rough pointers which can prove unreliable in particular cases. Thus modern physics is *highly* theoretical, and its theories are rivals to the theories (e.g., about space, time, and matter) advanced in the past by philosophers. Other areas of philosophy may rely on fairly specific factual assumptions (political and moral philosophers making assumptions about human nature, philosophers of art making assumptions about the nature of "aesthetic experience"). So the philosophical merges into the scientific: there is no sharp boundary between them (let us call this the continuity thesis). Hence scientific findings are in principle relevant to philosophical claims. Hence, more specifically, the claims of the epistemologist are not immune to revision in the light of empirical information. More positively, they can in principle be confirmed or overturned by advances in empirical knowledge. In other words, the naturalized conception of epistemology is the correct one.

It is important to remember in connection with this claim that the kind of "confirmation" and "overturning" envisaged can be very indirect. As we saw earlier (7.5 [iii]), the challenge to the law of the excluded middle did not come from, for example, observations of grass which was neither green nor not green. It came from *very* theoretical developments in quantum mechanics. Similarly, we should not think that epistemological theories about, for example, how people ought to reason will be overthrown *just* by the finding that many people do not reason in that way. The relationship between how people do reason and how they ought to reason is a very complicated one. What is characteristic of NE and what distinguishes it from TE, is that it does recognize the potential *relevance* of how people reason when it formulates theories about how they ought to reason.

12.7 Three Examples of Naturalized Epistemology

(i) Empiricism confirmed by science

So far, we have been suggesting that acceptance of universal coherentism implies acceptance of naturalized epistemology. But it is one thing to accept in theory that empirical findings can have a bearing on epistemological claims, and another to see in detail how this might be so. Quine does provide an example, though only a sketchy one. He says that the epistemological theory of empiricism is confirmed by science:

> The most notable norm of naturalised epistemology actually coincides with that of traditional epistemology. It is simply the watchword of empiricism: *nihil in mente quod non prius in sensu* [there is nothing in the mind which did not come through the senses]. This is a prime specimen of naturalised epistemology, for it is a finding of natural science itself, however fallible, that our information about the world comes only through impacts on our sensory receptors. (Quine, 1990, 19, translation added)

But we will focus on two different areas in which the traditional idea that philosophical theses are securely insulated against all empirical investigations has turned out to be untenable. The first concerns the ancient philosophical claim that man is a rational animal; the second focuses on Goodman's Paradox.

(ii) "Man is a rational animal": philosophy versus science

Aristotle declared that man was a rational animal, and a number of modern philosophers have sought to show by philosophical argument that in a sense this *must* be so. More specifically, they have tried to show that anyone who has beliefs about anything at all must be rational. They have tried, in other words, to establish a necessary connection between the concepts of belief and of rationality. The details of all these arguments need not concern us, but the main outlines of one of the arguments can be briefly sketched to give a flavor of what they are like.

One argument, due to Dennett (1971, 1978), goes as follows. Confronted by any creature (including a human being), one of the things we want to be able to do is to explain why it behaves as it does, and to predict how it will behave in a variety of possible future situations. We want to be able to say things like "It picked up the ball and threw it across the room because . . . ," or "If we put a glass of water in front of it when . . . , it will. . . ." With some kinds of creature (perhaps, e.g., with worms), we can explain the behavior in merely physical terms, without assuming that the creature has any beliefs or desires or preferences or perhaps even sensations. But with other kinds of creature (preeminently with humans), we cannot explain why they do what they do, nor predict what they will do, unless we can attribute beliefs to them. This is so because a large part of what we do, we do *because* of what we believe about our current environment and how it relates to the larger world in which we are situated. But (so the argument goes), these belief attributions could not perform this explanatory role unless the creature was rational in the way it formed its beliefs. If for example, it believes p, we may be able to use that fact to explain why it does one thing rather than another. But that possibility presupposes that if it believes p, it will not also believe not-p. If in general, for any given proposition p which it believed, it was as likely as not *also* to believe not-p, then we could not use its supposed belief in p to make any reliable predictions or explanations about its behavior. So, if the attribution of beliefs to a creature is to be justifiable, it must be the case that the creature is rational in the way it forms its beliefs.

There are many ways in which this argument can be qualified to take account of possible objections. But for our purposes, the crucial feature is the way in which it tries to construct an a priori proof that believers must be rational, by arguing that the concept of belief is essentially tied to the concepts of *explanation and prediction,* and that explanation and prediction of the relevant kind presuppose that the beliefs follow the canons of rationality.

In considering philosophical arguments of this sort, Stich draws attention to a range of empirical findings which indicate that many humans who are certainly believers

> . . . regularly and systematically invoke inferential and judgemental strategies ranging from the merely invalid to the genuinely bizarre. (Stich, 1990, 249)

Stich quotes a number of studies which support this claim. We will select one as an illustration. It is an elementary truth of probability theory that if the probability of one event is independent of the probability of another, then the probability of both of them happening must be less than the probability of either of them singly. The probability of both of them happening is in fact the product of their individual probabilities. For example, the probability of my picking a red card from a standard deck is 1 in 2 (i.e., a half) (since half the cards in the deck are red); the probability of picking a Queen is 1 in 13 (since there are 52 cards of which only 4 are Queens); so the probability of picking a card which is both a Queen and red *must* be less than either 1 in 2 or 1 in 13. It is in fact 1 in 26 (i.e., one-half times one-thirteenth).

So much is true and seems *obviously* true. And yet reflective people who are trying to reason carefully regularly violate this principle. Stich (1990), quoting work by Kahneman and Tversky, describes how subjects were asked to assess the probability that people with certain characteristics would be lawyers, the probability that they would be Republicans, and the probability that they would be Republican lawyers. What Kahneman and Tversky found was that if the subject judged that a person was unlikely to be a lawyer, but likely to be a Republican, she would then judge that the person was moderately likely to be a Republican lawyer. In other words, the likelihood of being a Republican lawyer was judged to be higher than the likelihood of being a lawyer, a judgment which an elementary grasp of probability tells us is absolutely impossible.

So, we have a philosophical argument for saying that it must be true that believers are rational, and empirical evidence for thinking that they are not rational. Of course, as we have presented the issue so far, it might be possible to find some compromise. For at best the philosophical argument shows that a believer must at least adhere to the law of noncontradiction on pain of ceasing to having *beliefs* at all; and this leaves open the possibility that she may still be a believer even if she regularly flouts the most basic principles of probability. But the attractiveness of looking for such a compromise is lessened by other empirical studies of people's reasoning capacities which shows that they are deficient in a variety of areas other than those concerned with probability judgments (see studies by P. C. Wason and P. N. Johnson-Laird quoted by Stich, 250).

(iii) Natural selection shows that "green" is preferable to "grue"

A third example of naturalized epistemology at work is provided by Quine himself. In his essay "Natural Kinds" (reprinted in Quine, 1969), he discusses how Goodman's Paradox should be solved (and also makes some comments on Hempel's Paradox of Confirmation). He argues that in confronting Goodman's Paradox, we need to focus on the concept of similarity. Speaking of Goodman's famous emeralds, Quine asks:

> ... why do we expect the next one to be green rather than grue? The intuitive answer lies in similarity, however subjective. Two green emeralds are more similar than two grue ones would be if only one of the grue ones were green. (op. cit. 116)

If this is so, then it would be natural for a traditional epistemologist to try to specify criteria for similarity by reference to which we could justify this claim of comparative similarity. What justifies the claim that all emeralds which are green are more similar to each other, than are emeralds which are green and blue and yet are all grue? Quine, however, does not address this question at all. Rather, he asks where our sense of similarity comes from. He asks about the origin, not directly about the justification, of our sense of similarity, and he declares that it is innate. But to say that it is innate is not a

> ... point against empiricism; it is a commonplace of behavioural psychology. A response to a red circle, if it is rewarded, will be elicited again by a pink ellipse more readily than by a blue triangle; the red circle resembles the pink ellipse more than the blue triangle. (op. cit. 123)

So it is an innate fact about us that pink is perceived as more similar to red than it is to blue, that ellipses are perceived as more similar to circles than they are to triangles, and so on. Each of us has what Quine calls an innate quality space, within which we have an innate tendency to range qualities as being more, or less, similar to each other.

Quine is not saying that pink *is* more similar to red than it is to blue, and so on. He is saying that we are so constructed that we have an innate tendency to see things in that way. And that leaves him with a gap in the argument so far. Briefly, why should we think that our innate tendency to see some things as similar and others as dissimilar corresponds to any objective similarities or dissimilarities. Might we not be so constructed that we perceive as similar things which are in fact dissimilar, and vice versa? Quine of course is aware of the gap, and indeed points it out himself:

> . . . why does our innate spacing of qualities accord so well with the functionally relevant groupings of nature as to make our inductions tend to come out right? Why should our subjective spacing of qualities have a special purchase on nature and lien on the future? (op. cit. 126)

To fill this gap, Quine appeals to Darwin and evolutionary theory:

> If people's innate spacing of qualities is a gene-linked trait, then the spacing that has made the most successful inductions will have tended to predominate through natural selection. Creatures inveterately wrong in their inductions have a pathetic but praiseworthy tendency to die before reproducing their kind. (ibid.)

In other words, our innate tendency to see some things as importantly similar to each other, and others as importantly different, is shown to be correct because if it were not correct, the species would not have survived. We would often have identified as edible, substances that were in fact poisonous, and vice versa; we would have judged situations safe that were in fact dangerous, and vice versa; and so on. In a word, we would have failed to learn from experience, and would have paid for such an incapacity with our collective death. So if *we* as survivors in the evolutionary struggle find it natural to use predicates like "green" and not to use predicates like "grue," that is some reason to think that the use of "green" in prediction and explanation is reliable, and the use of "grue" is not.

What is interesting about this from our present point of view is not so much whether Quine's remarks solve Goodman's Paradox, but rather the way in which he approaches the issue. He does not try to tackle it in the way that some traditional epistemologists have, by producing, for example, an a priori theory of confirmation, or by showing that "grue" and similar predicates violate some a priori constraints on legitimate predicate formation. Rather, he immediately invokes fairly detailed empirical considerations drawn from biology and human history. The implication is that it is only by appealing to facts that would traditionally have been classed as empirical, contingent, and synthetic (and hence entirely nonphilosophical) that we can make any progress in tackling the problem.

More specifically, we can see his remarks as part of the naturalizing of epistemic norms which we noted in section 12.5 (iii). Given a question of the form "Why *ought* we to prefer the hypothesis that all emeralds are green to the hypothesis that they are all grue?," Quine's answer appeals to such (naturalistic) facts as the psychophysiological construction of the "green"-users, their survival rate, and the best explanation of why they have survived. Just as "it is natural science that tells us that our information about the world comes only through impacts on our sensory surfaces"; just as psychological investigation bears on the question of whether people are rational; so too it is natural science which tells us that we ought to prefer "green" to "grue."

(iv) The interdependence of philosophy and science

According to NE, the moral we should draw from all this is that it is impossible to insulate empirical and philosophical concerns from one another. The relationship between belief and rationality needs to be determined in part by theoretical reflection (of the kind that philosophers have traditionally engaged in), but must also take into account the findings that emerge from empirical studies like those which we have quoted. To accommodate the empirical findings, we may need to loosen the link between belief attribution and the explanation of behavior which the philosophical argument relied on, or perhaps to develop a different conception of how beliefs explain behavior. But equally, in drawing conclusions from the empirical findings, we need to be sensitive to which kinds of reasoning they are focusing on, and to make sure that we do not overgeneralize the capacity for irrationality which they reveal. But what the NEist tells us we must not do is to assume that the two areas of study can sensibly be carried on in complete independence from each other.

Exercises

1. Without rereading the chapter contrast naturalized epistemology with non-natural epistemology in no more than one page. Assess your answer for clarity, accuracy, and completeness against 12.2.
2. Contrast the three different lines of argument which Quine appears to deploy concerning the existence of an external world (see 12.4[i], 12.5[i]). Write no more than one page.
3. Describe three ways in which Quine's naturalized epistemology seems to be radically different from traditional epistemology (write no more than one page). Assess your answer for clarity, accuracy, and completeness against 12.4.
4. Imagine that you are taking part in an experiment to check the rationality of some of your beliefs. You are asked to throw a die and to write down the sequence of results which is produced. Every so often you are asked to predict the likelihood of a particular result on the next throw. Psychologists report that most people believe that the longer a sequence of throws which

does not contain a six the more likely it is that a six will turn up on the next throw. But this is a fallacy, known as "the gambler's fallacy"—the likelihood of a six remains one in six with every throw. Discuss the question "How might questions about what we *ought* to believe be studied by science?" bearing this example in mind. (Cf. Stich, 1990, 83, 84.)

5. Explain and assess Quine's answer to Goodman's Paradox about the predicates "green" and "grue."

CHAPTER 13

Rorty on Philosophy and the Mirror of Nature

13.1 Rejecting a Traditional Conception of Philosophy

Richard Rorty has been very influential in undermining some of the philosophical ideas we have criticized in earlier sections of this book. He rejects the belief in incorrigible sense experiences and the traditional distinction between the a prior and the empirical and, partly for these reasons, he also rejects foundationalism. Besides holding these negative positions, Rorty also identifies with many elements in the pragmatist tradition, in particular with the coherentism and the "holism" we have been advocating (see Chapter 7). However, though he would probably agree with much of the reasoning we presented earlier about this general position, he also has some other reasons for adopting them and these have had a marked impact on philosophical thinking in recent years. In short, Rorty has argued that the belief in incorrigible sense experiences, the belief in the a priori/empirical distinction, foundationalism, the attempt to give necessary and sufficient conditions for "S knows that p," and so on, all belong to a general conception of philosophy which has to be abandoned. Just as Quine, in advocating naturalized epistemology, appears to repudiate a whole philosophical program, so Rorty rejects a widely held traditional conception of what philosophy is about. It is fair to claim that his views have been part of and have contributed to a revolution in philosophy in recent years, and we cannot leave the subject of epistemology without explaining them briefly.

13.2 Different Ways of Undermining Philosophical Positions

Rorty (1980) argues his case by first characterizing what is generally called the "modern" philosophical tradition, both its theses and its methods, and then showing how these have been discredited by the insights of certain philosophers during the present century. It is probably easiest to explain what is special about Rorty's contribution to the philosophical revolution of recent years by distinguishing different ways in which a philosophical position might be undermined.

On the one hand, a position might be shown to be flawed, or to lead to absurdity *in its own terms*. Thus, one classic attempt to give a definition of knowledge—by giving necessary and sufficient conditions for the truth of "S knows that p"—was shown to fail by Gettier's counterexamples. These counterexamples take seriously the attempt to provide a definition of "S knows that p" in terms of justified true belief and show that there are cases of justified true belief which we would not wish to count as knowledge. Notice that such a criticism does not necessarily challenge the general objective of attempting to define "S knows that p" by giving necessary and sufficient conditions—by providing an *analysis* of "S knows that p."

Another way to undermine a philosophical position is to show that a *general approach* to some philosophical question or range of questions is mistaken. Thus, the familiar approach to giving a definition of knowledge by stating necessary and sufficient conditions for the truth of "S knows that p" is rejected by Wittgenstein's arguments about the "family resemblances" which exist among the uses of a word like "know." In a famous section of his *Philosophical Investigations* (Pt. I, sec. 66), Wittgenstein argues that it is impossible to give necessary and sufficient conditions for the correct use of the word "game." He does not simply argue that some attempted definitions or "analyses" of the word "game" in terms of necessary and sufficient conditions fail because there are counterexamples. The argument is that we do not use general terms, like "game" and "know," in ways which can be captured by giving necessary and sufficient conditions at all. We use them in ways which resemble each other as the members of a family resemble each other (see Logic Appendix 2, exercise 4); each member of the family has some qualities in common with other members of the family, but there are no qualities which are common to every member. This way of attacking a philosophical position, if successful, means that a general problem or range of philosophical problems disappears. Thus, to return to the example of our previous paragraph, philosophers no longer try to give "analyses" or "S knows that p."

Another way of undermining a philosophical position is to describe an alternative way of looking at the world which gains the assent of listeners but which leaves a *whole conception of philosophy* on one side, and which thus makes the philosophical position of which it was a part seem unimportant or irrelevant. When a whole conception of philosophy is thus relegated to the history books, the problems which were central to it and the "solutions" within that tradition simply slip from view. For example, modern philosophy has long been seen as a discipline which attempts to answer eternal questions such as "What is truth?" and "What is knowledge?" (cf. Rorty, 1980, 3), which uses essentially a priori and analytic methods to attempt to answer such questions, and which has epistemology at its core. Someone who argues, as Quine does, that the main current problem is to explain how we generate such a "torrential output" from such a "meager input," and that the way to solve such a problem is to rely on the findings of science, leaves much that has been thought to be central to philosophy on one side. In that case certain "philosophical problems" may cease to be seen as problems at all.

This third way of challenging a philosophical position is the one to which Rorty attaches greatest importance and his own work mounts this kind of attack on "modern" epistemology.

As a matter of history, the twentieth century has seen the "modern" philosophical tradition attacked and undermined in all the ways we have just described. The modern tradition, which has been generally dominant for much of this century, stemmed largely from ideas and methods which originated in the seventeenth century with philosophers like Descartes and Locke. During the present century that tradition has been widely criticized *in its own terms*, witness the discussion of Gettier's counterexamples or of some attempts to justify induction. Besides such attacks, *general approaches* to philosophical issues have been challenged, witness the gradual abandonment of attempts to give "analyses" of concepts or to find foundations of knowledge. Finally, a *whole conception of what philosophy is about*, the "modern" conception of the problems and methods of philosophy, has been challenged. On Rorty's account in *Philosophy and the Mirror of Nature* (1980), some of the key figures who have brought about this change in the standing of the "modern" tradition are Dewey (1859–1952), Heidegger (1889–1976), and Wittgenstein (1889–1951). He sees them as key figures in this revolutionary change of attitude toward "modern" philosophy because they do not provide new philosophical theories, such as alternative theories of knowledge or philosophies of mind within the traditional framework. It is rather that they "set aside epistemology and metaphysics as possible disciplines" (op. cit., 6). Rorty explains that he says "set aside" rather than "argue against" because the philosophers he admires do not so much "devote themselves to discovering false propositions or bad arguments in the works of their predecessors (though they occasionally do that too)"; it is rather that they cease to regard the problems of "modern" philosophy and their "solutions" as being important, indeed these problems are seen as being in a certain sense "pointless." To explain the sense in which this is meant we need to explain a little of the history of philosophy.

13.3 The Emergence of "Modern" Philosophy

(i) The "scholastic" tradition challenged by science

In broad terms, the philosophical traditions which prevailed in Europe in the Middle Ages were mostly a combination of religious ideas, belonging to the Christian tradition, and ideas deriving mainly from the ancient Greeks and generally known as the "ancient" tradition. This combination is commonly referred to as the "scholastic" tradition. The ancient tradition contained many elements which we need not mention, but some are important for an understanding of the modern tradition in philosophy. First, the ancient tradition knew little or nothing of experiment or science. Secondly, it attached great importance to the certainty of mathematical reasoning and to the structure of mathematical knowledge, especially as exemplified in Euclid's geometry. Thirdly, especially in the part of the tradition deriving from Plato, it was much preoccupied with trying to find the "essence" of "truth," "knowledge," "virtue," and so on, and this often meant trying to find necessary and sufficient conditions for something to be "truth," "knowledge," "virtue." Fourthly and finally, it was very impressed by long-established "experts" or "authorities," especially ancient Greek and Roman ones; thus, for example, people believed that heavier bodies fall faster than lighter ones *because Aristotle said they did,* and physicians accepted that the blood ebbed and flowed in the veins like the tides in the ocean *because Galen said so* (Galen, A.D. 130–200, had been physician to the Roman emperors at the height of the Roman Empire)!

With the rise of science in the sixteenth and seventeenth centuries, some elements in this scholastic philosophical tradition were challenged and others took on a new lease of life. Clearly, religion was challenged in various ways, both with respect to its doctrines and its methods. Equally, the tendency to believe what ancient authorities said was challenged because experiments began to show that the ancients were mistaken about all sorts of things. For example, experiments showed that heavier bodies do not fall faster than lighter ones, *contrary to what Aristotle had said;* experiments also began to show that blood does not ebb and flow like the tides but flows around the body, *contrary to what Galen had said* (cf. Fisher, 1988, ch. 8).

(ii) The influence of mathematical ideas on philosophy

On the other hand certain elements in the ancient tradition were reinvigorated. For example, the certainty of mathematical reasoning became an ideal to aspire to in other domains too, and especially in philosophy. Furthermore, the structure of Euclid's geometry was widely admired and seemed to provide a model for other domains of knowledge, including philosophy. It seemed to show that if one wished to acquire knowledge in a given field there was much to be gained from defining one's terms very clearly and finding indubitable truths which could serve as foundations on which to build the whole edifice of knowledge in that field by deriving truths from the foundations, using absolutely reliable principles of reasoning. It is no exaggeration to say that science and philosophy were under the spell of Euclid's geometry in the seventeenth century. Thus, for example, Isaac Newton's theory of motion is propounded in his *Principia* (1687) on the model of Euclid's geometry: basic terms are defined, basic laws of motion are identified, and the rest is, generally speaking, derived from these by careful reasoning. Even Thomas Hobbes, writing on political theory in *The Leviathan* (1651) structured his political theory on the model of Euclid's geometry, and Spinoza (1632–1677), writing his *Ethics* (1677) derived moral principles using definitions, axioms, propositions, and demonstrations on the model of Euclid. Finally, and perhaps most importantly for modern philosophy, René Descartes (1596–1650) tried to derive all our knowledge from indubitable first principles, by indubitable principles of reasoning—on the model of Euclid's geometry. This is very clear in his *Arguments Demonstrating the existence of God and the Distinction between Soul and Body, Drawn up in a Geometrical Fashion* (1641), which is a partial summary of Descartes's *Meditations* (1641), which is itself widely regarded as the beginning of modern philosophy.

That part of the "ancient" philosophical tradition deriving from Plato, and concerned to find the "essence" of "truth," "knowledge," "virtue," and so on, complemented the tendency to present science and philosophy on the model of Euclid's geometry, since this tendency requires clearly defined terms or concepts on which to build. Plato, of course, had been impressed by the clarity and certainty of mathematical knowledge and aspired to comparable clarity and certainty in philosophy. In short, the search for essences was, in many respects, inspired by mathematics. For these reasons, it should come as no surprise to learn that the modern tradition gave a new lease of life to the Platonic search for essences. As we explained above, this often meant something very like trying to find necessary and sufficient conditions for the application of a concept. Hence, for example, the attempt to define "knowledge" as justified true belief, seems very natural within the modern philosophical tradition and quite central to it. Outside that tradition, it can seem positively bizarre. How on earth can it help anyone to understand what knowledge is to tell them that it is justified true belief? Surely this is to explain *one* familiar if problematic idea in terms of *three* which are at least as problematic, and it is surely ludicrous to suppose that someone might be ignorant of what "know" means while knowing the meaning of "justified," "true," and "belief." But, of course, the *point* of the definition of knowledge as justified true belief within the modern philosophical tradition is *not* to provide an explanation of the meaning of the word to someone who is unsure about it, but *rather* to establish a definition which can tie together some of our fundamental concepts in a philosophical edifice which resembles Euclid's geometry. The name of the game is "conceptual analysis," so that we can do for our conceptual scheme what Euclid did for geometry.

(iii) The importance of observation as a source of knowledge

The other side of the coin from these mathematically inspired ideas was that science emphasized the importance of observation and experiment. People were no longer to rely on what ancient authorities told them but were to rely, instead, on what their senses told them. This did not come at all easily to people at that time and there are many reports of scientists saying that they could not believe their senses when, for example, the evidence of their eyes contradicted what ancient authorities declared to be the case (cf. Fisher, 124). This led to a good deal of theorizing about the senses as a source of knowledge, and the main question concerned whether we could be certain of knowledge based on our senses. Given that people had relied for so long on the "wisdom" that had been handed down from generation to generation, it required radical new thinking to overthrow beliefs that were backed by greatly respected ancient authorities simply because these ideas didn't correspond to what our senses told us. The natural suspicion was that our senses were mistaken or were deceiving us; such was the stature of ancient authorities. For example, Galen was "the" authority on medicine for thirteen centuries, and medical students were taught his theories because they were "in Galen." Thus in the sixteenth century, students were taught anatomy not by doing dissections themselves but by watching assistants do dissections while the lecturer read the appropriate passage from Galen. If things turned out as Galen said they should then the assistants would be very proud of themselves, but if they didn't still Galen was to be believed. (See Herbert Butterfield, *The Origins of Modern Science 1300–1800*). Then in 1543, Andreas Vesalius (1514–1564) published his book *On the Fabric of the Human Body*, which challenged various of Galen's ideas and is now regarded as the beginning of modern anatomy. Even Vesalius said that he couldn't believe his own eyes, and the publication of his book provoked enormous opposition from the medical establishment.

Many similar stories can be told about scientists having difficulty in believing their own senses and generating fierce opposition by publishing ideas which conflicted with traditional beliefs, deriving from Aristotle and other ancient authorities. Nonetheless, science began to make rapid progress and observation, experiment—or experience as it was generally called—began to contribute more and more to our knowledge. Of course there were questions about the bases of this knowledge, whether it was our private sensations or more public objects of experience (cf. our discussion of the foundations of empirical knowledge in Chapter 5), but generally speaking, there was increasing confidence that here was another source of knowledge, besides the mental reflection which could supply us with knowledge of abstract matters like mathematics and philosophy.

(iv) The presumptions of modern philosophy

Thus, in the sixteenth and seventeenth centuries, modern philosophy emerged from the prevailing tradition of thought because that tradition was challenged in all the ways we described previously. As we explained, detailed work on anatomy challenged Galen's account of how the various organs functioned, and experiments with falling bodies challenged Aristotle's ideas on the subject. The general approach to answering a question by finding what some ancient authority had said on the issue was increasingly disregarded. And finally, the scholastic philosophical tradition was in certain respects, simply "set aside"—it simply gave way to a new conception of philosophy and a new set of philosophical problems. Modern philosophy, dating essentially from Descartes and Locke in the seventeenth century, generally accepted a distinction between truths known just by thinking about them and truths known on the basis of experience; it accepted the importance of our ideas and sensations as bases of knowledge, partly because of Euclid's influence it was predisposed to be foundationalist, and it had epistemology at its core. It had rejected much of the ancient philosophical tradition, in favor of a new problematic and a new way of thinking.

13.4 The Social Conception of Knowledge Outlined

Rorty contends that just as the ancient tradition of philosophy was superseded by modern philosophy in the seventeenth century, so has the modern tradition of philosophy been superseded in the twentieth century by something close to "pragmatism." As we explained earlier, elements of the modern tradition have been criticized in their own terms and have been found wanting. Furthermore, general approaches to problems have been repudiated. But most importantly, a large part of that conception of philosophy has been overthrown in favor of radical new perspectives. Just as in the case of the demise of the ancient tradition, this does not mean that everything from the modern tradition is abandoned, but rather that some of its fundamental problems and methods have fallen by the wayside, and new ideas about what is problematic and how these should be tackled have come into prominence.

Before we go into details about what has been repudiated and why, it will help if we summarize some of the key elements in the new view and the most important change. On the modern view, which obtained for the past three hundred years, every human being is, so to speak, "an island unto himself (or herself)." Such a being has "ideas" which are private to her own mind and of which she has privileged knowledge. The problem then is to explain how she knows anything about "the external world," whether there is an external world, whether it is as it *appears* to her, whether there are *other minds* or human beings besides herself, whether they experience the world as she does, and so on. The question is whether her ideas—of which she has *certain* knowledge—give her an accurate representation of reality. For example, suppose she has experience of a red flower, the question is whether the world is really like that (or are the apparent colors of flowers added by our minds to a world which is really colorless, say)? Thus, on the modern view, there is a radical distinction between the contents of the mind and the external world, and the problem is whether the mind's "picture" of reality is a correct representation of the way things are, whether it accurately mirrors reality. Rorty called his book *Philosophy and the Mirror of Nature* precisely to draw attention to this traditional conception of the problem that philosophy faces.

On the new thinking which has now come to the fore, the view of human beings as isolated individuals who have privileged knowledge of their own private ideas—an "atomistic" conception of human beings—has been replaced. It has been replaced by a conception of human beings as essentially parts of a social whole—the "holistic" conception of human beings—beings whose very way of experiencing the external world is not private to each of us, but is one we learn from others, partly by learning a shared language in which to talk about our experience, but also by simply learning how others see the world (for example, it is said that Eskimos have 40 different words for different kinds of snow). The ideas each of us have are now thought of as essentially public phenomena, given to us through a public language. The knowledge we each have is no longer thought of as being based on ideas which are private to each of us, but as being knowledge essentially because it is credited as knowledge by other human beings, because it has withstood the test of scrutiny by others.

Rorty articulates this alternative conception throughout his work and in many different ways. For example, in speaking of Dewey's conception of knowledge, he says we should see justification of a belief *not* as a "transaction between 'the knowing subject' and 'reality,'" but as a "social phenomenon" (1980, 9). Again, "justification is not a matter of a special relation between ideas (or words) and objects, but of conversation, of social practice" (op. cit., 170–171). There are many other such references, but the general idea is put to detailed use in repudiating many of the ideas which are central to modern philosophy, and which we have been criticizing in this book, so let us now look at how Rorty uses this general idea in particular contexts.

13.5 Incorrigible Sense Experiences Rejected

On the traditional "atomistic" view, each of us has privileged knowledge of the pains we feel and of the other sensations which we experience; no one else knows what is in our own mind in the way that we do. Furthermore, each of us is more certain about this knowledge than we are about our knowledge of the external world; we cannot be mistaken about the contents of our own mind but we could be mistaken about what we infer about the external world, on the basis of that experience. As Rorty puts it, "the tradition . . . [assumes] that reflections in the Mirror of Nature are better known than nature itself" (op. cit., 174).

On the alternative "holistic" view, what makes something we claim to know *certain* has to be decided by reference to *public* criteria—to criteria which refer to publicly observable behavior and not to something private, like sensations. In the present context, this means that what makes each of us certain about claims we make concerning our own inner states, for example, "I have a headache" or "I see a red rose," is that others generally accept that that is the best way of finding out someone's sensations. Yes, we each feel our own headache and each have our own "image" of the red rose, but what makes us *certain* that we have these experiences, correctly described in this language, is that others do not normally challenge claims about one's own inner states. It is not that we are certain of our sensations and that this explains why people don't challenge us about such claims, but the other way round. As Rorty puts it:

> It would seem enough for our peers to believe that there is no better way of finding out our inner states than from our reports, without their knowing what "lies behind" our making them. It would also seem enough for *us* to know that our peers have this acquiescent attitude. That alone seems sufficient for that inner certainty about our inner states which the tradition has explained by "immediate presence to consciousness," "sense of evidence," and other expressions of the assumption that reflections in the Mirror of Nature are intrinsically better known than nature itself. (op. cit., 173–174).

Some people may find it hard to grasp this idea, that what explains our certainty about our own experiences is *not* that we each have privileged access to them but that others do not normally challenge such claims. If one is to see any plausibility in this new position, it is essential to adopt the social perspective we outlined previously, the view that the legitimacy of ideas and beliefs has to be explained in terms of public criteria and in terms of what society lets us say, rather than the other way round (cf. op. cit., 173–174).

Rorty draws the following radical implication from this "social" perspective:

> . . . if assertions are justified by society rather than by the character of the inner representations they express, then there is no point in attempting to isolate *privileged* representations. (ibid.)

From the old perspective this is a very paradoxical thing to say. From the new perspective, it seems quite natural; the problem of identifying privileged ideas has simply dropped from view, because *all* our ideas are judged by similarly public criteria.

13.6 What Is the Source of Mathematical Certainty?

Rorty wishes to claim something quite similar about the certainty which is traditionally thought to attach to mathematical knowledge. Remember that on the traditional view, Euclid's geometry is seen as a model of well-founded mathematical knowledge, and on that model the basic axioms (the foundations) are believed to be self-evident and everything else is justified by being derived from them by equally self-evident principles of inference.

Just as the traditional atomistic view attaches great importance to the certainty of the knowledge each of us has about our own sensations of pain, color, and so on, in the same way it attaches great importance to the *self-evidence* of our mathematical ideas. As in the case of incorrigible sense experiences, the "self-evidence" of mathematical truths is something each of us can see alone—without essential reference to what others say. We see that a mathematical claim is true or false simply by the "light of reason," simply by reflecting on the ideas involved, and we each need only reflect on our *own* ideas to judge whether a mathematical claim like $1 + 1 = 2$ is self-evident.

However, on the new holistic view, what entitles us to be *certain* has to be something *public*, has to be explicable by reference to public criteria. In the case of mathematical knowledge, this means that what makes each of us certain about such claims as $1 + 1 = 2$ is that others are unable to find telling considerations against them. Of course, each of us may *think* that we alone can see that these truths are self-evident, but what *makes* us certain is that no one succeeds in challenging them. It is not that we are certain of the *self-evidence* of such basic claims and that this explains why people don't challenge us successfully, but the other way round.

Rorty articulates his position on mathematical thinking as follows:

> It is so much part of "thinking philosophically" to be impressed with the special character of mathematical truth that it is hard to shake off the grip of the Platonic Principle [that differences in certainty must correspond to differences in the objects known]. If, however, we think of "rational certainty" as a matter of victory in argument rather than of relation to an object known, we shall look to our interlocutors rather than to our faculties for the explanation of the phenomenon. *If we think of our certainty about the Pythagorean Theorem as our confidence, based on experience with arguments on such matters, that nobody will find an objection to the premises from which we infer it, then we shall not seek to explain it by the relation of reason to triangularity. Our certainty will be a matter of conversation between persons, rather than a matter of interaction with non-human reality.* So we shall not see a difference in kind between "necessary" and "contingent" truths. At most, we shall see differences in degree of ease in objecting to our beliefs. (op. cit., 156–157, italics added)

The italicized words clearly articulate the claim that our certainty about mathematical ideas is *not* due to their self-evidence, but is due to the fact that others are unable to persuade us that they are mistaken.

Slightly more general considerations than these relating to mathematics (considerations about our knowledge of meanings in general) undermine the traditional distinction between a priori and empirical knowledge or between necessary and contingent truths. Let us look briefly now at Rorty's views on this subject.

13.7 The Necessary/Contingent Distinction:
No Behavioral Differences

As we have explained earlier in many places in this book, it has been a central tenet of modern philosophy that there is a Great Divide between truths which we know by reflection alone and truths which we know on the basis of experience. As a matter of history, this distinction has been characterized in many different ways, but it has always been there in some form (see 5.2). The origin of this belief need not detain us now, though Rorty has many illuminating things to say on the subject. For us, what is important at this point is to explain how the social conception of knowledge contributes to undermining this traditional distinction.

Suppose we retain the old view of human beings as isolated individuals who have privileged knowledge of their own ideas but less certain knowledge of everything else. Then, as Rorty points out, the implications of a "post-modern" holism will probably sound pointlessly paradoxical. Someone who is still in the grip of the old philosophical presumptions will probably feel that Quine's attack on analyticity has simply "gone too far" and that he has allowed the arguments to sweep him off his feet and away from common sense (cf. Rorty, op. cit., 170). But, as Rorty insists, Quine's arguments have to be understood as arising from his "commitment to the thesis that justification is not a matter of a special relation between ideas (or words) and objects, but of conversation, of social practice" (170), and the crucial premise in the Quinean argument against the necessary/contingent distinction is "that we understand knowledge when we understand the social justification of belief . . ." (173).

So, suppose that instead of the old perspective, we think of human beings as creatures who learn everything from others, whose very way of experiencing the world is learned from others and for whom justification is essentially a social matter—a matter of convincing and being convinced by others—then Quine's arguments might seem more plausible. Assume that we learn from the publicly observable behavior of others, that we learn a language by learning to *use* it as others use it. Then if we are to sustain the analytic/synthetic distinction, we have to find differences in kind in the way people behave when considering the two kinds of sentence. But Quine argues that we do not find this. For example, he argues that we cannot distinguish "the sentences to which [native speakers] invariably and wholeheartedly assent, into contingent empirical platitudes on the one hand and necessary conceptual truths on the other" (cf. Rorty, op. cit., 173); the required differences in behavior just do not exist. Looked at from this behavioral perspective it is difficult to see a hard and fast distinction between sentences which are true solely in virtue of "meanings" and others which are not; indeed, it seems more natural to recognize a continuum of beliefs, some being hard for others to fault while others are much easier—some being deeply embedded in a conceptual scheme and others being more peripheral.

13.8 Foundations, Coherentism, and the Nature of Philosophy

Rorty argues that there are no "privileged representations," ideas which we know for certain and which can serve as foundations of our knowledge in the empirical and the a priori domains. He regards Sellars's arguments against the former and Quine's arguments against the latter as decisive and as proving that there are no foundations. Since Rorty thinks of epistemology as essentially foundational, he takes these arguments (along with many others criticizing modern philosophy) to show that there is nothing left for epistemology to be.

> I want to urge that [there is nothing for epistemology to be]. To understand the matters which Descartes wanted to understand—the superiority of the New Science to Aristotle, the relations between this science and mathematics, common sense, theology, and morality—we need to turn outward rather than inward, toward the social context of justification rather than to the relations between inner representations. This attitude has been encouraged in recent decades by many philosophical developments, particularly those stemming from Wittgenstein's *Philosophical Investigations* and from Kuhn's *Structure of Scientific Revolutions*. (Rorty, op. cit., 210)

It will be clear that in our view Rorty is right to reject privileged representations and foundationalism, but we do not agree that this leaves no scope for discussing the nature and grounds of our knowledge. If epistemology is essentially foundationalist, as Rorty often seems to imply, then he is right that there is nothing left for epistemology to be, but "holism" and "coherentism" are epistemological positions, in the broader sense of epistemology which sees itself as being concerned with the nature and grounds of our knowledge, and in our view Rorty is right to embrace these positions.

13.9 To Conclude

Speaking in general terms, modern philosophy was obsessed with the search for *certainty*. For reasons we outlined earlier (13.3 [ii]), its main concern was to find absolutely secure foundations for knowledge. Since there are no such foundations, it is right to put that epistemological tradition on one side. However, if we accept that coherence among our beliefs is the best we can hope for, and that justification is essentially social and holistic, there is still much theoretical work to be done in spelling out how our ideas do and do not hang together. Surely this is a worthy task for a new epistemology. Quine has argued that philosophy should give way to science, but science will still raise many theoretical problems of a kind which will still look very philosophical, in the broad sense of that word which does not identify it with the modern philosophical search for certainty (cf. Rorty, op. cit., 171).

What has to be abandoned is the search for certainty. What is left is the need to make sense of our experience, and this will take more than science alone. Even if a tradition has been shown to be wanting there are still problems about how or whether our beliefs and ways of thinking can be justified, how best to decide between conflicting conceptual schemes or ways of looking at the world, and which of our ideas need to be revised and on the basis of which criteria. Of course, just as we have to abandon the traditional Great Divide between necessary and contingent truths and between deductive and inductive reasoning, so we also have to abandon the traditional Great Divide between philosophy and science. There is no "purely conceptual" discipline, which deals only in timeless, a priori knowledge. However, if we are right that beliefs are justified by their coherence with other beliefs and that justification is essentially public and social, then there is still a great deal to be understood and explained. There will be no shortage of work for theoretically inclined scientists, even if traditional philosophers have to take a back seat!

Exercises

1. Without rereading the chapter, explain three different ways of undermining philosophical positions, giving illustrative examples of your own. Write no more than a page and a half.
2. Without rereading the chapter, explain briefly (in one page) how the rise of science in the sixteenth and seventeenth centuries affected philosophical thinking.
3. If public agreement is the source of certainty, what does that tell us about the incorrigibility of our knowledge of sense experiences? Write only one page and compare your answer with 13.5.
4. What entitles us to believe with certainty that 1 and 37 are the only whole numbers which divide 37 without leaving remainders? Compare your answer with 13.6.
5. "Among the sentences to which native speakers of a language wholeheartedly assent, we cannot find *behavioural* differences which enable us to distinguish between contingent empirical platitudes and necessary conceptual truths." What is the significance of this Quinean claim?

Logic Appendix

"For a complete logical argument," Arthur began with admirable solemnity, we need two prim Misses—"
"Of course!" she interrupted, "I remember that word now. And they produce—?"
"A Delusion," said Arthur. "Ye-es?" she said dubiously. "I don't seem to remember that so well. But what is the whole argument called?"
"A Sillygism."

—Lewis Carroll, *Sylvie and Bruno*

Some readers of this text will have taken a first level logic course and thus will be familiar with the kinds of things logicians say about reasoning and with some basic formal logic. This appendix is intended for those readers who are not familiar with the basic logic which is relevant to the arguments of this book or who would welcome a review chapter.

1. What Is the Subject Matter of Logic?

Logic is often described as the science of reasoning or argument. When we speak of "argument" in this context, we do not mean "argument" in the sense of a quarrel—in which disputants yell and scream at each other—but "argument" in the sense of a sequence of reasoning which is presented in support of some conclusion. Here are two passages, the first of which is not an argument (because it does not present reasons in support of a conclusion) and the second of which is:

1. Psychosemanticists are highly specialized therapeuticians. They should not be confused with psychosomaticists, who study the effects of mental weather upon the ramparts of the body. Psychosemanticists specialize in the havoc wrought by verbal artillery upon the fortress of reason. Their job is to cope with the psychic trauma caused by linguistic meaninglessness, to

prevent the language from degenerating into gibberish, and to save the sanity of persons threatened by the onset of polysyllabic monstrositis. (adapted from *Alarms and Diversions* by James Thurber. New York: Harper Brothers, 1957, 18.)

2. If there is a "private" language which only Hank understands, and Hank uses a word of this language, "plok," to refer to something which is private to him (say, a pain he has), then only Hank can know whether he is using the word "plok" in the same way on different occasions. But in this case neither Hank nor anyone else can tell the difference between using the word in the same way and *seeming* to use the word in the same way. If it is impossible to tell whether a word is used repeatedly in the same way, that word is meaningless. It follows that there cannot be such a thing as a "private" language (cf. 5.4 [ii]).

In the second passage, the author presents three reasons for accepting a conclusion; in this case, the conclusion is "there cannot be such a thing as a 'private' language" and each of the preceding sentences expresses one of the reasons which are presented as being sufficient to justify the conclusion if taken together. The reader who cares to look back through this book will find many "arguments"—in the sense in which we are using the term "argument." Following the ancient Greek philosopher Aristotle (384–322 B.C.), logicians usually call the reasons which are presented for a conclusion the "premises" of the argument. An argument, then, has premises and a conclusion, and the premises are presented as reasons to accept the conclusion. The term "argument" in our context is simply a convenient short expression for such a sequence of reasoning, and logic is the discipline which studies such reasoning or argument with a view to explaining which arguments are good and which are bad.

2. How to Recognize Arguments in Ordinary Language

In ordinary language contexts, it is not always easy to tell when an argument is being presented, but the use of certain words *often* gives a powerful clue. For example, the following words are commonly used to indicate that a conclusion is being presented:

> *therefore* . . . , *hence* . . . , *thus* . . . , *so* . . . , *consequently* . . . , *which proves that* . . . , *justifies the belief that* . . . , *allows us to infer that* . . . , *it follows that* . . . , *establishes the fact that* . . . , *demonstrates that* . . . , etc.

These words and phrases, and others which function like them, are called "conclusion indicators" because they are often followed by a conclusion in place of the dots. Though they commonly indicate the presence of a conclusion, they do not always do this, because such phrases are sometimes used in quite different ways; for example, "You shoot a basket *thus*," "You can only drive *so* far in a day," "There is no evidence which justifies the belief that miracles happen."

Besides conclusion indicators, there are also English words and phrases which indicate that reasons are being presented. Here are some examples:

because . . . , *since* . . . , *follows from the fact that* . . . , *the reason being* . . . , *firstly* . . . *and secondly* . . . , etc.

Again, we are not saying that whenever these words or phrases are used a reason is being presented, but that they are commonly used to indicate the presence of a reason in place of the dots.

Of course, reasoning is sometimes presented without using these reason or conclusion indicators at all. However, they are often present and they often help us to see that we are being presented with an argument. There are other argument indicators too, particularly "suppose for the sake of argument that . . ." and synonymous expressions (see Fisher, ch. 6, and also 86).

Exercise   The reader should now read through the following examples, which are mostly adapted from earlier sections of this book, deciding (a) which are presenting arguments and which are not, and (b) which sentences are reasons/premises and which are conclusions.

1. A few decades ago it was thought that the main task of philosophy was to provide logical analyses of philosophically puzzling concepts, such as the concepts of knowledge, free will, the self, and so on. In more recent times the pendulum has swung the other way, and many philosophers are now skeptical about the possibility of providing *any* philosophically illuminating analyses of this kind. (2.2[iv])

2. According to the "justified true belief" analysis of what knowledge is, there are possible cases which show that true belief is not sufficient for knowledge. For sometimes a person's belief is true just by chance or by luck. If a person bets regularly on the horses, and says one day, "I just know that I am going to have a big win," we would not say that she knew what she claimed to know, even if she did have a big win. (2.3)

3. If a method for acquiring knowledge is reliable, this means that it has a tendency or disposition to give the right answers *in general.* So the reliability of a method attaches to the *run* of answers which it yields; it cannot attach to any *individual* answer. Individual answers are *correct* or *incorrect*, whereas a method which is only reliable *in general* will—on occasion—give incorrect answers. (3.1[i])

4. If we consider the activities we call "games"—board games, ball games, Olympic games, and so on—we see that they do not have any one thing in common. They are not all "amusing" (think of chess or tic tac toe). There is not always winning and losing (think of a child playing a game with a ball against a wall). There is not always competition between players (think of patience). In fact we see a complicated network of similarities, overlapping and crisscrossing. A good expression which characterizes these similarities is "family resemblances," for the various resemblances between members of a family—build, features, color of eyes, gait, temperament, and so on, overlap in the same way. (see p. 49, and cf. Wittgenstein, Pt. I, sec. 66)

5. If the justification of a belief consists in part in its being caused by another justified belief, then that justified belief must itself have been caused by a third, and so on. Thus if we are trying to explicate the concept of justified belief, we are going round in a circle, invoking in our explanation the very concept that we are trying to explain. And if we were trying to acquire a justified belief, we would be faced with an infinite regress; to acquire one presupposes that you already have a second, which in turn presupposes that you have a third, and so on. (5.1)

6. The foundationalist uses the metaphor of a building—which has foundations—to picture the structure of justified belief. The coherentist uses other metaphors. One is to think of our set of beliefs like a wigwam of sticks. Each stick is supported by other sticks in the bundle, and each stick in turn provides some support to all the other sticks. There is no one stick (a sort of foundational stick, as it were) on which all the other sticks lean for support. (7.1)

7. The distinction between necessary and contingent propositions is easy to explain informally. The idea is that there are some propositions which not only *are* true—they could not possibly have been false (or which not only are false, they could not possibly have been true). These are the propositions which are *necessarily* true (or *necessarily* false). By contrast, there are other propositions which although true, could have been false (or which although false, could have been true); and these are contingent propositions.

It should be clear that in the preceding examples 2, 3, 4 and 5 contain arguments and the others do not.

3. Aristotle's Theory of the Syllogism

Once we can recognize arguments, we can address the problem of how to distinguish good ones from bad ones. It appears that the ancient Greeks were the first systematically to address this question and the most important philosopher who wrote on this subject was undoubtedly Aristotle, who is generally regarded as the "father" of logic. He wrote very widely on the subject of reasoning, and his ideas were the orthodoxy on the subject for two thousand years. Aristotle distinguished three aspects of reasoning, called "analytic," "dialectic," and "rhetoric." "Analytic" was the science of demonstrative reasoning, the kind of reasoning which absolutely guarantees the truth of its conclusion if its premises are true, as in mathematical reasoning. Dialectic was concerned with argumentative dialogue between disputants, as in legal disputes, and rhetoric was concerned with the language which would persuade different audiences. Modern logic derives from Aristotle's analytic and pays no attention to dialectic or rhetoric. What Aristotle called demonstrative reasoning is what we now call deductively valid reasoning (cf. Chapter 9).

The most famous element in Aristotle's analytic is probably his theory of the syllogism. Since the theory of the syllogism is an easy way to introduce some of the ideas which are fundamental to the tradition of logic as we now have it, we shall explain its elements very briefly now. The most important notion in this tradition is that of "logical form," and the reader should notice that logicians do not define deductive validity as we defined it in Chapter 9, but in terms of the notion of "logical form." We introduce this idea now in the context of syllogistic reasoning.

3.1 The Notion of Logical Form Introduced

Here is an example of a syllogism:

(1) All philosophers are people who argue logically.
     Some people who argue logically are very trying.
Therefore
     Some philosophers are very trying.

Notice that this little piece of reasoning has two premises and a conclusion (the conclusion is clearly signaled by the use of the word "therefore"); notice also that the premises have one term in common ("people who argue logically") and that the conclusion contains the other two terms; all syllogisms are alike in these respects.

However there is more to it than that. Here is another example of a syllogism:

(2) All students are intelligent people.
     Some intelligent people are very poor.
Therefore
     Some students are very poor.

Notice that this second syllogism has the same "shape," "pattern," or "form" as the first one. If we write A in place of the terms "philosopher" (1) and "student" (2), B in place of "people who argue logically" (1) and "intelligent people" (2), and C in place of "very trying" (1) and "very poor" (2), then both arguments exhibit the pattern:

     All A's are B's.
     Some B's are C's.
Therefore
     Some A's are C's.

Logicians say that both these arguments have the same logical form. Though their subject matter is quite different, if one abstracts from their subject matter to the underlying "logical skeleton" or "logical structure," it is the same in both cases. The same logically key words, namely "all" and "some," occur in the same positions within the same pattern in both cases. Here we have the beginnings of the idea of logical form which is central to modern logic, and the words "all" and "some" are what logicians call "logical constants." They are called logical constants because, however the subject matter of the argument varies, they always mean the same and always play the same logical role. Both these constants will figure importantly in what we say later (notice incidentally that there are synonyms for "all" and "some," like "every," "any," "each," "there are," and so on, so we are not speaking of these two words alone, but of all the logical words which function like them). And, as we shall see shortly, there are other very important logical constants than just "all" and "some."

Besides the examples we have already given, there are many other logical forms which a syllogism can exhibit; here are three more:

(3) Anyone who is sane can do logic.
    Anyone who can do logic should have the vote.
Therefore
    Anyone who is sane should have the vote.

(4) No one who reads the *Wall Street Journal* is stupid.
    Everyone who reads the *Wall Street Journal* is rich.
Therefore
    No one who is rich is stupid.

(5) All poets have long hair.
    Some students do not have long hair.
Therefore
    Some students are not poets.

Notice that example (3) has the logical form "All A's are B's and all B's are C's, so all A's are C's." (4) has the form "No A's are B's and all A's are C's, so no C's are B's. And (5) has the form "All A's are B's and some C's are not B's, so some C's are not A's."

All of these count as *syllogisms,* simply because a syllogism is defined as an argument which has two premises and a conclusion where all three sentences are of one of the following forms, (A) "All A's are B's," (E) "No A's are B's," (I) "Some A's as are B's," (O) "Some A's are not B's," and the two premises have one term in common. The terms which are common to the two premises in the examples we have given so far are (1) "people who argue logically," (2) "very intelligent people," (3) "one who can do logic," (4) "one who reads the *Wall Street Journal,*" and (5) "one who has long hair."

Syllogisms, then, are very distinctive kinds of argument. Indeed, you are very unlikely ever to encounter one in the course of ordinary language argumentation. However, Aristotle's theory of the syllogism has been taught in colleges and universities as a central part of logic ever since there have been colleges and universities. Its historical importance has been immense. However, it is obvious to anyone thinking about understanding and evaluating real reasoning, that the theory of the syllogism has almost no relevance to that issue. How logic, as the science of reasoning, could have been so sidetracked for centuries from studying real argumentation, is a fascinating story to which we shall return very briefly later.

3.2 Which Syllogisms Are Good Arguments? Deductive Validity Explained

Before we, too, get sidetracked, we need to say a little about how to decide which syllogisms are good arguments and which are bad, though we need say relatively little about this because syllogisms are so simple to handle. The first thing to say about evaluating syllogistic arguments is that, like any other argument, they may fail to establish their conclusion in two *quite different* ways. Every argument has premises which are presented as justifying (at least to some degree) its conclusion. It should be intuitively clear then, that an argument can fail to establish its conclusion *either*

because at least one of its premises is false or

because even if its premises were true, they would not justify its conclusion.

Here are two examples of syllogisms which fail to establish their conclusions in these two *different* ways:

(6) All American school children are well educated.
     Everyone who is well educated plays basketball.
Therefore
     All American school children play basketball.

Most informed people would dispute the truth of both premises in this example! However, the reasoning is deductively valid in the sense defined in Chapter 9, that is, *the truth of the premises absolutely guarantees the truth of the conclusion.* In this case then the argument fails to establish its conclusion because although the logic of the inference is faultless, the argument is based on false premises.

Moving to our second case, consider the following example,

(7) All newborn babies are illogical.
     No newborn babies can play chess.
Therefore
     No illogical people can play chess.

Presumably both of these premises are true, and presumably the conclusion is true too, but the question is whether the reasoning supports its conclusion, that is, in this case, could the premises be true and the conclusion false? Reason it through; if all newborn babies are illogical and none of them can play chess, does it follow that no illogical people can play chess? The conclusion may well be true, but that is not the issue; the question is whether the premises could be true and the conclusion false.

One of the commonest "moves" in ordinary argumentation, when you want to show that someone's reasoning is faulty is to say, "But you might as well say . . ." and then produce a *parallel* piece of reasoning which is clearly bad reasoning; this shows your listener that the first argument was faulty too. Here is a famous example due to Lewis Carroll:

> A. "I mean what I say because I say what I mean."
> B. "You might as well argue that you eat what you see because you see what you eat."

If we now look back to example (7) and replace the word "illogical" by the word "smelly," it is surely easy to see that the premises of the resulting argument could be true and the conclusion false! In doing this, haven't we shown that (7) is not a safe pattern of reasoning, that there are parallel examples—displaying the same pattern of reasoning—where the reasoning does *not* support its conclusion because it has true reasons and a false conclusion?

Logic builds on the intuition that a parallel argument can show that a given argument is unsound and redefines the notion of deductive validity in terms of this idea. In short, logicians say that

> an argument is deductively valid if and only if it exhibits a deductively valid logical form, and a logical form is deductively valid if and only if there is no argument of that form which has true premises and a false conclusion.

Thus, on this conception of deductive validity, if we want to check whether an argument is deductively valid, we do not simply inspect the argument itself to see if the premises could be true and the conclusion false. We have to check that there is *no* argument of that form which has true premises and a false conclusion; and so we have to look at the form rather than the substantial argument itself. To put it another way, on this tradition a particular argument is deductively valid provided it accords with a valid principle of inference, and a principle of inference is valid provided there are no inferences of that form leading from true premises to a false conclusion.

Looking back to example (7), it is clear that the argument with "smelly" inserted in place of "illogical" has the same logical form as (7) and clearly argues from true premises to a false conclusion. Thus it shows that the logical form of argument (7) is invalid, hence we can conclude that argument (7) is not deductively valid. Hence, (7) fails to establish its conclusion in the second of the ways we mentioned above; in this argument its premises do not justify its conclusion.

In general, logicians since Aristotle have not been much interested in discussing how one might decide the truth or falsity of the premises of an argument. Traditionally, they have focused on the reasoning step, the inference that is made from the premises, and on whether that is logically compelling. In the case of syllogisms, this means, "Could the premises be true and the conclusion false?" or "Is this syllogism deductively valid?"; these are the questions which have interested logicians.

There are several routine procedures which can decide this question for syllogistic arguments—which enable us to check the logical form of syllogistic arguments for validity. We do not need to go into these procedures, which include, for example, the use of Venn diagrams. It is sufficient for present purposes to ask the reader to reflect on the meanings of the logical constants "all," "some," "no," and so on, and to think the arguments through. In our examples (1) and (2), this will soon convince the reader that if the premises are both true, then the conclusion must also be true (picture it in your mind's eye: "if every A is a B and some B's are C's, then some of the A's—the ones which were also B's—must be C's). If our reasoning is correct (and it is), this shows that arguments (1) and (2) have a deductively valid logical form.

If now we look at one of our other examples, number (4), we shall see that the premises could be true and the conclusion false (again, picture in your mind's eye); "people who read the *Wall Street Journal*" and "stupid people" are groups which do not overlap; however, if it is true that everyone who reads the *Journal* is rich, there could be rich people (who don't read the *Journal*) who are stupid. Alternatively, to show that an argument is invalid one can construct a parallel argument which obviously has true premises and a false conclusion. For example, consider the following argument:

No women are men.

All women are human.

Therefore

No men are human.

As these preceding examples suggest, generally speaking it is not difficult to decide whether a syllogism is deductively valid or not.

3.3 Basic and Derived Syllogisms: The Beginnings of Foundations?

Aristotle systematized the theory of the syllogism, identifying some valid syllogisms as basic (cf. Kneale and Kneale, 73ff.) and others as derivable from the basic ones. It requires very little reflection to see that our examples (1), (2), and (3) are valid; example (5) is less obvious, but its validity can be derived from (3) (Kneale and Kneale, 76). This has been a pattern which logicians have followed ever since; some logical principles are identified as basic and others as derived from the basic ones; it has long seemed natural in logic to organize our knowledge of logical principles in a way which suggests that it is derived from foundations. Though Aristotle organized our knowledge of the principles of syllogistic logic in this kind of way, we do not need to go into the details here, because it will be more instructive to do this with what is called "propositional logic." For those who wish to know more about Aristotle's theory of the syllogism, see Prior, which contains an excellent account.

3.4 Concluding Comments and Questions on the Syllogism

As we already remarked, you will almost never meet a syllogism in the course of real, ordinary, everyday reasoning (we don't think there are any in this book, even though some people who have had a philosophical education occasionally use this form of argument!). However, if we want to theorize about reasoning, syllogisms are easy arguments to handle, so they are a good place to start. They have introduced us to the idea of logical form, to some logical constants, to the logicians' notion of "deductive validity," and to the idea of "basic" versus "derived" principles of reasoning, and these are all fundamental ideas in the tradition of formal logic.

Exercise   Identify which of the following are syllogisms and decide which of these are deductively valid. Comment on which you think establish their conclusions.

(Ex. 1) All wine drinkers are very talkative.
          No wine drinker can be trusted to keep a secret.
Therefore
          No one who is very talkative can be trusted to keep a secret.

(Ex. 2) All diligent students are successful.
          All drunken students deserve to fail.
Therefore
          No diligent students deserve to fail.

(Ex. 3) All cool cats understand French.
          Some lazy dogs are cool cats.
Therefore
          Some lazy dogs understand French.

Aristotle's theory of the syllogism has been of immense importance in the history of logic and is interesting so far as it goes. However, most arguments are not syllogistic in form, and Aristotle's theory says little or nothing about arguments which exhibit other forms. So let us now move on to the beginnings of what is called "sentential" or "propositional logic."

4. The Beginnings of Sentential or Propositional Logic: The Stoics

Here is an example of an argument which is not syllogistic at all:

  (i) Either the ancient Greeks invented logic or the scholars of ancient India did. The scholars of ancient India said nothing about logic. So, the ancient Greeks invented logic.

This argument has the form, "Either A is true or B is. B is false. So A is true." Let us look now at three more examples of reasoning in ordinary English:

(ii) If the ancient Greeks invented logic then the scholars of ancient India didn't. But the scholars of ancient India constructed elaborate logical theories long before the ancient Greeks, so the ancient Greeks didn't invent logic.

(iii) If induction can be justified at all then the justification will rest either on deductive reasoning or on inductive reasoning. The justification of induction cannot rest on deductive or on inductive reasoning. Therefore induction cannot be justified at all.

(iv) If there is a private language which only one person can understand then it must be possible for one person to decide (alone) whether a word is always used in the same way. It is impossible for one person to decide (alone) whether a word is always used in the same way. Therefore there is no such thing as a private language which only one person can understand.

These three examples are all expressed quite naturally and one can easily envisage contexts in which they might actually be used (for example, see 9.7 and 5.4[ii] for two of them). Furthermore, it is also clear when they are placed next to each other like this, that they exhibit the same pattern of argument; each has the same logical skeleton or what we just called logical form. Though they are about quite different subjects, each is saying, "The first thing implies the second. The second is mistaken or false. So the first thing is mistaken or false," where "the first" and "the second" refer to sentences (or propositions) about quite different subjects. It should be clear to anyone who understands English (in particular who understands the use of "implies" and "is false") that any argument of this form is deductively valid—if its premises are true, its conclusion must be true—whatever the subject matter. So we have here a principle of inference (or principle of logic) which is true for any subject.

4.1 Some Principles of Inference

Though Aristotle said nothing about such patterns of reasoning, the Stoics (ancient Greek philosophers who lived about a hundred years after Aristotle) did extract the principles of what we now call sentential or propositional logic from the context of their use in argument. They recognized that in the course of reasoning and arguing we assume principles of inference like the ones we mentioned in the last section—without considering or questioning them at all. Though we normally take them for granted and use them without thinking about them, clearly we can easily make them explicit if we choose to—as indeed the Stoics did. The logical principles which the Stoics identified as underlying everyday reasoning were the following, where the phrases "the first" and "the second" refer to whole sentences:

1. If the first then the second; but the first; therefore the second.
2. If the first, then the second; but not the second; therefore not the first.
3. Not both the first and the second; but the first; therefore not the second.
4. Either the first or the second; but the first; therefore not the second.
5. Either the first or the second; but not the second; therefore the first.

This collection of basic principles of logic is the beginning of what is needed if one is to axiomatize logic as Euclid axiomatized geometry. Indeed, they will probably remind the reader of Euclid's axioms (for a brief discussion of axiomatization and of Euclid's axioms, see Chapter 6). Furthermore, for those who believe in "foundations" of knowledge, principles like these are very plausible candidates as foundations for logic; we shall have more to say about this later.

Strangely, though the beginnings of this branch of logic were first expounded by the Stoics over two thousand years ago, the subject remained largely undeveloped until about two hundred years ago. Then, in the nineteenth century, several philosophers and mathematicians, including Bernard Bolzano (1781–1848), Augustus De Morgan (1806–1871), George Boole (1815–1864), and others, made important contributions to the subject, until finally Gottlob Frege (1848–1925), the father of modern logic, completely systematized the subject, very much as Euclid had systematized geometry over two thousand years earlier. The result was what we now call "classical" propositional logic, and it is this tradition, deriving essentially from Frege, which we shall now explain (since this is the logical tradition which is of central relevance to the arguments of this book).

This is perhaps the point to note that Frege was very careful to distinguish between a sentence and the *thought* it expresses, because different sentences could express the same thought, for example "Tom chased Jerry" and "Jerry was chased by Tom." Since it is the thought which is expressed by a sentence (rather than any particular way of expressing it) which is relevant to the validity of any argument in which the sentence occurs, and since logicians have generally called such thoughts "propositions," they have tended to speak of propositions and of propositional logic rather than of sentences and sentential logic. Since this usage is so common, we shall generally follow it.

4.2 Logical Form and Deductive Validity Again

Before we expound Frege's system, let us return to what we were saying about the logical form and deductive validity of propositional arguments and let us explain these ideas more fully. To simplify the process of explanation, let us agree that, instead of referring to "the first" proposition and "the second" proposition, and so on, we can use capital letters to stand in place of such propositions (as we did briefly at the beginning of section 4 of this Appendix). This is the first step toward making the presentation of the principles of inference which belong to the logic of propositions—to propositional logic—much easier to read. Allowing this then, the Stoics identified the following principles of propositional logic:

1. If A then B. A (is true). Therefore B (is true).
2. If A then B. B is false. Therefore not-A.
3. Not both A and B. A (is true). Therefore not-B.
4. Either A or B. A (is true). Therefore not-B.
5. Either A or B. B is false. Therefore A (is true).

Their contention was that any argument exhibiting one of these forms was deductively valid, both in the sense that *if its premises were true its conclusion must also be true,* and also in the sense that *there are no arguments of these forms with true premises and a false conclusion.*

Some explanation of these forms, as we have expressed them, is probably necessary.

1. We put the phrase "is true" in parentheses because it is not really necessary—or as logicians like to say in this context, it is redundant. Let us explain: if, in the course of ordinary conversation, I say that "Madonna is a mega-star," then I am presenting this claim as true; I do not need to add "is true" because everyone will understand that when one makes such a claim in normal circumstances, it is being presented as true, so "Madonna is a mega-star" and " 'Madonna is a mega-star' is true" or "It's true that Madonna is a mega-star" mean the same (except perhaps for rhetorical force). In future then, we shall omit the parenthetical phrase "is true," and it will always be understood that a proposition (A, B, or whatever) is being presented as being true unless otherwise stated.

2. There are several ways of saying that a proposition is false. For example, consider the proposition "The Dallas Cowboys are the richest football team in the United States." To deny this claim one could say "The Dallas Cowboys are *not* the richest football team in the United States" or *"It's false that* the Dallas Cowboys are the richest football team in the United States" or "The claim that the Dallas Cowboys are the richest football team in the U.S. is false (untrue)," etc. The important point here is that for any proposition A there is always an opposite claim, which logicians usually call "the negation" of A and write as "not-A." If A is true then "not-A" is false, and if A is false then "not-A" is true. We shall follow the practice of logicians in speaking of "not-A" when we wish to refer to the negation of a proposition.

Notice that negation is a more complicated idea than might appear from what has just been said. Consider the proposition C, "All Canadians love the United States"; what is the negation of this proposition C, that is, the proposition which is false if C is true and true if C is false? Is it "All Canadians do not love the United States" or "Not all Canadians love the United States" or "Some Canadians do not love the United States" or "No Canadians love the United States"? We leave this as an exercise for the moment. It is sufficient for present purposes to note that every proposition A has a negation, that is, a sentence which is false if A is true and true if A is false. A little reflection will soon convince the reader that there may be many different ways of articulating "not-A" in ordinary English, but logicians always express it in the same way, as "not-A."

3. Accepting what has been said so far, it is clear that there are certain key words and phrases which occur in the principles of inference identified by the Stoics. These are the key logical words which occur in such inferences; they are such words and phrases as "not," "if . . . then . . .," "and," and "either . . . or . . . ." These are the words which determine whether such inferences are deductively valid, just as "all," "some," "no," and so on, determined this for syllogisms. Of course, these words and phrases have many equivalents in ordinary English. For example, "A but B" and "A however B" often mean the same as "A and B" for logical purposes; one sometimes uses "but" to signal that, given A one might not expect B, but otherwise "A but B" means that both A and B are true. Similarly, "If A then B" may be expressed by saying "A implies B," or "Given A, B follows," and so on. We shall not discuss all these equivalents here. All we need to notice is that we have identified *some* of the key words in English which play a crucial role in reasoning. Whatever the subject matter of the argument, whether it is about football or philosophy, these words function in the same way so far as the logic of the reasoning is concerned; as we explained in connection with Aristotle's theory of the syllogism, they are called logical constants for this reason.

4.3 Comparisons between Propositional Logic and Syllogistic Logic

What are we to say, in summary, about the logic of propositions as we have introduced it so far? As in the case of the syllogism, it is easy to see that there are some basic principles of reasoning which are true of whole sentences, that there are some propositional arguments which are deductively valid, and that there are logical constants other than those we already introduced in our account of Aristotle's theory of the syllogism. We shall also shortly see that there appears to be a distinction between basic (foundational) principles of propositional logic and more complex, derived ones.

5. Deciding Which Principles of Propositional Logic Are Deductively Valid

In dealing with the arguments and logical principles we have encountered so far, we have relied on the intuitive judgment of readers to "see" whether the arguments are deductively valid or not. In many ways there is nothing wrong with relying on our intuitions. At least where relatively simple arguments and principles are concerned, our intuition seems to be quite reliable. But what should we do in more complicated cases, and can we do anything to supplement or support our intuitions? Traditionally, logicians have proceeded in two different ways in attempting to answer these questions. We'll call these the "proof method" and the "meaning method." Let us look at the proof method first.

Notice that, given the logicians' conception of deductive validity, if we wish to judge the validity of arguments we must attend to the logical principles which lie behind them, so in what follows the focus of interest will be on how to assess the validity of *principles* of propositional logic rather than particular arguments.

5.1 The Proof Method: Basic and Derived Principles of Inference

On this approach to justifying our judgments about which (arguments and) principles are valid and which are not, the logician proceeds in the following way. First, choose some "basic" principles which seem incontrovertible (self-evident), and then show how more complex principles may be "derived" from these using only basic principles—principles which have been chosen precisely because they seem absolutely safe and reliable. Here is the outline of a simple example, which takes as its "basic" principle the first principle in the Stoics' list, generally known as modus ponens:

> Suppose that you accept the principle known as modus ponens (namely, given that "A implies B" and that A is true), we can draw the conclusion that B is true. But suppose also that you are not sure whether it is true that if A implies B and B implies C then A implies C, that is, whether "implies" is *transitive*. We can prove the transitivity of "implies" from modus ponens as follows. Let us first assume that A implies B, and B implies C are both true. If we now assume that A is true, it follows by modus ponens (from A, and A implies B) that B is true. But now if B is true, again it follows by modus ponens (from B, and B implies C) that C is true. So, if we first assume that A implies B, and B implies C, and then we assume A, we can infer that C must be true, so if A implies B, and B implies C, then A implies C.

This derivation mainly uses modus ponens to prove the transitivity of "implies" (it actually assumes some other very obvious logical principles too, but we need not delay over these here). This kind of procedure, then, derives more complex logical principles from simpler ones; it provides reasons for accepting more complex principles in terms of simpler ones.

Exercise   The reader might like to try to construct a similar "proof" of the principle of *reductio ad absurdum* using the first two Stoic principles and whatever other principles seem necessary and correct. *Reductio ad absurdum* is the principle which says that if *A* implies a contradiction *(B* and not-*B)* then *A* is false. (This is not an easy exercise.)

Provided such a proof procedure starts from deductively valid principles and uses only deductively valid principles to derive further results, then only deductively valid principles will be derived. It may be difficult, however, to be *absolutely sure* that one's basic principles and inferential procedures are deductively valid. For this reason, you have to scrutinize the derived principles carefully. If the derived principles all seem to be deductively valid, this increases your confidence that your basic intuitions are right. On the other hand, if a derived principle does not seem to be deductively valid, then you either have to change one or more of your basic principles or you have to accept that your intuitions are unreliable where more complex principles are concerned. The point is that it is very difficult to be sure that your basic principles are correct except by deriving a significant number of other principles from them and scrutinizing these, but as you succeed in deriving principles from one another, the way they all hang together gives you increasing confidence that your basic intuitions are right. (Notice that what we are saying here mirrors what was said in Chapter 6 when we explained the case for foundationalism in the case of a priori knowledge and in Chapter 7 when we argued in favor of a coherentist position.)

One final point is worth making here; it might be that the basic intuitions of which we were just speaking allow you to prove *all* the principles which you accept as applying to arguments of a particular kind, say syllogistic arguments or propositional arguments or whatever. In that case, you have good reason to think that you have captured the notion of deductive validity for those kinds of arguments. Suppose you try to think of principles of propositional reasoning which cannot be derived from your "basic" theory. Suppose that you try very hard, but that you fail. Then you can feel confident that your theory is, in an intuitively clear sense, complete. The position here is exactly as it was with Euclidean geometry.

5.2 The Semantic Method

On this approach to justifying our judgments about which logical principles are valid and which are not, the logician focuses on the meanings of the logical constants. Let us begin to explain this procedure, then, by explaining how logicians see the logical constants.

5.21 The Logical Constants

The logical constants we have so far identified in the context of propositional logic are "if . . . then . . . ," "and," "either . . . or . . . ," and "not" (or their ordinary language equivalents). Of course, these phrases are not used only in the course of reasoning of the kind we are discussing. They may be used in many other contexts. For example, they may be used to issue a threat, "Either you hand over the money or I shoot"; to ask a hypothetical question, "If I loan you my car, will you write my essay?"; to declare a position, "Bush for President, NOT!"; and so on. But what interests us is how they function in factual argumentative contexts in which reasons are presented to support a conclusion. If we look back at some of the examples we have given and some of the principles we have identified, or simply reflect on the way we use these phrases in reasoning, it is fairly easy to see that they function as follows.

"Not-P" is the easiest logical constant. We have already accepted that, for every proposition P there is an opposite one—its negation—which is false if P is true and true if P is false. In fact, we can represent this in what is called a "truth table," where the truth or falsity of P (its "truth value") is placed under P and the corresponding truth value of not-P is placed under "not-P":

P	Not–P
T	T F
F	F T

"P and Q" is quite straightforward too. If P is true and Q is true then the whole proposition "P and Q" (the whole "conjunction" as it is called), is true too. Otherwise—if P or Q or both are false—then the whole conjunct is false. If this is not absolutely clear, think of an example: "Clint Eastwood is the mayor of Carmel, and President Clinton is a personal friend of Clint Eastwood"—this conjunction is true if both the "conjuncts" are, otherwise it is false. One might be tempted to say that the conjunction is "half true and half false" but there are no "halfway houses" in classical logic; a proposition is either true or it is false. Another way of putting this point would be to say that logic interprets "P and Q" to mean that *both P and Q* are true, and clearly if only one of them is true, it must be *false* to say that both of them are true. Again we can represent the position in a truth table. This time we write the truth value of P and of Q under each letter respectively, and the truth value of the whole conjunction under "P and Q." Notice that this time, however, the truth table has four lines and not two, because we have to tabulate all possible combinations of truth values of P and of Q (when P is true, Q may be either true or false, and when P is false, Q may also be either true or false).

P	Q	P and Q
T	T	T
T	F	F
F	T	F
F	F	F

"*P* or *Q*" is a little more complicated, though not much. The problem here is that in ordinary language we use "either . . . or . . ." in two different ways. Here are two examples to illustrate the different usage. First, "Either Carl Lewis is the fastest man in the world or Linford Christie is" where the suggestion is that the two alternatives ("disjuncts" as they are often called) cannot be true together. Second, "Either we shall go swimming or we shall have a picnic" where there is nothing to prevent both disjuncts being true—we go swimming *and* take a picnic. The first use of "or" is called by logicians the "exclusive" use—because it intends to exclude the case in which both disjuncts are true—and the second use is called the "nonexclusive" or the "inclusive" use of "or"—because it allows that both disjuncts are true. Logicians have nearly always preferred to work with the inclusive use of "or," so the standard truth table for "*P* or *Q*" is:

P	*Q*	*P* or *Q*
T	T	T
T	F	T
F	T	T
F	F	F

The truth table for the exclusive "or" simply has F under "*P* or *Q*" when both conjuncts are true (in the first line of the truth table). It is an easy exercise to define the exclusive use of "or" using the inclusive "or," "and," and "not," so logicians who prefer to work with the inclusive "or" remain able to express both senses of "or" within their logical systems. (See section 5.23, Stoic principle 4.)

"If *P* then *Q*" is the most difficult case. We shall not go into all the arguments about how this phrase works in reasoning. We shall simply explain the standard view. Let us do this by reference to a simple example: "If the future resembles the past (*P*), then induction is a safe method of inference (*Q*)." One thing is surely clear: if *P* is true (the future resembles the past), but *Q* is false (because induction often leads us astray and is *not* a safe method of inference), then the whole hypothetical claim (as it is often called) "if *P* then *Q*" must be false. We shall not discuss the other three cases at any length; logicians have long agreed that, in the cases where *P* and *Q* are both true, or where *P* is false, the whole hypothetical is true (for a classic discussion see Quine [1952] who explains that on this account *a true proposition is implied by any proposition* and *a false proposition implies any proposition,* but that these paradoxes should not worry us!). The basic justification for the classic view is that our main concern is to guarantee that we never infer something false from something true, and this "ruling" about the truth value of "if . . . then . . ." has precisely that effect—in short, it works! The truth table for "if *P* then *Q*" then looks like this:

P	Q	If P then Q
T	T	T
T	F	F
F	T	T
F	F	T

For present purposes, it doesn't matter whether this truth table seems natural to you or puzzling. The point is that we have just identified what are universally treated by logicians as some of the most basic logical constants, and we have explained the meaning they are given within the tradition of modern logic. (Incidentally, this is the tradition which underlies the operation of all modern computers, so one might argue that it is vindicated to a considerable extent by their success.)

5.22 Using Logical Symbols

Mathematicians find ordinary English too cumbersome for doing mathematics, so they employ a symbolic language with clearly defined symbols, like + and =. In the same way, logicians find ordinary English both cumbersome and unclear, so they too employ a symbolic language for expressing logical ideas. In particular they use the following symbols to stand for the logical constants we just introduced; not-$P = \neg P$; P and $Q = P$ & Q; either P or $Q = P$ v Q; and if P then $Q = P \supset Q$. The meaning of these symbols is given by the truth tables associated with their English equivalents, so their meaning is, like + and = in mathematics, very clearly defined. Besides these symbols, logicians commonly use the sign $\vDash$ to stand for the word "therefore"; since it will simplify some of our subsequent exposition we shall use this sign too. One advantage of using such symbols is that their meaning is unambiguous; the corollary of this is that, when translating ordinary English into logical symbolism, we have to be careful not to lose the real meaning of what is said. This is not a trivial problem, though we shall leave it on one side here.

One remaining point needs to be made. It is clear that

Phil pondered and Quinn questioned or Randy replied

is ambiguous. Does it mean "either (Phil pondered and Quinn questioned) or Randy replied"? Or does it mean "Phil pondered and (either Quinn questioned or Randy replied)"? Using an obvious notation, does it mean $(P$ & $Q)$ v R or does it mean P & $(Q$ v $R)$? These are different because if Phil did not ponder (P is false) and Quinn did question and Randy did reply (Q and R are both true), then the first is false and the second is true. Thus, in order to express the logical form of sentences using the symbols we have just introduced for various logical constants, and in order to do this unambiguously, we shall need to use parentheses in the way we have just indicated. Thus our basic logical notation will be ¬, &, v, ⊃, (,), and *P, Q, R*, and so on, to stand for propositions which are either true or false.

5.23 Deciding Which Logical Principles Are Valid: Using Truth Tables

Now that we have introduced the notation of propositional logic, we can express the logical form of arguments symbolically; to put it slightly differently, we can now express the logical principles which underlie arguments in the symbolism of formal logic (i.e., a logic which focuses on the *logical form* of propositions). If we look back to the principles of Stoic logic, we can see that they can be expressed as follows in the notation of formal logic using the comma "," to separate the premises of the argument:

1. $(A \supset B), A \vDash B$.
2. $(A \supset B), \neg B \vDash \neg A$.
3. $\neg (A \ \& \ B), A \vDash \neg B$.
4. $((A \ v \ B) \ \& \ \neg (A \ \& \ B)), A \vDash \neg B$.
5. $(A \ v \ B), \neg B \vDash A$.

As we have indicated, there may be difficulties about translating some reasoning into this symbolic notation partly because of the meanings which the truth tables give to the logical constants, and to ⊃ in particular. But there is a great advantage to using this symbolism, which is that it yields a very simple, and quite mechanical procedure for deciding whether a principle of inference belonging to propositional logic—a propositional logical form—is valid or not. Suppose we have an argument which has two premises with the logical form *P*, and ¬*P* v *Q*, and the conclusion *Q*; the question we have to answer if we are to decide whether the argument is deductively valid is whether there is any argument of that form in which the premises are true and the conclusion false. One intuitively obvious way to do this is to assume that there is an argument of this form which has true premises and a false conclusion and then to use the truth table for the logical constants to see if that is really possible. Two things may happen: either it is possible or it isn't; if it is, the initial assumption is true, and if it isn't, the initial assumption is false. To spell this out a little more: if the initial assumption is true, then the argument form is not deductively valid. But perhaps as we work through the implications of our initial assumption we find that it is impossible for it to be true. In that case we know that the argument form is valid, because there can be no argument of that form with true premises and a false conclusion. Let us talk this idea through with our example.

Here we display the logical form of the premises of the argument and its conclusion; the numbered steps are then explained.

P,	¬ P v Q	⊨	Q
T	T F T F		F
(1)	(3) (4) (1) (2)		(1)
X	X		

Step number (1) is simply our starting position; we begin by *assuming* that there is an argument of this form in which the premises are both true and the conclusion is false. Step (2) records the fact that if Q is false in the conclusion, the same proposition must also be false elsewhere in the reasoning. Step (3) is then computed by using the truth table for v; if the whole premise ¬P v Q is true and Q is false, then by the truth table for v, ¬P must be true. Step (4) is now computed by using the truth table for ¬; if ¬P is true, then P must be false.

Notice that in working out what *must* be the case if the premises of this reasoning are to be true while the conclusion is false, we find that P must be both *true and false at the same time*. Since this is clearly impossible, our original assumption (that there was an argument of this form with true premises and a false conclusion) *must be false*. Hence, arguments exhibiting this logical form must be deductively valid—if they have true premises, then they must have a true conclusion too.

The method we have just used will enable the interested reader to check the validity of many argument forms belonging to propositional logic and variations on this method will enable *any* such argument form to be tested.

Exercise   Use the method just explained to test the validity of the following inference forms:

1. $P \supset Q, \neg Q \vDash P$.
2. $P \supset Q, \neg Q \vDash \neg P$.
3. $P \supset \neg Q, R \supset Q \vDash R \supset P$.
4. $P \supset Q, P \supset \neg Q \vDash \neg P$.
5. $P \supset \neg Q, R \supset Q, P \vDash \neg R$.

An alternative way of testing to see if such argument forms are valid is to construct what is called a truth table for the formula which expresses the logical principle which underlies the argument. In the case of our example above the principle we consider is $(P \ \& \ (\neg P \ v \ Q)) \supset Q$. Immediately below we display the steps by which a truth table is constructed, and below that we explain the process in full.

	P	Q	¬P	¬P v Q	P & (¬P v Q))	(P & (¬P v Q)) ⊃ Q
(i)	T	T	F	T	T	T
(ii)	T	F	F	F	F	T
(iii)	F	T	T	T	F	T
(iv)	F	F	T	T	F	T
	(1)	(2)	(3)	(4)	(5)	(6)

The columns numbered (1) through (6) show the six successive steps which have to be taken to construct a truth table for the whole formula $(P \,\&\, (\neg P \,v\, Q)) \,Q$, from the truth tables for the logical constants $\neg$, $\&$, v, and $\supset$. Columns (1) and (2) display all the possible combinations of truth values which P and Q could have (if P is true, Q may be either true or false, and if P is false, again Q may be either true or false, so there are four possible combinations in all—displayed in lines [i] through [iv]). Column (3) is computed from column (1) by using the truth table for $\neg$, which says that if P is true, then $\neg P$ is false and if P is false, then $\neg P$ is true. Similarly, column (4) is computed from columns (3) and (2) using the truth table for v. Then column (5) is computed from columns (1) and (4) by using the truth table for $\&$. Finally, column (6) is computed from columns (5) and (1) using the truth table for $\supset$. The order in which these steps are taken is determined as follows: first assign truth values to the proposition letters which occur in the formula; then assign truth values to the negations of proposition letters; next assign truth values to logical constants which connect expressions whose truth value has already been determined; continue this process until there are no more logical constants to deal with.

Notice that in the example we have just discussed, column (6) contains only the truth value T under the logical constant $\supset$. This means that *whatever* combination of truth values the premises have, the claim that the premises imply the conclusion comes out true. In other words, there can be no argument exhibiting this pattern of reasoning which has true premises and a false conclusion: this is because the truth table effectively considers *all possible arguments*, since only the truth or falsity of the propositions which occur in an argument really matters to its validity. Such a truth table then shows that the logical principle it expresses must be deductively valid.

Exercise   Construct truth tables for the following formulas of propositional logic and decide which are deductively valid logical principles:

1. $((P \,v\, Q) \,\&\, \neg \,(P \,\&\, Q)) \supset \neg \, Q$.
2. $(P \,\&\, Q) \supset \neg \,(\neg \, Q \,v\, \neg \, R)$.
3. $(((P \,v\, Q) \,\&\, \neg \,(P \,\&\, Q)) \,\&\, \neg \, P) \supset \neg \, Q$.

The *most important fact* about the procedures we have just explained is that they provide an entirely mechanical way of deciding whether an inference exhibiting such a logical form is deductively valid or not. Given the definitions of the logical constants which we have explained above, then the process of deciding whether a principle of propositional logic is valid is an entirely routine one—requiring no imagination or intelligence. Indeed a machine could carry out.

5.3 Summarizing the Position So Far

Let us summarize the position we have reached, especially concerning propositional logic. On the classical logical view which we have been expounding, whether an argument is deductively valid depends on its logical form. *A particular piece of reasoning is valid if and only if it exhibits a valid logical form, and a logical form is valid if and only if there is no argument of that form which has true premises and a false conclusion.* Hence, if we wish to decide whether a given argument is deductively valid we have to exhibit its logical form and then test that form by some suitable means. In the case of principles of propositional logic (propositional logical forms) there are procedures employing the truth tables for the logical constants which enable us to check quite mechanically whether a principle is deductively valid or not. Alternatively we can attempt to derive such principles from simpler, more basic ones, which are thought to be self-evident.

6. Alternative Propositional Logics

In the previous section we described the so-called classical logical tradition deriving from Frege and others. Not all logicians have accepted that the classical tradition is correct. In this section we explain an alternative view and its significance.

At the beginning of this century, a Dutch mathematician called Brouwer (1881–1966) challenged various principles of logic which the classical tradition accepted. For example, he argued that the law of excluded middle, the principle which says that a proposition is either true or false ($P \vee \neg P$), is not universally true. He also argued that other classical logical principles failed to hold universally, for example he rejected the principle which says that not-(not-)P implies P, ($\neg \neg P \supset P$), and many others. How could Brouwer challenge logical principles which had seemed so certain to so many for so long? If we look back at our exposition of classical propositional logic it is very hard to see how ($P \vee \neg P$) or ($\neg \neg P \supset P$) could fail to be true. Just look at the meanings of the logical constants; given that not-P is true when P is false and false when P is true, how could these principles fail to be universally true?

The short answer is relatively obvious when the question is put like that; the logical constants must be understood differently from the way in which they are understood in the classical tradition. This is not to say that they are no longer regarded as logical constants—they are still seen as meaning the same thing wherever they occur in reasoning—the point is that the meaning which is ascribed to them is different from that spelled out in the truth tables. This was precisely Brouwer's position; he did not accept that the truth tables accurately spelled out the meanings of the logical constants, and he spelled these out differently. Brouwer's ideas came essentially from mathematics (as did the classical ideas about the meanings of the logical constants) and especially from considerations about the infinite. However, we shall not go into the details of Brouwer's mathematical ideas but we shall try instead to give their flavor with nonmathematical examples.

An easy way to explain the essential idea which lay behind Brouwer's thinking is to say that he believed there was a "middle way" between a proposition's being true and its being false. This is not wholly accurate however, and a better way of explaining it is to say that he believed one should explain the meanings of the logical constants *not* in terms of a notion of truth which regards what is true as something which may lie beyond anything we could possibly find out, but in terms of epistemological notions, in particular in terms of what we can know. Thus for Brouwer, the meaning of "if P then Q" is *not* to be explained in terms of the classical truth table (which few readers will regard as very natural anyway). Rather, it is saying, in the context of mathematics, "we can convert a proof of P into a proof of Q"; and in nonmathematical contexts, "we can convert a justification of P into a justification of Q," where these proofs and justifications refer *only* to things which we as human beings can do and know. So, for example, a justification which required us to check infinitely many numbers separately to see if they had some property would not count as a justification because this is something that is in principle impossible for human beings to do.

Turning to another logical constant, "not-P," for Brouwer its meaning is *not* given by the classical truth table; on his account, to say "not-P" is to say "there is a proof or justification in terms which we as human beings can do and know, which shows that P is not true." Consider the following example. Imagine some very big, perhaps infinite, class of objects like "the class of human beings with a different genetic make-up" and consider the sentence P "Some human being has had or will have 40 natural teeth" (the normal human mouth has 32 teeth). On the classical view this sentence is either true or false regardless of whether we shall ever be in a position to know which, thus (P v $\neg P$). On Brouwer's view, we have to recognize that P is shown to be true if we ever find someone with 40 natural teeth (perhaps with the help of a little genetic engineering), and not-P is shown to be true (or P is shown to be false) if we can show that this has never happened and never will. Of course, we may never be able to settle this matter—perhaps we never find anyone with 40 natural teeth and never prove that this is impossible. Hence, on Brouwer's view, we cannot say "Either P or not-P," we are not entitled to believe that (P v $\neg P$) in all cases.

Whether you find the view we have just expounded plausible or not, many mathematicians and philosophers have taken it sufficiently seriously to grant that perhaps the classical principles of logic are open to challenge. The most important of these for our purposes is Quine. As we mentioned in 7.5(iii), Quine has argued that some of the problems associated with quantum theory (in physics) might be alleviated by abandoning the law of excluded middle—despite its impressive pedigree. Roughly speaking, Quine's argument is that the so-called laws of logic, though central to our web of beliefs, are revisable like any of our other beliefs if this leads to an overall simplification of our system of beliefs. His position is made quite comprehensible provided one grants that it makes sense to explain the meanings of the logical constants in ways which are significantly different from the way in which the classical tradition does it. We suggest that the discussion above indicates how this is indeed possible and indicates that it *can* make perfectly good sense to challenge principles of classical logic and to take seriously talk of "alternative logics."

7. Predicate Logic and Beyond

We explained the ideas which belong to classical propositional logic in some detail because an understanding of these is central to the argument of this book. This is also why we explained the challenge which can be mounted against these ideas from people like Brouwer and Quine. Propositional logic is only the simplest part of classical logic, and there are many arguments which cannot be dealt with formally by the apparatus which we have so far developed. For example, consider the following simple piece of reasoning:

> Suppose everyone is taller than someone else. In that case, there cannot be a shortest person.

Whether this piece of reasoning is valid cannot be determined by using the theory of the syllogism or by using propositional logic. This, and similar but more complex reasoning, would require us to look more deeply into the logical structure of the reasoning if we wished to judge its validity by reference to its logical form. Of course, it is easy to see that our particular example is valid (the conclusion must follow because if there were a shortest person *that* person would have to be taller than someone—a contradiction!), but it is not difficult to construct rapidly more complicated examples where a formal language quickly becomes necessary if we are to judge their validity.

We shall not go into detail about the formal language which is required to articulate the logical form of arguments like our preceding example. We shall just note that in addition to the symbols for whole propositions and the logical constants "and," "or," "not," and "if . . . then . . . ," we would need symbols for quantity words (called *quantifiers*), "all," "everyone," "some," and "someone" (etc.), for *names*, like Socrates and Plato, and for *predicate expressions*, like "is a person," "is taller than," and so on. This is the beginning of what is called first order predicate logic, and it is much more complicated than propositional logic.

Though we do not need to go into details about first order predicate logic, we do need to note one major difference between it and propositional logic. As we noted earlier there is a quite mechanical procedure, namely the truth table procedure, for deciding whether a formula of propositional logic is deductively valid. The most important fact to note about predicate logic is that there is no such mechanical procedure for deciding on the validity of formulae of first order predicate logic (this is generally known as Church's Theorem, after the logician who proved it). Although we can often decide whether a formula of predicate logic is valid, as we could in the case of our simple example, there are infinitely many formulae of predicate logic for which there is no simple decision procedure and it may require great ingenuity to decide on their validity. What this means is that there are many principles of inference whose validity is anything but self-evident. Far from being self-evident, it can be extremely difficult to decide the logical validity of many inferences and inferential principles at the level of predicate logic.

Further Reading

References in the following reading lists are to books and papers, full details of which are given in the bibliography at the end of the book. If authors have just a single entry in the bibliography, the entry is referred to using only the author's name. If the authors have two or more entries, the relevant text is referred to by the author's name followed by the year of publication.

Chapter 1: What Is Epistemology?

Surprisingly few texts provide any comprehensive outline of what epistemology covers. Rather, they tend to focus at once on some favored epistemological topic, such as skepticism, or empirical knowledge, without providing a general overview. One exception to this rule is Chisholm (1966—but not 1989). A brief but interesting discussion is in Stich (1990). An excellent survey of individual topics in epistemology is provided by Dancy and Sosa.

Chapter 2: Propositional Knowledge as Justified True Belief

Ryle has an extended examination of the types of knowledge. There are also clear though much briefer discussions in O'Connor and Carr, and in Lehrer (1974 and 1990).

Baker and Hacker (pp. 76–85) examine in passing the idea of philosophical analysis as consisting in the discovery of necessary and sufficient conditions. An early discussion of whether knowledge is adequately justified true belief can be found in Plato. Modern versions of the view can be found in Russell (1964), Chisholm (1989), and Ayer (1956).

Gettier's criticisms of the JTB analysis appeared first in Gettier, and have been reprinted in A. Phillipps Griffiths, ed., Roth and Gallis, eds., Pojman, ed., and Goodman and Snyder, eds. An insightful recent discussion is to be found in Sturgeon.

The idea that knowledge requires conclusive justification is defended by Dretske (1971), and criticized by Pappas and Swain. Both articles are reprinted in Pappas and Swain, eds. (1978).

An indefeasibility approach is defended by Lehrer and Paxson, by Annis, by Swain (1974 and 1981), and by Moser (1989). It is criticized by Pappas and Swain, eds. (1978), in their Introduction.

Chapter 3: Further Attempts To Define Propositional Knowledge

An early version of reliabilism is found in Armstrong, and later descendents are discussed by Swain (1981), Goldman (1979 and 1986, the latter being reprinted in Goodman and Snyder, eds.). Pollock and also Lycan criticize the theory.

Goldman (1967) propounds a causal analysis of knowledge, though he takes the causal analysis to be a supplement rather than a rival to the JTB account. Goldman's paper is reprinted in Pappas and Swain, eds., Pojman, eds., and Goodman and Snyder eds.

Nozick expounds the "tracking" account, and the relevant part of Nozick's book is reprinted, together with a selection of critical essays on the tracking account and a very useful introduction, in Luper-Foy.

Brief but useful discussions of both reliabilism and causal theories can be found in Dancy and Sosa, eds.

Chapter 4: When Is a Belief Adequately Justified?

Lycan contains a useful discussion exploring the relation between conscious and unconscious belief. Armstrong touches on this issue and also considers whether beliefs are dispositions or states. Fodor provides a difficult but rewarding study.

The link between justification and norms is explored in the works cited in the text, especially in Goldman (1986).

Chisholm (1989) has a good discussion of the relations between justification and probability, a topic which is also discussed by Lehrer (1990) and Pollock.

A number of works regard justification as closely linked with inference (although without necessarily agreeing on how the concept of inference should be understood). These include Russell (1964) and Harman (1973).

Works which provide a non-inferential account of justification include those which define justification in terms of production by a reliable method, such as Goldman (1979) and Papineau, or in causal terms, such as Armstrong, Goldman (1967), Swain (1974 and 1981), and Dretske (1981). But it should be noted that the dividing line between reliabilists and causal theorists is not sharp.

Chapter 5: Foundationalism about Empirical Beliefs

A classic formulation of foundationalism about empirical beliefs can be found in Ayer (1936). More recent defenses include Chisholm (1989), Alston, Moser (1989), and Audi. An early attack on the "deep" foundationalist conception of experience is in Barnes, while Sellars (ch.5) provides a further, difficult but very influential attack.

The conception of the self which foundationalism presupposes is addressed indirectly in Shoemaker and Swinburne, Shoemaker implicitly supporting the line of argument presented in the text, and Swinburne attacking it.

The antiprivate language argument first appeared in Wittgenstein. A sympathetic discussion of this difficult text is found in Fogelin.

Bonjour (1976 and 1985) defend the claim that experience cannot itself justify any of our beliefs, as does Davidson, but the thesis is rejected by Sosa and by Pollock.

Chapter 6: Foundationalism about A Priori Beliefs

Dancy and Sosa, eds., contain useful discussions under the headings "a priori knowledge," "analyticity," "foundationalism," "coherentism," "geometry," and "mathematical knowledge," each with useful associated bibliographies. Quine and Ullian contains a critical discussion of self-evidence.

The classic exposition of Euclidean geometry is in Heath, while Bell, De Long, Swinburne, and Musgrave all provide simple nontechnical explanations of non-Euclidean geometries. Delong includes some interesting historical background information about the development of non-Euclidean geometries.

The modern classic treatment of the foundations of arithmetic is found in Frege. This is not an easy text, and Russell (1919) (still not simple) is a little more accessible.

The idea that certain logical truths are self-evident has a long history. Early defenses of the claim can be found in Descartes, Locke, and Leibniz. Twentieth-century defenses are Russell (1964) and Hollis and Nell, though the latter operates with a narrow conception of self-evidence.

The most thorough but nontechnical explanation of Godel's theorems is in Nagel and Newman. Other accessible discussions of Godel can be found in Penrose and in Hofstadter. Crossley's treatment is more formal though still intended as an introduction.

Chapter 7: Coherence Theories of Justification Explained

A classic defense of coherentism can be found in Blandshard, and the doctrine is sympathetically considered by Ewing.

More recent defenses can be found in Lehrer (1974) and Bonjour (1985), the former being partly modified in Lehrer (1990). The views of both Bonjour and Lehrer are subjected to close scrutiny in Bender, which also contains replies by both authors to criticisms. Lehrer's epistemology is also examined in Pastin, and further criticisms of Bonjour are in Sosa and in Moser (1989).

The origins of Quine's very influential position are to be found in Quine (1951), reprinted in 1953, and also in Sumner and Woods eds. in Sleigh ed., and in Moser, ed. (1987).

Quine's position, which he has never spelt out in very much detail, appears to have altered slightly in his 1970. Harman (1973) provides a version of coherence which is Quinean in spirit, and which emphasizes the importance of inferences to the best explanation. He adds refinements in Harman (1985).

Chisholm has been a steady critic of all forms of coherentism, and a typical statement of his position can be found in Chisholm (1989). More nuanced criticisms of coherentism can be found in Sosa.

Chapter 8: An Assessment of Coherentism

Among those advancing the claim that coherentism cannot cope satisfactorily with perception are Moser (1986) and Pollock, and variants of the objection can be found in papers by Moser, Mattey, Silvers, and Lemos in Bender, ed. The origins of the usual line of reply can be found in Sellars, a line of thought more fully developed by Bonjour (1978 and 1985).

The "plurality" objection has been voiced by Lewis, Firth, Goldman in Bender, ed. and Sosa, and attempts to meet it can be found in the replies by Lehrer and Bonjour in Bender (ed.). The claim that only beliefs can justify beliefs is ably defended by Davidson, and also by Rorty (1980), but challenged by Swain (1981).

Chapter 9: Problems with Identifying Deductive Inferences

Dancy and Sosa, eds., contains an entry on "Intuition and deduction" which addresses some of the issues in this chapter.

Dummett (1973) is a classic consideration of the problems of justifying deduction, and his ideas receive more extensive and difficult elaboration in

Dummett (1991), which also considers such related matters as holism and coherentism.

Quine (1970) discusses deviant logics in an interesting assessment of some good and bad arguments against the law of the excluded middle. Haack (1976) examines some parallels between the problems of justifying deduction and induction. Haack (1978) discusses some epistemological questions associated with deductive inference, and covers such topics as the revisability of logic, necessity, analyticity, self-evidence, and the relationship between logic and thought.

Chapter 10: The Traditional Problem of Induction

Swinburne, ed. (1974) is a good collection of articles on induction, with a helpful introduction.

The inductive justification of induction is defended by Black and by Braithwaite, and criticized by Achinstein (all in Swinburne op. cit.). Van Cleve has recently revived the argument, which has also been defended by Papineau.

Popper's views on induction are given in Popper 1959, 1963, and 1972. The claim that he is a closet skeptic is well made in Stove.

Goodman's Paradox was first propounded in Goodman 1973, which also contains Goodman's own solution. Blackburn has an excellent discussion, arguing that Goodman's "new" problem about induction is not significantly different from the old one. Hollis 1969–70 offers a delightfully witty attempt at *reductio ad absurdum* of Goodman, while Poundstone also provides a discussion with a light touch.

Hempel's Paradox was first presented in two uncompromising papers in Hempel 1945, and reprinted with some changes in 1965. An excellent discussion of Hempel is in Ayer 1972, and in Cohen (which also examines the traditional problem of induction and Goodman's Paradox). Poundstone again supplies a more light-hearted look at the problem.

Chapter 11: A Continuum of Inferences

Rawls first used the term "relective equilibrium" in connection with political philosophy, though the concept he was naming had previously guided Goodman (1973). For a clear account of the concept, see Stich (1990), who denies however that the method can yield the results claimed for it.

Kantian transcendentalism originates in Kant's extremely difficult *Critique of Pure Reason*. Useful aids in the task of understanding Kant's ideas are Strawson (1966), Bennett, and Melnick. Blackburn focuses specifically on the link between induction and the possibility of self-knowledge, and Strawson (1959) on the link between self-knowledge and objectivity.

Chapter 12: Quine and Naturalized Epistemology

The classic text is Quine's essay "Epistemology Naturalised," reprinted in Quine 1969, though this needs to be supplemented with his 1970, 1974, and 1990, and also with his brief but important remarks on the subject in Barrett and Gibson (eds.).

Papineau provides a general defense of naturalized epistemology. Kornblith (1985) is a good collection of articles, with a very extensive bibliography. Kim (reprinted in Goodman and Snyder, eds.) argues that Quine's naturalized epistemology must exclude normative considerations, a view apparently shared by Goldman (1986). Hookway focuses on the relation between naturalized epistemology and the traditional problem of skepticism, while Stroud (1981 and 1984) argues at length that naturalized epistemology evades the traditional problems of epistemology. Cherniak provides an interesting defense of the claim that naturalized epistemology undercuts itself. Putnam gives a powerful critique of naturalized epistemology.

Dennett's argument about the essential rationality of all believers can be found in a number of his writings, but one of the most accessible is his 1971, reprinted in his 1978. Similar claims are defended in Hollis (1969–70 and 1982).

Chapter 13: Rorty on Philosophy and the Mirror of Nature

The key text is of course Rorty's (1980). But the ideas that led up to that text can be found in Rorty (1982), a collection of essays written in the 1970s; Rorty's subsequent reflections can be found in Rorty's three collections of papers (1988, and 1991). The latter are given an extensive review by Bernstein. A standard collection of useful readings is Malachowski (which also contains a full bibliography of Rorty's other writings).

Bibliography

Achinstein, Peter. "The Circularity of Self-Supporting Inductive Argument." *Analysis* 23 (1963): 43–44. Reprinted in Swinburne, ed., 1974.

Ackerman, Robert J. *Belief and Knowledge.* London: Macmillan, 1973.

Amundson, R. "Epistemology Naturalised." *Inquiry* 26 (1983): 333–444.

Alston, William. *Epistemic Justification.* Ithaca, N.Y.: Cornell University Press, 1989.

Annis, David. "Knowledge and Defeasibility." *Philosophical Studies* 24 (1973): 199–203. Reprinted in Pappas and Swain, eds.

Armstrong, D. M. *Belief, Truth and Knowledge.* Cambridge: Cambridge University Press, 1973.

Audi, Robert. "Fallibilist Foundationalism and Holistic Coherence." In Pojman, ed.

Ayer, A. J. "Truth by Convention." *Analysis* (1936–37).

———. *The Problem of Knowledge,* Harmondsworth, England: Penguin, 1956.

———. *Language, Truth and Logic.* London: Gollancz, 1936 (2nd ed. 1946).

———. *Probability and Evidence.* London: Macmillan, 1972.

Baker, G. P., and P. M. S. Hacker. *Wittgenstein: Understanding and Meaning.* Oxford: Blackwell, 1980.

Barnes, Winston. "The Myth of Sense Data." *Proceedings of the Aristotelian Society* 55 (1944–45). Reprinted in Swartz, ed.

Barrett, Robert B., and Roger F. Gibson eds. *Perspectives on Quine.* Oxford: Blackwell, 1990.

Bell, E. T. *Men of Mathematics.* New York: Simon & Schuster, 1961.

Bender, John W., ed. *The Current State of the Coherence Theory.* Dordrecht: Kluwer Academic Publishers, 1989.

Bennett, J. F. *Kant's Analytic.* Cambridge: Cambridge University Press, 1966.

Bernstein, J. M. "Richard Rorty's Philosophical Papers." *Journal of the British Society for Phenomenology* 23 (1) (1992): 76–83.

Black, Max. "Self-supporting inductive arguments." *Journal of Philosophy* 55 (1958): 718–725. Reprinted in Swinburne, ed., 1974.

Blackburn, Simon. *Reason and Prediction.* Cambridge: Cambridge University Press, 1973.

Blanshard, Brand. *The Nature of Thought,* 2 vols. London: Allen and Unwin, 1939.

Bogdan, Radu J., ed. *Keith Lehrer.* Dordrecht: D. Reidel, 1981.

Bonjour, Laurence. "The Coherence Theory of Empirical Knowledge." *Philosophical Studies* 30 (1976): 281–312. Reprinted in P. Moser (1986).

———. "Can Empirical Knowledge Have a Foundation?" *American Philosophical Quarterly* 15 (1978): 1–12.

———. *The Structure of Empirical Knowledge.* Cambridge, Mass.: Harvard University Press, 1985.

Braithwaite, Richard. *Scientific Explanation.* Cambridge: Cambridge University Press, 1953.

Butterfield, Herbert. *The Origins of Modern Science 1300–1800.* London: G. Bell and Sons, 1949.

Carroll, Lewis. *Sylvie and Bruno.* London: Macmillan, 1889.

Cherniak, Christopher. *Minimal Rationality.* Cambridge, Mass.: MIT Press, 1986.

Chisholm, Roderick M. *Perceiving: A Philosophical Study.* Ithaca, N.Y.: Cornell University Press, 1957.

———. *The Foundations of Knowing.* Brighton, England: Harvester, 1982.

———. *Theory of Knowledge.* Englewood Cliffs, N.J.: Prentice Hall, 1966; 3rd ed., 1989.

Cohen, Jonathan L. *An Introduction to the Philosophy of Induction and Probability.* Oxford: Clarendon Press, 1989.

Cornford, F. M. *Plato's Theory of Knowledge.* London: Routledge, 1964.

Cresswell, M. J. "Can Epistemology Be Naturalised?" In Robert W. Shahan and Chris Swoyer, eds., 1979.

Crossley, John, *et al. What Is Mathematical Logic?* Oxford: Oxford University Press, 1972.

Dancy, Jonathan. *Introduction to Contemporary Epistemology.* Oxford: Blackwell, 1985.

Dancy, Jonathan, and Ernest Sosa, eds. *A Companion to Epistemology.* Oxford: Blackwell, 1993.

Davidson, Donald. "A Coherence Theory of Truth and Interpretation." In Ernest LePore, ed.

Delong, Howard. *A Profile of Mathematical Logic.* Reading, Mass.: Addison-Wesley, 1970.

Dennett, Daniel. *Brainstorms.* Cambridge, Mass.: Bradford Books, MIT Press, 1978.

———. "Intentional Systems." *Journal of Philosophy* 68 (1971): 87–106. Reprinted in Dennett, 1978.

Descartes, R. *The Philosophical Writings of Descartes.* Trans. John Cottingham, Robert Stoohof and Dugald Murdoch. (*Rules for the Direction of the Mind* in vol. 1, *Meditations* in vol. 2) Cambridge: Cambridge University Press, 1984.

Dretske, Fred I. "Conclusive Reasons." *Australasian Journal of Philosophy* 49 (1971): 1–22. Reprinted in Pappas and Swain, eds.

———. *Knowledge and the Flow of Information.* Oxford: Blackwell, 1981.

Dummett, Michael. "The Justification of Deduction." *Proceedings of the British Academy* 59 (1973).

———. *The Logical Basis of Metaphysics.* London: Duckworth, 1991.

Edwards, Paul. "Bertrand Russell's Doubts about Induction." *Mind* 68 (1949): 141–163. Reprinted in A. Flew, ed., and in R. Swinburne, ed., 1974.

Ewing, A. C. "The Linguistic Theory of A Priori Propositions." *Proceedings of the Aristotelian Society* (1939–40).

———. *Idealism: A Critical Survey.* London: Methuen, 1934.

Firth, Roderick. "Coherence, Certainty and Epistemic Priority." *Journal of Philosophy,* 1964.

Fisher, Alec. *The Logic of Real Arguments.* Cambridge: Cambridge University Press, 1988.

Flew, Antony, ed. *Logic and Language.* First Series. Oxford: Blackwell, 1951.

———. *David Hume.* Oxford: Blackwell, 1986.

Fodor, Jerry. "Propositional Attitudes." *The Monist* 61 (1978). Reprinted in Fodor's *Representations,* Brighton, England: Harvester Press, 1981.

Fogelin, Robert. *Wittgenstein.* London: Routledge, 1976.

Frege, G. *The Foundations of Arithmetic.* Trans. J. L. Austin. Oxford: Blackwell, 1974.

French, Peter. Theodore Uehling, and Howard Wettstein, eds. "Causation and Causal Theories." *Midwest Studies in Philosophy IX.* Minneapolis, Minn.: University of Minnesota Press, 1984.

Gettier, Edmund. "Is Justified True Belief Knowledge?" *Analysis* 23 (1963): 121–23. Reprinted in Phillips Griffiths, ed., and in Roth and Galis, eds.

Gillies, David. *Philosophy of Science in the 20th Century,* Blackwell, Oxford, England, 1993.

Goldman, Alvin. "A Causal Theory of Knowing." *Journal of Philosophy* (1967): 355–72. Reprinted in Pojman, ed., Goodman and Snyder, eds., and Pappas and Swain, eds.

———. "What Is Justified Belief?" Reprinted in George Pappas, ed.

———. *Epistemology and Cognition.* Cambridge, Mass.: Harvard University Press, 1986.

———. *Empirical Knowledge.* Berkeley: University of California Press, 1988.

Goodman, Michael, and Robert Snyder, eds. *Contemporary Readings in Epistemology.* Englewood Cliffs, N.J.: Prentice Hall, 1993.

Goodman, Nelson. *Fact, Fiction and Forecast* (1st ed. 1955) 3rd edition, Indianapolis, Ind.: Bobbs-Merrill, 1973.

Grice, H. P. "The Causal Theory of Perception." *Proceedings of the Aristotelian Society,* Supp. Vol. 35 (1961). Reprinted in Swartz, ed.

———. "Presupposition and Conversational Implicature." In *Radical Pragmatics.* Ed. P. Cole, New York: Academic Press, 1981.

———. "Logic and Conversation." In *The Logic of Grammar.* Donald Davidson and Gilbert Harman. Encino, Calif.: Dickinson, 1975.

Haack, Susan. "The Justification of Deduction." *Mind* 85 (1976): 112–119.

———. *Philosophy of Logics.* Cambridge: Cambridge University Press, 1978.

Hahn, Hans. "Logic, mathematics and knowledge of nature." Reprinted in *Logical Positivism.* Ed. A. J. Ayer. Glencoe, Ill.: The Free Press, 1959.

Hare, R. M. *The Language of Morals.* Oxford: Oxford University Press, 1961.

Harman, Gilbert. *Thought.* Princeton, N.J.: Princeton University Press, 1973.

———. "Positive versus Negative Undermining in Belief Revision." In Hilary Kornblith, ed.

———. *Change in View.* Cambridge, Mass: MIT Press, 1986.

Heath, Sir Thomas. *The Thirteen Books of Euclid's Elements.* 3 vols. New York: Dover Publications, 1956.

Hempel, Carl G. "Studies in the Logic of Confirmation." *Mind* 54 (1945): 1–26, 97–121 (reprinted with some changes in Hempel, 1965).

———. *Aspects of Scientific Explanation.* Glencoe, Ill.: The Free Press, 1965.

Hofstadter, Douglas. *Gödel, Escher, Bach: an eternal golden braid.* Harmondsworth, England: Penguin, 1980.

Hollis, Martin. "The Limits of Irrationality." *Archives Europeenes de Sociologie* 8 (1967): 247–64. Reprinted in *Rationality.* Ed. Bryan Wilson. Oxford: Blackwell, 1970.

———. "Monadologue." *Analysis* 30 (1969–70): 14–147.

———. "The Social Destruction of Reality." In *Rationality and Relativism.* Ed. Martin Hollis and Steven Lukes. Oxford: Blackwell, 1982.

Hollis, Martin, and Edward Nell. *Rational Economic Man.* Cambridge: Cambridge University Press, 1975.

Hookway, Christopher. *Quine*. Stanford University Press, Stanford, CA, 1988.

Hume, David. *A Treatise Of Human Nature*. Ed. L. A. Selby-Bigge, Oxford: Clarendon Press, 1960 (1st ed. 1739).

———. *Enquiry Concerning Human Understanding*. Ed. P. H. Nidditch. Oxford: Clarendon Press (1st ed. 1748) 1975.

Kant, Immanuel. *Critique of Pure Reason*. Trans. Norman Kemp Smith. London: Macmillan, 1963 (1st and 2nd eds. 1781 and 1787).

Kim, Jaegwon. "What is 'Naturalised Epistemology'?" *Philosophical Perspectives 2, Epistemology*. Ed. James E. Tomberlin. Atascadero, Calif.: Ridgeview Publishing Co., 1988, pp. 381–405. Reprinted in Jaegwon Kim. *Supervenience and Mind*. Cambridge: Cambridge University Press, 1993, and in Goodman and Snyder.

Kitcher, Philip. "A Priori Knowledge." *Philosophical Review* 76 (1980): 3–23. Reprinted in Hilary Kornblith, ed.

Kneale, W. C. and M. *The Development of Logic*. Oxford: Oxford University Press, 1962.

Kornblith, Hilary. "Justified Belief and Epistemically Responsible Action." *Philosophical Review* 92 (1983): 33–48.

———. *Naturalising Epistemology*. Cambridge, Mass.: Bradford Books, MIT Press, 1985.

Kripke, Saul. "Identity and Necessity." In *Identity and Individuation*. Ed. M. K. Munitz. New York: New York University Press, 1971.

———. *Naming and Necessity*. Oxford: Blackwell, 1980.

Leibniz, G. W. F. *New Essays on Human Understanding*. Trans. and ed. Peter Remnant and Jonathan Bennett. Cambridge University Press, Cambridge, England, 1981 (1st ed. 1765).

Lehrer, Keith. *Knowledge*. Oxford: Clarendon Press, 1974.

———. *Theory of Knowledge*. London: Routledge, 1990.

Lehrer, Keith, and T. Paxson. "Knowledge: Undefeated True Belief." *Journal of Philosophy* 66 (1969): pp. 225–37. Reprinted in Pappas and Swain, eds.

LePore, Ernest. *Truth and Interpretation: Perspectives on the Philosophy of Donald Davidson*. Oxford: Blackwell, 1986.

Levin, Michael E. "Quine's view(s) of logical truth." In Shahan and Swoyer, eds.

Lewis, C. I. "The Given Element in Perception." *Philosophical Review* 61 (1952).

Locke, John. *An Essay Concerning Human Understanding*. (5th edition) Ed. John W. Yolton. London: Dent, 1961 (5th ed. 1706).

Luper-Foy, Steven. *The Possibility of Knowledge*. Totowa, N.J.: Rowman and Littlefield, 1987.

Lycan, William G. *Judgement and Justification*. Cambridge: Cambridge University Press, 1988.

Malachowski, Alan, ed. *Reading Rorty*. Oxford: Blackwell, England, 1990.

Melnick, Arthur. *Kant's Analogies of Experience*. Chicago, Ill.: University of Chicago Press, 1973.

Mill, John Stuart. *A System of Logic* (1st ed. 1943), London: Longmans, ____.

Moser, Paul K. *Empirical Knowledge*. Totowa, N.J.: Rowman and Littlefield, 1986.

Moser, Paul K. ed. *A Priori Knowledge*, Oxford: Oxford University Press, 1987.

———. *Knowledge and Evidence*. Cambridge: Cambridge University Press, 1989.

———. "Some Recent Work in Epistemology." *Philosophical Papers* 19 (1990): 75–98.

Musgrave, Alan. *Commonsense, Science and Scepticism*. Cambridge: Cambridge University Press, 1993.

Nagel, Ernest, and James Newman. *Gödel's Proof*. London: Routledge and Kegan Paul, 1959.

Nathan, N. M. L. *Evidence and Assurance*. Cambridge: Cambridge University Press, 1980.

Nielsen, Kai. *After the Demise of the Tradition: Rorty, Critical Theory and the Fate of Philosophy*. Boulder, Colo.: Westview Press, 1991.

Nozick, Robert. *Philosophical Investigations*. Oxford: Clarendon Press, 1984.

O'Hear, Anthony. *What Philosophy Is*. Harmondsworth, England: Penguin, 1985.

O'Connor, D. J., and Brian Carr. *Introduction to the Theory of Knowledge*. Brighton, England: The Harvester Press, 1982.

Papineau, David. *Reality and Representation*. Oxford: Blackwell, 1987.

Pappas, George, ed. *Justification and Knowledge: New Studies in Epistemology*. Dordrecht, Holland: Reidel, 1979.

Pappas, George S. and Marshal Swain. "Some Conclusive Reasons against 'Conclusive Reasons.'" *Australasian Journal of Philosophy* 51 (1973): 72–6. Reprinted in Pappas and Swain (eds).

Pappas, George S., and Marshal Swain, eds. *Essays on Knowledge and Justification*. Ithaca, N.Y.: Cornell University Press, 1978.

Pastin, Mark. "Social and Anti-Social Justification: A Study of Lehrer's Epistemology." In *Keith Lehrer*. Ed. Radu J. Bogdan. Dordrecht, Holland: Reidel, 1981.

Penrose, Roger. *The Emperor's New Mind*. Oxford: Oxford University Press, 1989.

Phillipps Griffiths, A., ed. *Knowledge and Belief*. Oxford: Oxford University Press, 1967.

Plato. *Theaetetus*. Published under the title *Plato's Theory of Knowledge*, by F. M. Cornford. London: Routledge and Kegan Paul, 1960.

Pojman, Louis P., ed. *The Theory of Knowledge: Classic and Contemporary Readings*. Belmont, Calif.: Wadsworth, 1993.

Pollock, John L. *Contemporary Theories of Knowledge*. London: Hutchinson, 1987.

Popper, Karl. *The Logic of Scientific Discovery*. London: Hutchinson, 1959.

———. *Conjectures and Refutations*. London: Routledge, 1963.

———. *Objective Knowledge*. Oxford: Clarendon Press, 1972.

Poundstone, William. *Labyrinths of Reason*. New York: Doubleday, 1988.

Prior, Arthur. *Formal Logic*. Oxford: Clarendon Press, 1955.

Putnam, Hilary. "Why Reason Can't Be Naturalised." In *Realism and Reason: Philosophical Papers*. Vol. 3. Cambridge: Cambridge University Press, 1983.

Quine, W. "Two Dogmas of Empiricism." *Philosophical Review* 60 (1951). A slightly amended version was reprinted in Quine 1953, in Sleigh, ed., in Sumner and Woods, ed., in Moser, ed., 1987.

———. *Methods of Logic*. London: Routledge and Kegan Paul, 1952.

———. *From a Logical Point of View*. Cambridge, Mass.: Harvard University Press, 1953. 2nd ed.: New York: Harper and Row, 1961.

———. *Word and Object*. Cambridge, MA: MIT Press, 1960.

———. *Ontological Relativity and Other Essays*. New York: Columbia University Press, 1969.

———. *Philosophy of Logic*. Englewood Cliffs, N.J.: Prentice Hall, 1970.

———. *The Roots of Reference*. La Salle, Ill.: Open Court, 1974.

———. *The Pursuit of Truth*. Cambridge, Mass.: Harvard University Press, 1990.

Quine, W., and J. S. Ullian. *The Web of Belief*. New York: Random House, 1970.

Quinton, Anthony. "The a priori and the analytic." *Proceedings of the Aristotelian Society* (1963–64). Reprinted in *Philosophical Logic*. Ed. P. F. Strawson. Oxford: Oxford University Press, 1967.

Rawls, John. *A Theory of Justice*. Oxford: Oxford University Press, 1973.

Romanos, George D. *Quine and Analytic Philosophy*. Cambridge, Mass.: MIT Press, 1984.

Rorty, Richard. *Philosophy and the Mirror of Nature*. Oxford: Blackwell, 1980.
———. *Consequences of Pragmatism*. Brighton, England: Harvester Press, 1982.
———. *Contingency, Irony, and Solidarity*. Cambridge: Cambridge University Press, 1988.
———. *Objectivity, Relativism and Truth: Philosophical Papers*. Vol. 1. *Essays on Heidegger and Others: Philosophical Papers*. Vol. 2. Cambridge: Cambridge University Press, 1991.
Roth, Michael D., and Leon Galis, eds. *Knowing: Essays in the Analysis of Knowledge*. New York: Random House, 1970.
Russell, Bertrand. *Introduction to Mathematical Philosophy*. London: Allen and Unwin, 1919.
———. *The Problems of Philosophy*. Oxford: Oxford University Press, 1964.
Ryle, Gilbert. *The Concept of Mind*. London: Hutchinson, 1949.
Sellars, Wilfred. *Science, Perception and Reality*. London: Routledge, 1963.
Shahan, Robert W., and Chris Swoyer, eds. *Essays on the Philosophy of W. V. Quine*. Brighton, England: Harvester Press, 1979.
Shope, Robert K. *The Analysis of Knowing*. Princeton, N.J.: Princeton University Press, 1983.
Shoemaker, Sydney, and Richard Swinburne. *Personal Identity*. Oxford: Blackwell, 1984.
Sleigh, R. C., ed. *Necessary Truth*. Englewood Cliffs, N.J.: Prentice Hall, 1972.
Sosa, Ernest. *Knowledge in Perspective*. Cambridge: Cambridge University Press, 1991.
Stich, Stephen. "Could Man Be an Irrational Animal?" In Kornblith ed., 1988.
———. *The Fragmentation of Reason*. Cambridge, Mass.: MIT Press, 1990.
Stove, D. C. *Popper and After: Four Modern Irrationalists*. Oxford: Pergamon Press, 1982.
Strawson, P. F. *Individuals*. London: Methuen, 1959.
———. *Introduction to Logical Theory*. London: Methuen, 1963.
———. *The Bounds of Sense*. London: Methuen, 1966.
———. ' "If" and " " ' In *Philosophical Grounds of Rationality*. Ed. Richard E. Grandy and Richard Warner. Oxford: Clarendon Press, 1986.
Stroud, Barry. "The Significance of Naturalised Epistemology" in *Midwest Studies in Philosophy*. Vol. 11. University of Minnesota Press, Minneapolis, Minn. 1981. Reprinted in Kornblith, ed. 1988.
———. *The Significance of Philosophical Scepticism*. Oxford: Clarendon Press, 1984.
Sturgeon, Scott. "The Gettier Problem." *Analysis* 53 (1993).
Sumner, L. W., and John Woods, eds. *Necessary Truth*. New York: Random House, 1969.
Swain, Marshall. "Epistemic Defeasibility." *American Philosophical Quarterly* 11 (1974). Reprinted in Pappas and Swain, eds.
———. *Reasons and Knowledge*. Ithaca, N.Y.: Cornell University Press, 1981.
Swartz, Robert, ed. *Perceiving, Sensing and Knowing*. New York: Anchor Books, Doubleday, 1965.
Swinburne, Richard, ed., *The Justification of Induction*. Oxford: Oxford University Press, 1974.
———. *Space and Time*. London: Macmillan, 1981.
Unger, Peter. "A Defence of Skepticism." *Philosophical Review* 80 (1971). Reprinted in Pappas and Swain, eds.
Van Cleve, James. "Reliability, Justification and Induction." In P. French, T. Uehling, and H. Wettstein, eds.
Wittgenstein, Ludwig. *Philosophical Investigations*. Oxford, England: Blackwell, 1963.

Permissions Acknowledgments

Index